Good Indian Daughter

How I Found Freedom In Being A Disappointment

Ruhi Lee

16pt

Copyright Page from the Original Book

Published by Affirm Press in 2021
28 Thistlethwaite Street, South Melbourne,
Boonwurrung Country, VIC 3205
affirmpress.com.au
10 9 8 7 6 5 4 3 2 1

Text and copyright © Ruhi Lee, 2021
All rights reserved. No part of this publication may be reproduced without prior permission of the publisher.

 A catalogue record for this book is available from the National Library of Australia

Title: Good Indian Daughter / Ruhi Lee, author

Cover design by Karen Wallis, Taloula Press
Cover image by Agnieszka Murphy/Shutterstock
Typeset in 12.5/20 Adobe Garamond Premier Pro by J&M Typesetting
Proudly printed in Australia by Griffin Press

TABLE OF CONTENTS

1: The wrong kind of homework	1
2: Just desserts	10
3: Dharwad	19
4: Unhappy little Vegemite	52
5: Pseudoscience	89
6: Not that kind of Indian	126
7: Feeling myself	153
8: Thanks for the panic attacks. Here's a heart attack in return.	175
9: Rite of passage	205
10: The Good Indian Daughter	229
11: A baby shower fit for a queen who hates parties	264
12: Unsolicited advice	299
13: Funeral plans	322
14: Atithi Devo Bhava	357
INTERMISSION	383
15: God vs. family counselling	388
16: Following in the footsteps of Blinky Bill	405
17: Birth and death	417
18: Birds	447
Author's Note	469
Acknowledgements	477
Glossary	483
Sources	489

Praise for Good Indian Daughter

'This book left me reeling – for all the right reasons. A torrent of conflicting emotions oscillating between shock, laughter, rage, resonance, solidarity and awe. Above all else, though, gratitude; I am so grateful for Ruhi Lee's tenacity that has delivered a memoir as hilariously on point as it is, at times, horrifying. Her courage and grit are matched squarely with a wry humour so wickedly timed. Further, Lee's wordsmithing prowess conquers the complexity of cultural idiosyncrasies of Indian households with a deftness that is pure art. It was impossible to put this book down, and not declare "I KNOW, RIGHT!" numerous times while reading it. To every desi girl who has felt the struggle of being a good daughter, combating the weight of expectations, self doubt and familial angst, this book will hit home.'
Tasneem Chopra OAM, author, broadcaster and director

'Told with humour and a light touch, *Good Indian Daughter* lays bare the

experience of growing up in a family and culture that requires its daughters to be dutiful, compliant and silent. It is a story about the intergenerational consequences of those expectations and about one woman's refusal to continue being "good". *Good Indian Daughter* is a book for our times – a reminder that respect for women starts at home.'
Pip Williams, bestselling author of The Dictionary of Lost Words *and* One Italian Summer

'A love letter to the child she was, a reckoning with trauma, and a promise to her own daughter – Ruhi Lee's memoir made me laugh hard and then catch my breath with hurt. Unflinching in her examination of herself and her family, Lee tells this difficult story with clever, playful prose and fills it with anecdotes that made me snort with laughter. It is a privilege, as a reader, to be taken deep into Lee's experiences and past, and to understand all the ways in which she both tries to be and rails against the notion of a Good Indian Daughter.'

Kate Mildenhall, author of The Mother Fault *and* Skylarking

'Absorbing from the first page, *Good Indian Daughter* lays out the complex expectations of immigrant parents who made sacrifices for the sake of family, yet thwart their children's attempts to live lives of their own. The laugh-out-loud moments make Lee's accounts of childhood trauma and her fierce and intelligent observations on Indian culture – particularly with regard to girls and women – all the more powerful as she searches and finds who she really is beneath the guise of the Good Indian Daughter.'
Katherine Tamiko Arguile, author of The Things She Owned

'Forthright and heartfelt, *Good Indian Daughter* is a book for anyone who's ever been a child, for anyone who's struggled with family expectations, for anyone who needs to do the hard work of setting boundaries and cultivating self-love. Lee's story is deeply personal, intensely relatable, often hilarious and ultimately joyous.'

Ashley Kalagian Blunt, author of How to Be Australian *and* My Name Is Revenge

'Another important memoir about lives at the convergence and friction between two homes, *Good Indian Daughter* reflects on identities, history, and what it means to be a brown woman, daughter, and mother. We see Australia and India from Ruhi Lee's observant and loving yet critical eyes. She gives breath to the past and turns the everyday and the mundane in the present into a curious, exciting story. *Good Indian Daughter* is funny and moving, and within the first few pages you know you would care about the characters, yet it also has moments of discomfort in which you interrogate your assumptions and boundaries.'
Intan Paramaditha, author of Apple and Knife *and* The Wandering

'Warm and wry, with moments of crackling beauty; Ruhi Lee writes with humour and grace. Inside each story of *Good Indian Daughter* is another story

unfurling, memory by memory peeling back to a nugget of truth laid bare.'
Emily Clements, author of The Lotus Eaters

'I chuckled, I laughed, I teared up, I cried. A riveting tale of being a good Indian daughter has been carefully and honestly told by Ruhi – a terrific writer! It took my heart back to India and to the love and anxiety it brings that never truly leaves our bodies. Even beyond borders. Every Indian "disappointing" daughter must read this one!'
Dilpreet Kaur Taggar, founder and editor-in-chief of South Asian Today

Ruhi Lee writes on Boon Wurrung land. Her articles, poetry and book reviews have been featured in *The Guardian, ABC Life, SBS Voices, South Asian Today* and *The Big Issue* among other publications. In 2019, she was a recipient of the Neilma Sidney Literary Travel Fund and her manuscript was shortlisted for the Penguin Random House Write It Fellowship. In 2020, she was one of the commissioned writers for the Multicultural Arts Victoria's Shelter program. *Good Indian Daughter* is her first memoir. Ruhi loves to hear from readers. You can find her online at ruhilee.com.

For every difficult, disappointing daughter who continues to push back against the patriarchies she faces for a life that will not disappoint her.

And for my daughter; my jalebi baby.

This book is a memoir. It reflects my present recollections of experiences over time. Pseudonyms have been used and some characteristics have been altered to protect the identity and privacy of people mentioned in the book. Some events have been compressed and some dialogue has been recreated. While every effort has been made to recall past events accurately, the memories contained within this book are my own and may differ from those of others.

*'The English lesson was that I am
is a complete sentence.*

*And just before the afternoon bell, she
made the math equation look easy.
The one that proves that hundreds of
questions,*

*and feeling cold, and all those nights
spent looking
for whatever it was you lost, and one
person*

add up to something.'

– Brad Aaron Modlin,
'What You Missed That Day You Were Absent From Fourth Grade'

1

The wrong kind of homework

Early in the millennium, I set myself a new goal: to one day be able to tell my parents things they wouldn't like hearing, without shitting myself. At that point in time however, my backbone was so close to non-existent, I may as well have been classified as an invertebrate. This was not an ideal condition to be in on the day Pa had the biggest explosion I'd experienced in those first eleven years of my flaccid existence. It happened on Boon Wurrung land, about forty minutes south-east of Melbourne's city centre, in a suburb where the pharmacy, Vietnamese bakery, Hair Panache, Hot Potatoe's DISCOUNT SUPERSTORE, Chandu's Sweetmeats and Spices and the local Club X sex shop, were all conveniently located on the same shopping strip — it seemed, just to make family errands awkward for us.

Our house was a double-brick basket of stone fruit. A secondhand velveteen sofa the colour of pluot flesh was the pride of the lounge room, its upholstery surprisingly taut for its age. Peach venetians hung on the windows. The kitchen benchtop was the colour of apricot, naturally. And we always kept a cardboard crate full of ripe mangoes, selected by Pa according to the sweetness of their scent, in the place we pragmatically referred to as the 'kitchen cupboard'. We didn't know yet that it had a special name: pantry.

The lounge was the nucleus of our square home. A corridor wrapped all the way around it from the front door to the kitchen, joining the dots between the three bedrooms, bathroom, toilet and laundry. Children did not jump on furniture in this house, hence the undefiled sofa, and shoes were not allowed indoors. Devoted to the meticulous preservation of all things his sweat-soaked money had bought, Pa had also spread plastic protectors along this corridor, lest the filthy soles of our bare feet ruin the frieze carpet forever.

On the evening of the explosion, I stalked along this plastic-covered corridor in search of Ma, clutching two sheets of folded-up paper in my small brown hands. I found her in her bedroom, reorganising her wardrobe. Again. It was an unusual hour of tranquility in our home as the radio played SBS Hindi; only the sound of the radio host's voice floated through our open doorways between old Bollywood ballads that sounded like they were being broadcast through a thick woolly sock.

I could hear Pa crooning along as he did the laundry. Detergent. Cottons. Cold. Start. No fabric softener. No delicates. Ma sat cross-legged on the ground, a bindi on her forehead and a knitted sweater over her bandhani nighty, surrounded by piles of folded clothes. Melbourne's winter always snapped its metallic fangs at immigrants from warmer climates, but to Ma, it was worth enduring for her daughters to receive 'a better education' than she believed we would have had in her hometown, Dharwad. She and Pa were raising two very good girls out here in

Australia: girls who would become accomplished women, and make their parents proud and their in-laws prouder. Girls whom they'd done an exemplary job of protecting from the satanic forces ruling the outside world – until this particular moment.

'Ma?' I murmured from around the corner.

'YA?!' she shouted into her cupboard. I shuffled closer.

'Shh!' I was embarrassed.

She popped her head out from behind her cupboard doors and made a poor attempt at a whisper. 'What?!'

'I've got some homework that my teacher said to do with you.'

'Ask your pa.' She shooed me away.

'NO! I mean, no. Can you please just have a look?' I unfolded the two large sheets of paper, shuddering as I took one fatal step after another toward her.

Earlier that day at school, I'd had my first sex-education class and the teacher had sent us home with diagrams of the male and female reproductive systems. We were to discuss what we learned with our parents and label the anatomy together. My gut told me Ma and Pa weren't likely to take to the exercise, but my teacher's naive optimism must have rubbed off on me. As I packed the papers into my schoolbag I thought, *Well, you never know. Ma and Pa might surprise me and actually want to talk about this stuff ... because...*

But really there was no precedent I could draw on to complete that thought.

'Give it here,' Ma said with a sigh. She snatched the sheets of paper, male bits first, from my now-trembling hands. Then she looked down and gasped.

'Ayo.' Her palm went to her forehead. 'What is this?' The blood drained from her face. Then she called out for Pa. *Oh no.*

Pa heard the panic in her voice and arrived promptly. Ma handed him the diagrams. It was as though they had seen a ghost. Or a ghost's dick, to be precise. They looked at the labels I'd already filled out in class: *vas deferens, urethra, epididymis, prostate.* I'd left the easier ones for my parents to spare them at least a fraction of the embarrassment – things like *scrotum* and *testicles.* Also, deep-down, I just wanted to hear someone in our household say the word 'penis'.

Ma was on the verge of tears. The tectonic plates beneath Pa's face shifted as horror turned into rage. 'What is this?!'

'My homework...'

'THIS? *THIS* is homework? WHO the HELL is the teacher giving you this?'

'Mrs Fitzsimmons.'

Pa glared again at the rudimentary depictions of male and female private parts. 'Maya! Go turn the radio off please!' he shouted to my little sister, who had been busy playing with her toys – or pretending to, by this point – in our shared bedroom down the hallway. The intermittent screams of the pressure cooker in the kitchen now began to pierce the silence. I found a speck of solace in the knowledge that – at least this time – I wasn't in trouble for my own actions. Still, even though Pa's fire-breathing was aimed at my teacher, my hair was sure to be singed; I was still a guilty, if mostly unwilling, participant in something so veritably *un* Indian.

'What is the need for this?! *WHY* does an eleven-year-old child need to know this rubbish?! They call this "homework" here?!'

So much for a better education. In Pa's eyes, my teacher, the school and the entire Department of Education had failed his daughter, who had neither the maturity nor the required wariness around boys to be asked to label a penis and its neighbouring unmentionables. Until this point, I'd understood the bits between my legs as just the front section of the general bum area, responsible solely for urination. My parents were happy to leave this conclusion unchallenged until I was married to a man of their choosing, who would explain the rest to me at the appointed time. Even before this new information penetrated my carefully curated consciousness, myriad obstacles had already threatened my ascent into a successful, career-driven woman. Boys equipped with the necessary parts would be the architects of my ruination, and needed to be pulled out of my path like weeds.

To add insult to Pa's injury, the teacher had photocopied these pictures of sexual organs on enormous A3 pieces of paper. How was this allowed when maths homework was only ever printed on tiny A5 sheets or hidden inside a textbook? My parents might have considered it marginally more admissible if, in the name of biological studies (not 'sex-ed'), Mrs Fitzsimmons had used an overhead projector to light up the images on the wall, just for a few seconds, before they could sear into our minds. Instead, she handed out what was, as far as my parents were concerned, gigantic, two-dimensional black-and-white porn for students to take home and drool over. Never mind that the work sheets looked more like mazes from an activity book to me.

Pa nearly blew the walls off our Stone Fruit House with his diatribe about the debauched syllabus that Year 6 kids all over Victoria had to endure. I expected him to tear my homework to shreds, but what he did instead petrified me. He folded the papers slowly and precisely, corners and sides accurately lining up, and placed them in his pocket. Then he assured Ma and me that he wouldn't let this go unaddressed. My teacher was in for a firm talking-to about this depraved so-called 'curriculum'.

But Pa's efforts were wasted. The penis got to me in the end. And not via some rando chosen by my parents.

2
Just desserts

To be pregnant is to become accustomed to search parties in your vagina. First it's the sperm gunning for its Fabergé egg, each swimmer as lustful and single-minded as Matthew McConaughey on a treasure hunt. Then it's the transducer probe assaulting your innards during an ultrasound.

I had my first extensive ultrasound on a Monday morning a couple of months after I'd turned twenty-seven. 'Do you seriously not care if it's a boy or a girl?' I asked Jake (the husband of English, Irish, Welsh and definitely not Indian descent – oops! – who I chose against my parents' wishes) in the moments just before our appointment.

'Nope. Happy with either.'

'Yeah, me too.' I feigned cheerfulness.

In the hospital's vast foyer, sunlight shone through generous skylights, some bouncing off the smooth grey walls, some being absorbed by the lush indoor greenery around us.

'Okay, for real now. You're not leaning more toward one gender than the other?' I asked again.

'Alright, yes, but only by the slightest fraction. Don't go making a big deal of it.'

'Yes, yes, yes! I won't! Tell me!'

'As you know, I'll be happy with either. But I sort of imagined myself more with a girl, at least for the first child.'

'Oh?' I had not expected that.

'I guess because I don't see myself as a camping or fishing dad. I'm not sure I'd be great at the activities that boys typically expect their dads to do.'

'You didn't expect your dad to do those things.'

'True.'

'Besides, who cares about that? If we have a boy who's into those things, we can just teach ourselves along the way. And he might end up liking baking and reading as much as we do! Regardless, I think you'll be an awesome dad whether we have a boy or a girl.'

'Thank you. What about you?'

'So ... I'd be grateful for either a boy or a girl too,' I began, already guilty and aware that this conversation was a luxury in the unpredictable land of the pregnant. 'But I don't think I would be as good a mum to a little girl.'

'Why not?' Jake's brow furrowed.

'Because!' I couldn't put my finger on it. 'So, listen. I have a confession to make before we go in.'

'Yes?'

I blurted it out at breakneck speed: 'You know how I didn't bring the heater into the room where we 'made the baby'? Well, this stupid website – and you know I don't believe in these scientifically unproven methods but I had to try – this website said that if we kept our bodies cold, we could increase our chances of conceiving a boy. And I know it's ridiculous! Because another website said that doing exactly those things would result in a girl. I just went with the site that was more visually appealing. Anyway, I feel like an idiot and I'm sorry. I'm sorry! Okay?!'

Jake burst into laughter.

'Ruhi?' the sonographer called. It was time to find out if the pretty website was right.

***

It was proving difficult for the sonographer to locate the private parts of the blob inside me. According to my pregnancy tracker app, my baby, now at nineteen weeks, was the size of a mango and was developing his or her five senses as well as the ability to suck and swallow. The app warned me to expect more changes on my end too, including abdominal aches and pains, dizziness or lightheadedness, leg cramps and maybe even hip pain. Wonderful.

What the app *didn't* tell me was that my brain would start to process my surroundings in terms of food. Looking around at the equipment in the room set off a craving for sweets; the computer and ultrasound machine resembled a tower of marshmallows, while the examination couch reminded me of a creamy glazed entremet. (Can you tell I'd been watching *The Great British Bake Off?*) The downlights created soft, golden circles on the carpet like slices of candied orange on dark chocolate cake. Beside me, sitting on a caramel fudge chair, Jake was tilting his head, studying the screen to make out his offspring's body parts. The dim lighting made his stormy blue eyes look grey. He was the first and only person I'd known who believed clouds, rain, hail and lightning were as beautiful as clear skies. Perhaps this was what made him so perfect for me.

It took forever to find out the sex of our baby. At this moment, I was blissfully unaware that this would only be the first of a whole pregnancy-worth of failed jelly-on-the-belly scans. Each time, our hermit baby would turn away from the transducer, no matter how much I leaned to the left or right, until the sonographer gave up and switched to an even more inelegant vaginal ultrasound. I shouldn't have been surprised; Jake and I were reserved too. We were staunch homebodies — recluses, even. So, as his or her mother, it was my duty to dack myself, spread my legs and wear the guilt of an entire bottle of ultrasound gel emptied on and inside my body.

The sonographer probed deeper, causing me to dig my heels into the vinyl examination couch and involuntarily push myself upward.

'See these three lines on the screen here?' she asked.

'Yeah,' I replied.

'They're suggestive of a little girl.'

'Really?'

'Just roll away from me one more time. Let's see if we can turn bubs over so we can see *her* heart.'

'So, it's definitely a girl?'

'Well, as definite as I can be.'

'Oh. Cool.'

The obstetrician passed me some tissues – nowhere near enough – to mop up the ultrasound gel on my belly and in my crotch. Instead of receiving the news with joy, some deep-down part of me recoiled at the word the obstetrician had cooed: *girl*.

As I emptied the tissue box, I glanced over at Jake, who was smiling.

A few nights before, we had played Monopoly. Unfortunately for Jake, I acquired the lucrative yellow, green and blue properties and promptly built hotels on them. I used a phrase from family Monopoly games in my childhood to gleefully trash-talk him: 'You're going to sut your kundi!' A mix of Kannada and English, it meant: 'You're going to burn your bum.' In other words, 'This is going to hurt.'

Jake burned his bum *a lot,* and even though he collected $200 every time he passed GO he lost too much money to recover. Shuffling his cards and paper bills into a pile, ready to pack up, he said, 'There's no coming back from this. You win.' Having jeered at each other down to the last moment, I was overcome with childish pity and I refused to let him formally concede defeat.

'No, no, no! Hold on, let's mortgage your properties and see if that helps!'

'Doesn't matter, I'm still going to lose.'

'No, you won't! I'm making a donation to you. Here!' I said in all seriousness.

'Babe! It's okay! It's just a game!'

'No! I have to go to the toilet now and before I do I am going to bequeath all of my fortune to you. Now we both win.'

The emotion that came with giving my wealth away to be able to see Jake 'win', contrived as his triumph was, revisited me in the ultrasound room. I tried to stop the callous thoughts that followed. *Having a daughter is not a matter of losing or drawing!* I told myself, appalled by my gut reaction. *Oh God, can she hear me?* I knew my baby couldn't perceive my thoughts, but could she feel my cortisol levels rising? *Hello?* I called out telepathically. *Just in case I'm wrong and you can, in fact, hear my thoughts, I want you to know that I'm not stressed because of you. It's not that I won't love you or I don't want you. I am just so afraid of messing up your life.*

I tried to focus on Jake, who was grinning at the thought of fathering a girl, and open myself up to the idea. I knew it shouldn't matter if my baby was a boy or a girl – or both or neither, though I'd barely paused to consider that possibility. But I couldn't ignore the feeling of a stalactite protruding from the bottom of my throat downward into the centre of my being, precariously suspended above my baby. Clearing my throat, I directed my awareness back to the obstetrician.

As far as she could tell, the baby looked healthy, so we were to come back in a few months for the next major ultrasound. I thanked her and excused myself. Then I turned to Jake. 'I have to go to the toilet now. Meet you in the foyer?'

'No worries. Take your time,' he said.

3

Dharwad

A month before the ultrasound, Jake and I had braced ourselves at our dining table.

'What the ... WHAT?' Maya stood up with such force that she almost knocked her chair over. Tears spilled down her face as she backed up against the wall. 'Guys, don't lie to me. Guys, I swear! If you're playing a joke it's not funny!'

Jake and I just laughed.

'Stop it! You know I'm gullible!'

'Nah, it's true, we're having a baby' Jake said.

I gave my overwhelmed baby sister – twenty-one at the time – a cuddle and because she was slightly shorter than me, I patted the top of her head. Her lustrous satin hair was like our mother's. I, on the other hand, had inherited our father's dense, wavy locks along with most of his physical features: 'mund moog' – blunt nose – as Ma called it, fleshy lips and rounded eyebrows framing big, circular eyes on an almost perfectly spherical head. Everything as round as round could be. He was Jupiter and I, Ganymede.

In contrast, Ma's sharper, more delicate features made her a more eligible candidate for the crown of Indian femininity than me. Maya had all of our mother's daintiness, from actual edges on her face down to her narrow feet: the whole shebang except for Ma's aquiline nose – a fact that Ma and her sisters openly teased Pa about. One thing the four of us did have in common was our smallness, and we all overcompensated for it in some way. Our tiny Ma spoke with volume and gusto that defied the laws of physics. Though I stopped growing upward in Year 6, my unrealistic daydreams unfurled hundreds of kilometres in every direction and kept going, much to the chagrin of my super-pragmatic father. Pa bore cultural and familial burdens as a son, son-in-law, older brother, husband and father that his shoulders and certainly his heart were not equipped to carry. And Maya was in a permanent state of emotional overflow: a waterfall throwing out rainbows,

Disney music, smiles and happiness. 'Maya has a wet face again,' we'd always joke, because she processed every emotion through her tear ducts. Sad? Cry. Happy? Cry. Ma and Pa called Maya their 'delicate darling', and though they told her to harden up at times, we all admired the extravagance of her empathy.

'When are we telling Ma and Pa you're preggers?' Maya asked, once the waterworks had somewhat subsided and she was capable of coherent speech again.

'Eventually...' I said. 'You know what it's like. We can't tell Pa and ask him to keep it a secret from Ma. And when Ma knows, all of Melbourne and Dharwad will know in a matter of hours.'

***

I'd travelled to India throughout my childhood and into my mid-twenties – through Maharashtra, Karnataka and Kerala – but by the time I was pregnant, it had been more than a decade since I'd set foot in the town where I was born, Dharwad; the town where I spent my first year of life before emigrating to Melbourne.

To my child self, Dharwad was a whimsical, bustling place of dirt roads, sinewy trees, bright bougainvilleas and colourful houses. Paan wallas, coconut wallas and ice-cream wallas were beacons of refreshment amid the ceaseless, turgid flow of people, scooters, motorbikes, trucks and auto-rickshaws. Women strolled around in vibrant cotton and silk chudidhars and sarees, often with sweet-scented jasmine in their hair. Every morning and afternoon, a flurry of students, all in white shirts, spilled out onto the roads like the wind had blown thousands of dandelion parachutes into the air.

During my school holidays at the end of 1998, before I started Year 4, my family left Melbourne summer behind for an Indian winter – hardly an adjustment – and made our way to Ajji's bungalow in Dharwad. Every few years, my grandmother's home became the epicentre to which her children and grandchildren returned from all over the world – a change that was all the more welcome after my Ajja passed away.

My favourite part of Ajji's place was the indoor courtyard, around which the rest of the house was built. Overhead was a vast light well that let fresh air and sunlight in from the terrace. My parents once recorded me dancing to *Muqabala* under the light well on a sweltering day, wearing nothing but my chuddie. Other recordings catch me harassing Ricky the cat, coddling her to near-death, hoping that my blithe rendition of 'There were Ten in the Bed' would ease her distress. When I wasn't choking the shit out of poor Ricky, I ran up and down the cement staircase that wrapped around the outside of the house with Maya and our cousins. The terrace overlooked a floral part of the town among churches, hospitals and schools. Up there, we made up games in the company of Ajji's palm tree, whose coconut water we enjoyed from time to time before drifting along swells of heat toward our next adventure in the humidity.

During the holidays, the sleepy kitchen below us transformed into a heaving food-manufacturing plant, churning out fresh snacks and meals at all hours for the children and husbands of Ajji's three daughters.

After two long flights between Melbourne and Mumbai, my body greeted the hot, rich air of India like an old friend. It was a physical sense of recognition: of my boundaries – the very pores of my skin – opening to absorb the world around me. That feeling was rare during my childhood in Melbourne, but about fifteen degrees north of the equator, just under the Tropic of Cancer, it was as though my spirit heaved a sigh of repose. *Ah. I was born here.* Exiting the airport's customs area was always a nerve-wracking exercise. I kept my head down and pretended not to see or hear my squealing aunties, Helen and Sybil. But when I finally stood in front of them, my heart would somersault as the welcoming ceremony began with much hugging, cheek-squeezing and repeated exclamations of 'Ayo! I missed you *so* much!'

My aunties lived with their in-laws in Maharashtra, slightly north of

Karnataka. So it made sense for our family of four to fly to Mumbai instead of Bengaluru, then hire a van with Helen, Sybil and their three kids for a riotous Dharwad-bound road trip. Most importantly, Ma wanted to inject her biennial stimulus package into Mumbai's retail economy before she faced the more limited shopping options in Dharwad (not that this stopped her from going shopping almost every single day in Dharwad).

    Ma dropped off her bags at the hotel and made a beeline to the shops, where she left a trail of freshly exchanged rupees at the clothing, homewares and jewellery stores in her wake. Everything was so much cheaper in India. Ma's affinity for gold was the bane of my existence and I'd be climbing the velvet walls of her favourite jewellery stores while she admired the goods. Meanwhile my aunties, though weary from travelling, remained ebullient. They were more content to bask in their indomitable eldest sister's rare presence than in the glow of the yellow metal she hungered for.

The saree boutiques were a different story: nowhere else could I lounge on a daybed with my aunties and mum, *in a shop,* with a fan blowing in my face. As we reclined, our own personal customer service assistant unfurled resplendent sarees before us, one by one, as selected by the women. Sometimes I was allowed to choose ghagras if they stocked children's sizes. Us kids followed Ma around, buoyed by bribes of Pepsi, Limca, Amla Supari and Alpenliebe toffees. Only when she was satisfied with her purchases (and the rest of us were dying from exhaustion) could we embark on our journey to Ajji's kingdom of chapatis, chucklies, ladoos and karchikais in Dharwad.

Ajji's house never got old – literally. In the same way that the human body replaces most of its cells every seven to fifteen years, her bungalow underwent a thorough rejuvenation whenever her descendants were due home. She hired tradies to give the whole interior *and* facade, including the decorative iron bars on the windows, a fresh coat of paint. She even had the living area retiled several times. The most vocal dissident to Ajji's renovations was Ma, despite the fact she was the only daughter to have inherited Ajji's ability to make money combust as soon as she touched it. 'MOMMY! You don't need to change the house every time we come back to Dharwad! Stop wasting your pension money!' They'd shout and argue until Ajji wanted to commit arson on her own property for all the wasted effort. Even when my pugnacious family wasn't yelling in disagreement, they yelled because it was their standard means of communication.

Evening was the only time of day when the yawping quietened down, the women's eyes glued to the television in the corner of the sunken lounge. On those balmy nights the warm breeze floated in through the open doors, windows and light well. The grown-ups would recline after a day of feverish shopping before or after visits to family and friends, their brains melting into the TV. Whenever Helen Aunty's husband, Manoj Uncle, took a break from running the interstate family business to join us in Dharwad, he was in charge of preparing paan for the adults. If Uncle hadn't picked up some from a paan walla while on his daytime errands, he would make them himself. He once explained to me that paan was the Indian equivalent of an after-dinner mint. That night I followed him into Ajji's kitchen and watched him lay out a betel leaf and slaked lime on top, followed by a sprinkling of spices, areca nuts and a spoonful of candied rose petals. He made one for me too. I declined but he insisted. He was a kindred shouty spirit to my mother, able to overpower others with sheer vocal volume.

'Try! Just try, Ruhi! If you don't like, then, okay! But you must try!' To someone unaccustomed to eating paan, doing so felt like biting down on sweet and spicy glass shards wrapped in a leaf. I spat it out immediately and hyperventilated over my bleeding mouth. Turns out, areca nuts will challenge your teeth to a duel to the death and slaked lime just turns your spit red.

My cousins and I played on the floor among the adults, who sat around us like a caravan of camels, chewing paan for what seemed like an eternity. At the risk of setting off the cacophony again or having something thrown at us, we smugly pointed out the plot holes and implausibility of their TV series, especially with Ajji's favourite, *Kyunki Saas Bhi Kabhi Bahu Thi.* Afterward, we hung up Christmas decorations as carols played in the background. We would eat dinner at around nine o'clock and we got used to late nights. It was a bummer going to bed after all the fun with my cousins, but even sleep was eventful. Sometimes all the grandchildren crowded into Ajji's huge bedroom for a slumber party, at the cost of enduring her snoring, which sounded like an oversized bee stuck inside a dagga.

Ajji woke up at 5am sharp daily, while it was still dark. Before she ate or did anything else, she lit her kerosene lantern and read her Bible at the dining table. Then, she lowered herself to the floor, onto her knees and forearms. With her hands in prayer and her head bowed, she fervently presented to God her list of needs, which covered every one of her relatives' lists of needs too. With a family as populous as ours, it's no wonder she regularly ran out of breath as she prayed.

Ajji was a boulder of a woman – even more so when she was curled up on the floor. Her exterior had hardened over her years spent with an alcoholic, violent father, then with a psychologically and verbally abusive mother-in-law whom Ajji cared for in her own home until my great-grandmother died in her nineties. Though Ajji was rock-hard to everyone else, she was more like crème brûlée to her grandchildren; we could crack through her thin, burnt-sugar skin and inside was sweet, milky custard.

The walls in the section of the house where Ajji would pray were painted two colours: the bottom half was cornflower-blue and the top mauve – just like Ajji was one colour when in a submissive prayer position on the floor and another when she was upright, ready to face the day as a powerful matriarch. I couldn't always wake up in time to join Ajji for her morning prayers but I felt deeply accomplished whenever I did, as though I'd fulfilled an important duty as her eldest granddaughter. Enduring the cold of the newly installed tiles next to her became my offering, after the decades of dark mornings she had spent interceding for us. Soon, the first rays of dawn streamed in through the light well. In the morning air, flavours from Ajji's cooking the day before mixed with the aromas of deep-fried street food, coffee, spices and, at times, cows passing by. When I was with Ajji, she wrapped up with a short, simple prayer that I could repeat after her in Kannada. *God, please bless my family. Keep us safe. Give us good health. Help me obey my mother and father and help me with my studies.* Amen was said. Ajji stood up and the day commenced.

The milkman would arrive shortly afterward, handing out one-litre sachets of fresh milk. Ajji would purchase seven to ten, depending on whether her sons-in-law were staying as well. She'd instruct me to cut open the sachets and empty them into a huge cauldron-like pot, ready to transform into fragrant masala chai. She threw in the tea leaves, ginger, cardamom, cinnamon, cloves and unbelievable amounts of sugar. She then made preparations for breakfast, whether we were having Bombay toast, Anda Boorji, Uppit Sheera or Idli Sambar. Her servants would soon arrive, ready to mop the floors, make the beds and help her with the rest of the day's cooking.

'Ajji, isn't it bad to have servants? Like slaves?' I once queried.

'No, Ruhi, they are not slaves. They are workers. Poor ladies. When they come and work, I give them money and they can send their children to school.'

I was relieved: I knew Ajji was a benevolent person who usually wouldn't take advantage of others. Although, I never did ask her how much she paid them. And I didn't appreciate the way they weren't allowed to sit on any of Ajji's furniture, instead forced to relax only on the kitchen floor or outdoors during lunch breaks. Whenever I questioned the inequality, I was reminded about how the servants in Ajji's house worked in vastly better conditions than those in other homes, where they were most likely abused. 'God knows how they treat those poor ladies, worse than animals!' Still, the way my family saw Ajji's servants and spoke to them was disconcerting – ordering them around as if they were lesser and undeserving of the same dignity a privileged little 'foreigner'[1] kid, like myself, enjoyed. I noticed India's hierarchies within hierarchies. Even those of us in Ajji's Protestant middle-class household, precariously exempt from India's violent caste system as part of the vastly outnumbered Christian community, enjoyed social superiority because of the servants who worked there.

Once the servants were deployed on the day's to-do lists, Ajji would fire up the stove while the rest of the household remained in a fog of slumber. I could hear the Islamic morning prayers in the distance. I found it comforting to listen to their graceful chanting as it floated over the morning birdsong and the growl of hefty trucks on the nearby highway. I had no clue

---

[1] Family and friends who lived in India often jokingly referred to Maya and me as 'foreigners'.

where it was coming from or how they projected the sound but I liked to imagine a Muslim man at the top of a minaret, singing into a loudspeaker, serenading all of Dharwad during Fajr Namaz. Other family members didn't appreciate the songs of worship as much as I did. But if someone had asked Ajji to get up into a tower and sing her heart out to Jesus at five o'clock in the morning, she would have snatched up the opportunity and the whole family would have supported her. In our home, an unabashed intolerance – subtle in the presence of 'outsiders' – of other belief systems coloured our worldview, even though in some ways we *were* a microcosm of the religiopolitical tensions in our country.

Ajji and Ajja were staunch Protestants and had raised their children accordingly. Oh to be a fly on the wall when my brave Lingayat father waltzed in demanding their precious daughter's hand in marriage. Okay, he didn't demand. He requested. I knew this because, when I wasn't cooking with Ajji or playing with my cousins, I followed Helen Aunty and Sybil Aunty around, asking them all of my unanswered questions about the famous story of my parents' union in a time when 'love marriages' were even more taboo than they would be when I reached my twenties. I was drip-fed small details over time, like how Ma was eighteen and Pa was twenty-two when they first met in Dharwad. How Pa wrote romantic letters to Ma and she went to a secret location to pick up his phone calls every Friday from Germany, Saudi Arabia or wherever he was working at the time. My chest puffed up every time I heard stories about my once idealistic parents, fighting to preserve their love in the face of adversity. But as much as I relished the sagas of their amorous youth, even as a young child, I'd wonder how and when the plug was pulled to drain out all of the affection. Given that I was so often the topic of their arguments, I felt responsible for reversing the damage and helping them restore their marriage to its original glory. I often took it upon myself to plead with each of them to speak to one another again after hours or days of silence. As I got older, my role was expanded to include mediation and adjudication when either wanted an ally. And I was too afraid to find out what would happen if I didn't take the initiative to 'fix things'.

My aunties told me that after much ado, my parents defied distance and courtship traditions to finally marry. But not before a bloodbath of egos. It began when Pa moved away from his family in Hidkal Dam to Dharwad for further studies after Year 10. He'd hoped to become an engineer but he and his family were unable to fund his dreams of a university education. So he settled for a trade: toolmaking. Still, wherever he went to school, he was a top-ranked student who skipped entire year levels. He eventually joined the teaching staff at the college he graduated from, which stood opposite the primary school where Ma was a teacher. One day, he caught sight of the beauty that was Ma, a peacock among pigeons as far as he was concerned.

In Dharwad, everybody knew everybody. Ajji was a headmistress at another local school and she'd heard of

Pa's academic excellence – and his elegant penmanship, which saw her recruit him as a scribe in her home. Unbeknownst to Ajji, Pa was checking out her eldest daughter between sentences. He and Ma met in secret and got to know each other when Ajji and Ajja weren't around. Time passed and Pa worked up the confidence to tell Ma that he loved her and wished to marry her. After some initial trepidation, she decided she felt the same way and was all in.

When Ma and Pa confessed their feelings for each other to Ajji and Ajja, my grandparents mowed down each fresh, green blade of hope my parents had for their life together right down to the dirt. Though my dad was fit to work for my Ajji, he was not fit to marry her daughter, not with his lower-class, non-Christian background. Ajja, an influential man with friends in high places – for example, the board of my father's college – threatened to have Pa thrown out of work. It mustn't have helped that Ajja's rifle hung on the wall behind him when he ordered Pa to leave his daughter alone.

When Pa accepted that he couldn't realise his dream to marry Ma without unthinkable collateral damage to both families, he told her to move on and forget him. He wanted their relationship to work, but it was too risky in a society so viciously hostile toward not only 'love marriages', but also to interfaith and interclass marriages. If he dragged his family's honour through the dirt, he risked jeopardising his younger sisters' eligibility to marry into 'good' families. If Pa eloped with Ma against her parents' wishes, they may have disowned her, which he didn't want either. Ma's sisters would end up in the same predicament as his; once a family's name was tarnished, the only thing that could make it shiny again was status and wealth – things neither family possessed, especially Pa's much poorer side.

Ajji was merciless, pushing Ma to just *pick* a suitable guy (read: Christian, reasonably affluent) and marry him. Ajji and Ajja brought Ma proposals from several suitors, all dismal compared to Pa. Ma refused to bow down. Then one day, a divorcé ten years older than Ma had the opportunity to meet her. When asked what he thought of her, he said, to her face, that she was 'okay but a little too short' for his liking.

Ma fulminated. She had been teased for her compact stature in the schoolyard. She wasn't going to marry someone who judged her for her height like a primary schooler. She told Ajja and Ajji that if they wanted her to get married at all, they'd have to let her pick the skinny Lingayat dude in bell-bottoms who did Ajji's writing for her.

Ajji and Ajja had hoped she'd fall into line, like a good Indian daughter was expected to do. Ma, on the other hand, had calculated that keeping the peace in those moments wasn't worth the lifetime of regret she'd face if she let go of Pa. Ajji and Ajja reluctantly ceded, knowing that an unmarried first daughter reflected worse on their family than one married to an undesirable man. Their caveat? Pa was to be baptised before marrying their daughter in a traditional Protestant ceremony at their church. Looking at their wedding photos, I could detect the artificial joy on Ajji and Ajja's defeated faces. As for my parents, they hid the fireworks going off inside them from the cameras – Pa in his soft-grey suit and Ma in her elegant lavender and silver reshmi saree, thick floral garlands weighing on their chests and around their necks. They weren't about to flaunt their glee and rub their salty victory into Ajja and Ajji's wounded pride. On the next page in the album, my parents' limbs were looser and their facial muscles more relaxed in photos of their honeymoon in the hill station of Ooty, safely folded within rows and rows of burgeoning tea leaves, away from their parents.

My paternal grandparents knew nothing of their son finding himself a wife. They continued with business as usual in a faraway village. Pa intended to keep it that way until he'd fulfilled his responsibility to get his younger siblings educated and married. All that my paternal Ajji and Ajja knew was that Pa was earning money from his job and sending most of it back home to support the family. They had no idea just *how* productive their son was, especially on his honeymoon. For exactly nine months and nine days later, I arrived. And Pa's parents were clueless about their new grandkid on the block for several years.

Pa didn't like to talk about his choice to keep me a secret from his parents, or how they found out long after we'd left for Australia. My aunties had made it sound like Pa's parents had accepted my existence without a problem when they inevitably did find out. That may well have been the case: Pa was the fifth child in a litter of nine – surely no one was still counting grandchildren on his side of the family at that point. Still, I found it difficult to believe that their reaction was naught but a smile and nod.

Helen Aunty and Sybil Aunty could only tell me these exciting stories when Pa wasn't around to hush them or change the subject – when he'd dropped us off in Dharwad and set off to make the rounds to branches of his extended family without us. (I supposed he was concerned about us kids not being able to cope with the extensive travel across potholed dirt roads, especially since a slight bump was all it took for young Maya to vomit her guts out).

On one trip to Dharwad, when I was eight years old, I became obsessed with Indian money. I figured: if one Australian dollar was equivalent to thirty Indian rupees, I was rich in this country. I pestered my parents for a few rupees for trips to the milk bar or the ice-cream parlour across from Ajji's house. When they gave me a few coins here and there, I devoutly placed them in a small brown leather zip-pouch Ajja had given me when he was still alive.

Early one morning, I was woken by Pa. I opened my eyes to find him kneeling beside the bed, his silhouette fuzzy in the dark. He whispered goodbye to me and I asked a final time, 'Pa, can you please stay, or at least take me with you?' I felt safer and calmer when he was around in Dharwad; after Ajja's death – and given that I wasn't close with my aunty's husbands – Pa being 'the man of the house' provided a sense of security in this place where women were believed to be in need of male protectors. He shook his head, saying it would be best for me to stay there and look after Ma and Maya. He told me he'd return in a few weeks and that I could speak to him over the phone in the meantime. He then handed me a roll of notes amounting to five hundred rupees and told me I could spend it however I wanted, but to do so wisely. Then he stood up, turned and left. I squeezed his gift in my palm. My sleepy eyes welled up with tears and my heart with gratitude. It was an infinitesimal point in time when the chasm between us closed. Though I soon grew out of my rupee-collecting hobby, it was one of those rare times my father gifted me something I wanted, rather than something he thought was best for me. And it would be a long time before I would ever unpack my feelings around this, because I was supposed to be grateful that I had a father who gave me gifts in the first place or had a father at all.

As soon as I got out of bed, I stowed the wad of notes in my pouch and continued to take my money requests to Ajji, as I was unwilling to cut into my new stash and knew she would cave in a matter of seconds. She was thrilled to drop her poo change into my greedy little hands and I was ready to make it rain on our next escapade to the shops.

The auto-rickshaw stand was at the base of the sloping road that Ajji lived on. Autos were parked in a single file like a line of gleaming black-and-yellow bumblebees. Whenever we made our way to the stand, the drivers addressed me first because I ran ahead of the pack, secreting gullible-little-foreigner pheromones. One time, when we set out on a family excursion to the movies, I rushed down to the rickshaw stand. The driver parked at the front spotted me and hollered in Kannada, 'Yelle honti?!' *Where to?!*

'Lakshmi Talkies!' I shouted over the frenzy of the adjacent highway, as the wheels of passing vehicles catapulted chalky dirt into the air.

'Okay, hop in!'

'How much?' I asked, by way of imitating the grown-ups and not because I actually cared.

'One twenty rupai!'

'Okay! Thank you!' I spun around to the adults waddling down the hill and waved at them to hurry up. 'Ma! I got us an auto!' I called, chuffed with myself and ready to jump in.

'Wait!' Ma yelled back. 'How much?!'

'He said one hundred and twenty!'

She caught up and pierced the driver with an icy look. 'Make it fifty.' Embarrassed by her preposterous attempt at negotiation, my smile dropped. The man needed to fuel his vehicle and feed his family. He wasn't handing out free balloons.

'Sorry, madam, nobody will take you for fifty. Make it one hundred.'

I squeezed her arm and muttered, 'Ma! It's just three bucks. Give it to him!'

'Fifty or we'll take another auto.'

'Please, madam! Okay, eighty!'

'*Eighty?* Goodbye.' The woman was ruthless.

'OKAY, MADAM, OKAY! FIFTY!' he cried after her as she turned her back.

Ma nodded at the rest of us. It was okay to board.

Seven of us – three adults and four kids – piled into the petite vehicle designed to transport two adults at a time. It was exhilarating to ride around in doorless autos on treacherous Indian roads, exposed to the open, dusty air. They zipped and darted between the roaring, colourful freight trucks that snailed along the highways, painted like Chinese dragons and adorned with tinsel. When at first I was not used to autos, each ride felt like a near-death experience; indicators were optional, speed limits were only a guide and traffic signals were mostly decorative. And every time we disembarked, the grown-ups made fun of me for thanking the drivers so profusely as compensation for my mother's bartering.

Going to the movies in Dharwad back in the nineties was pandemonium. I'd forgotten that the enormous theatres at Lakshmi Talkies were built to accommodate hordes of fans. All of them were as keen as my mother to see their favourite Bollywood star with a six-pack – shirtless, oiled and glistening – open his arms wide to welcome the next big actress into his sexy embrace as fake wind, rain and smoke machines raged around them.

No wonder my parents thought the standard Village and Hoyts cinemas in Melbourne were puny. From the back, drunkards catcalled and smashed their glass bottles against the concrete steps whenever the female lead showed some skin while dancing. As they carried on, audience members in the front and middle rows would yell back at them to shut up. Subtitles didn't just bridge the language gaps for me; they meant I could follow the plot over the disturbances of a highly participative audience.

At the conclusion of every film at Lakshmi Talkies, the jostling began. Like an enormous shoal of tuna, the crowd stood up and swam toward the doorway in unison. Unless there was a male family member with us, we made our way to and from our seats huddled together, kids in the middle of the circle guarded by our mums. At times like these I especially missed Pa. Ma, however, loved reliving her teen years – albeit with a couple of dependents in tow – with weekly visits to the talkies, where her troubles dissolved and she became engrossed in the murder mysteries or stories of star-crossed lovers. She was in awe of the latest fashion and jewellery adorning the actresses, the male lovers whose tenderness and passion she'd once hoped her future husband would emulate, the choreography and the foreign locations.

Back in Melbourne, she regularly complained that Pa didn't take her out to the movies enough. To my chagrin (because I was the self-appointed moral police of the family at the time) she compensated by purchasing pirated DVDs.

'You do realise these DVDs are illegal, Ma?' I'd say scornfully.

'No, they're not! I bought them!'

'Just because you bought them doesn't mean they were sold legally.' Those anti-piracy ads before every Hollywood movie at Australian cinemas were lost on Ma. Then again, she might have got the message if Pa took her every week, like she wanted him to.

'I paid for it! I didn't steal it!' she'd insist.

'How much did you pay?'

'$2 or $3.'

'Yeah, well you basically paid for someone else to steal it for you and make copies.'

'EH! HOGA!' HOGA was her staccato sound of dismissal, a mangled version of the 'proper' word, hōga (with an elongated 'o') which, in Kannada, meant 'Go'. When Ma shouted it, HOGA (pronounced hog-AH!), it meant 'Stop spewing rubbish. Bugger off and make yourself useful.'

Pirated or not, Hindi movies brought my family together. Even the ones Pa could point to and say, 'What rubbish is this behaviour?' in the hope that Maya and I would learn what *not* to do. We'd all turn to one another during the bits that made us laugh and wheeze until our bellies ached, our conspiratorial eye contact throwing more joy on the bonfire. And when we all stared into the screen during the sombre scenes, blue light illuminating our faces in the dark, I'd glance over and see shiny tears surreptitiously spill from my parents' eyes. I saw so much more of them in those moments than their sorrow for the characters. My parents barely processed the heartache from their own lives, unless it came out in an explosion. Instead, their hurt pooled into a heavy goblet inside each of their chests. During these tearful moments in front of the TV, they tilted forward and seemed to pour a little grief out over the place where their wedding garlands once sat. I knew because I felt the same way. We all saw ourselves in the characters who desperately yearned for what they couldn't have: freedom, respect, unconditional love or, most unattainable, a future that followed a script.

***

Back in Dharwad in 1991, my parents had thought their prayers were answered when they received a letter saying that their Australian visa application was approved. They believed the grass was infinitely greener across the Indian Ocean, blissfully unaware of how prickly it was going to be. I was one year old, Ma was twenty-three and Pa was twenty-seven when we boldly bade farewell to Dharwad. As they took their last footsteps on their motherland before boarding their flight, they dug their fingernails into their Indianness, willing themselves to hold on no matter what came. The only things heavier than their luggage were their ambitions for the fledgling little non-resident Indian (NRI) in their care.

They probably thought that the distance would defuse the family drama. Alas, they were severely underprepared for the sequel to their own Bollywood epic.

4

Unhappy little Vegemite

Jake and I bought our house a month before our wedding day and almost five years before the pregnancy. Our parents showed up to support us at the auction, except for Pa, who unsurprisingly didn't approve of our decision to buy a house at the time. Though Pa's absence stung, once we'd signed the papers I still had to stop myself from twirling with glee around our new beach cottage, as I called it, in front of the real estate agents. It couldn't have been more perfect, with its sixties redwood flooring, white walls and ornate timber brackets framing the doorways. The exterior was also white with a charming front door, embellished with blue stained glass and an old painted floral tile displaying our house number.

The house sat on a rainbow street of pink Japanese magnolias, flaming red canna lilies, vibrant birds of paradise, hibiscus and a hundred varieties of roses. From our place, the street snaked downhill and opened its mouth wide to the bay at the end. Mynas, magpies, lorikeets and rosellas serenaded us daily through the open kitchen window, a pleasant soundtrack over the buzz of the exhaust fan and appliances. That is, until our dog Panda ruined it. Panda had strong beliefs: no birds allowed in or near our courtyard; anything that fell to the ground immediately became property of Panda; all farts were to be investigated; singing or dancing wasn't allowed (except for the times one of us picked up our twenty-five-kilo ball of fluff and included her in the dance); and sneezing was a sin. Needless to say, we let her down on a daily basis.

Four years and a few months of daily disappointments later, Jake and I committed the ultimate betrayal: our family was about to grow, which meant our wilful, sassy Panda would have to share the spotlight.

***

Fairness and equality: the values that underpinned every Friday movie night in our household. If Jake chose the genre, I selected three movies from that genre, from which Jake would take the final pick, and vice versa. Pregnant and wanting a trigger to release the surfeit of emotion dammed up inside me, I gave him these options within the drama category: *Baabul, Veer-Zaara* and *Kal Ho Naa Ho.* All well-known tearjerkers.

Veer-Zaara it was. My face, chest, sleeves and Jake's shoulder were all drenched that night. Even as someone who almost never cried, Jake was moved to tears by the end. Seeing Zaara accompany Veer back to his home, a village in Chandigarh, made me wonder if I might ever take my little family back to Dharwad after the birth of our baby. But I didn't get very far with that thought before painful memories set in.

It was still on my mind the following morning while I grabbed breakfast. As I waited for my toast, I leaned against the kitchen bench and stared out the window at the overgrown ivy along our back fence. I was sipping from a glass of coconut water I'd bought to satisfy my weekend craving – or to at least come close with a packaged and shelved substitute. Indulging in the tastes of my early youth, it was a perfect moment of peace – if only a moment. All I could think about was the pinging in my head, like strings breaking on a harp. Something inside me was coming undone as I contemplated one day showing my daughter around the small wonders of the world as I knew it, things like fresh coconut water.

My daughter.
A girl.

This inconvenient truth quietly scissored its way through my mental and emotional stability which were already in tatters. Exercise was supposed to be helping with my stress levels but even that was proving too little now. A couple of years before the pregnancy, Jake and I decided to join a gym together. During our first session with our personal trainer, Jenn, we learned that she was a competitive bodybuilder intent on two things: turning us into bodybuilders and making us vomit. Despite having my guts in my throat at the end of most sessions, I thrived on weight training: anything that meant I didn't have to run, do burpees or any sort of cardio that involved getting smacked in the face with my own boobs. I found myself wanting to be less like the slender female models mainstream media worshipped and more like Arnold Schwarzenegger and Dwayne Johnson. I focused on the larger-than-life murals of Arnie and the Rock painted on the gym's brick walls as I breathed and growled through my circuits. My traps were popping, my hamstrings almost gained sentience and though I used to relish the delightful little spanks on my bottom when Jake walked past, I enjoyed it even more when he hurt his hand on my rock-hard glutes.

At Jenn's insistence, she wrote up a meal plan for us. She spat a mouthful of sandwich out when we told her we wanted it to be plant-based. So in the two years leading up to the pregnancy, I filled up on blueberries, tofu, black beans, sweet potato, whole carbs and an abundance of greens. Knowing that it was only a matter of time, I read Dr Michael C Lu's book, *Get Ready to Get Pregnant,* in which he asserted that, 'Even early prenatal care is too late.' So with a head-start of two years, which, technically, was still not enough for Dr Lu, I increased my intake of omega-3 fatty acids, antioxidants and anti-inflammatory foods and did everything possible to decrease stress, toxins and those dreaded dioxins. Eventually deciding that Jenn's diet was a tad too restrictive and unbearably bland (even with its 'cheat days'), I regularly incorporated other flavoursome meals in, at times asking Malee Aunty for Thai recipes and other times calling Ma for her South Indian recipes, which was a radical exercise in patience on any given day.

***

'*Please* – how many times do I have to ask you to show your daughter how to cook?' Pa asked Ma in the kitchen of the Stone Fruit House, flashing me a look of frustration.

'She can sit here and watch me!' Ma shouted over the whistling idli steamer and the exhaust fan, which was on full blast.

'No, you need to involve her! Make her do some of it. Only then will she learn properly,' he insisted.

'HOGA! I don't have time! It will all be delayed if I have to teach her on top of preparing everything!'

Pa sighed.

To placate him, she called me over, rushed me through making oollies (small round balls of chapati dough), then said, 'Okay, go back to your studies. I will quickly finish the rest.'

Pa shook his head.

'She will not learn properly this way. We must teach her now, while she is young. Otherwise, what will she do after marriage? Come here, Ruhi.' Pa appointed himself my culinary tutor.

I was about midway through primary school when Pa gave me my first chapati-making lesson. He pulled me aside to a small section of bench that Ma wasn't using and showed me how much water to add to the atta. He then sprinkled in a pinch of salt and demonstrated the kneading before leaving it to sit for a while. Next, he divided it into oollies, then rolled them into flat circles. He used a miniature spoon to measure sunflower oil from a matching miniature bowl and spread some over each doughy circle. He folded each circle in half, and half again, to create a triangle. This step gave the final chapati its padhar (layers), he told me. Then he showed me how to press down on the corners with a rolling pin and, making sure to keep the middle slightly thicker than the edges, roll the triangle out into a larger, thinner circle. I was mesmerised by the care he took with each step. He approached most activities in life in this way.

In contrast, Ma cracked whips and ripped every chore off like a bandaid.

'Lagoo, lagoo!' she'd shout. *Hurry, hurry!*

Relatives on my mother's side of the family were likely to tack 'Lagoo, lagoo!' onto the end of most sentences, because to them *everything* in life was urgent. Somehow, it failed to increase efficiency in pretty much any scenario.

When Pa made toast, he spread the butter to each edge in an even layer before he cut down the middle, ensuring that both pieces were of equal proportion. Ma, however, would slather on the jam and shove the toast at whichever child needed feeding, simultaneously investigating the fridge for leftover cheesecake. When restaurants served buffets, she always collected her dessert platter before starting her entree. Pa was a vegetarian – initially for religious reasons then due to preference when, upon arriving in Australia, he decided he wasn't a fan of the McChicken burger Ma persuaded him to try – and always began with a plate full of salad. Ma was a woman who savoured the pleasures of life and rushed through the valleys between the summits. To her dismay, Pa resided in the valleys and looked up at mountaintops with suspicion.

With patience levels like that, I couldn't imagine how Ma managed the early days of her career as a teacher in Dharwad. It blew my mind to think about her facing a classroom of seventy students. Then again, teachers in Dharwad were allowed to use corporal punishment. It was easier to picture her at work once I knew that her job involved beating the crap out of any kid who dared to cross her boundaries. On the rare occasions when she did show me how to cook, the lessons were a flurry with no time for me to commit anything to memory and certainly no time for me to gauge a clear idea of measurements.

'Just half a finger,' she'd say, helpfully holding up her smaller-than-average fingers.

'So, one teaspoon?' I'd ask, writing it down.

It was too late; she was already onto the next step.

'Okay – one spoon jeergi, one spoon chilli powder.'

'Ma, wait! What's jeergi?'

'Cumin. Okay next, some poppy seeds. You must fry quickly.'

'Ma! Hold on! Is it a tablespoon or a teaspoon?'

'EH! You're asking too many questions! Just look at how much I'm putting with my hands!'

'But I won't remember how much you held in your hand when I make it on my own. Plus, your hands are tiny compared to mine!'

'Yawa! I'll teach you another time! Go study!' End of lesson.

No matter how tricky it proved to be, absorbing the art of Indian cooking from one's mother was a rite of passage for many Indian girls my age. If parents were progressive enough, it was part of an Indian boy's upbringing too. But this was rare. In Pa's case, he had learned by necessity; with so many mouths to feed in his family, everyone was expected to pitch in. He gleaned his gastronomical education from watching his mother and sisters, as well as from Kannada cookbooks he brought over from India.

Of Ajji's three daughters, Ma was the only one who didn't inherit their mother's obsession with cooking, nor did she retain any knowledge Ajji tried to impart to her when she happened to saunter through the kitchen between games of Kabaddi or Khō-Khō with her friends. Ajja wasn't much help to Ajji either. According to Ma, she was his favourite child. When she complained about having to cook, Ajja gladly intervened, maintaining that his darling girl should be allowed to play or study instead. So Ajji ended up giving up on Ma and diverting her efforts toward her younger sisters instead.

This meant Ma started from scratch when she arrived in Melbourne without her mother and servants and had to learn to cook. Pa taught Ma how to make chapatis to get her started; everything else was self-taught. Still, Ma loathed cooking. She did it entirely out of a sense of duty toward her young family. Despite her late start, she became a truly accomplished South Indian cook. Apart from Malee Aunty, who both my mother and I revered for her unmatched Southeast Asian dishes, none of my many aunties measured up to Ma when it came to cooking.

Though Ma never looked forward to preparing dinner every day after work, I *always* looked forward to eating it. Pa was also magnificent in the kitchen – a fact I only registered when Ma was overseas with Maya and he cooked for us both. When Ma returned, Pa went back to being her assistant: chopping vegetables and preparing rice and other components of the meal. He enjoyed cooking, but he and Ma initially eschewed a fairer divide of household labour in favour of traditional gender roles. Each day she pushed herself to overcome her disdain for domesticity in order to put food on the table, as Indian women were expected to do in India. She didn't want the shame of her husband cooking for us: that was her job and she held to it tightly. Even back then, it saddened Maya and me to know that if they'd had it in them to resist some of their cultural norms, Pa might have delighted in cooking for his family and Ma in maintaining the garden instead. But any role-swapping, unless a spouse had taken ill, reflected poorly on the family. Or so they believed.

Unlike Ma, cooking and baking genuinely intrigued me. I was fascinated with all the flavours, smells, colours and textures that raw ingredients could be transformed into. On Saturdays, when Pa went to work and Ma slept in, I'd sometimes break the rules and use the stove unsupervised to rustle up pancakes the way my cousin, Jia, and her mum, Vaani Aunty, had once showed me on a sleepover. We would have milk and eggs but I'd have to mix in the atta we used for chapatis instead of self-raising flour. One morning Ma woke up to find atta and milk all over the bench. She hunted me down to find something even worse than just her kid eating lumpy, unauthorised pancakes in front of the TV: snips of paper and tiny balls of discarded sticky tape were strewn across the floor. I'd made a full-body Care Bear costume entirely from paper. Ma found me shoving pancakes through the mouth hole of my Tender Heart paper mask while I watched the *Care Bears* on video.

Given my propensity for mess-making and predictable unwillingness to tidy up afterward, I soon learned it was safer to watch TV chefs. But the more I watched, the more I became disheartened: Geoff Jansz, Huey and Fast Ed possessed a huge variety of kitchen tools that I didn't have access to. I was captivated by the sound and movement of their neat wooden spoons in a hundred different sizes of Pyrex glass bowls; each ingredient being poured from a smaller glass bowl to a larger one. At home all of our utensils were steel or aluminium, apart from two wooden spatulas that were yellowing from turmeric on the handles and charred black at their ends. The TV chefs used herbs I'd never heard of. What on earth were parsley and tarragon, rosemary, oregano and ... time? The only herbs we used at home were kothambari (coriander) and sabasgi (dill). *One day, I thought. One day I'll have 'proper' cooking utensils and all the herbs – especially t-h-y-m-e!*

On our weekly trips to the shopping centre, I would look into windows of homewares stores and pine for flat non-stick pans, muffin trays, whisks and loaf and cake tins. No one else in my family cared for baking; we always bought birthday cakes from the local cake shop. Even though Ma was a bakery assistant during her first couple of years in Melbourne and brought home the most delectable croissants, our own home oven was relegated as a storage place for large platters.

My family's apathy toward baked goods and my desire to enjoy food from other cultures, instead of the usual South Indian meant I would overcompensate whenever I had the chance to eat anything beyond our household's norm. I developed an uncontrollable impulse to gorge on these unusual, exciting foods. Every time I went to a friend's house, I'd go to town on the chips, spring rolls, pizza, pasta, lollies, cupcakes and party pies their parents made available to us. To town! *Probably going to be ages before I get to have this again,* I would tell myself.

I'd later learn these binge-fests were more than a bid to quench my taste buds' wanderlust.

***

The feeding (fattening) had begun early. I was an 'overweight' baby because in our culture, the chubbier babies were, the healthier they were considered.

One day in a Year 2 maths class, we students had to weigh ourselves and measure our height. Upon realising that I was one of the heavier kids in the class at twenty-seven kilos (and not accounting for the fact that my build was stronger and stockier than most of the other children's) my new year's resolution that year and every year thereafter was to lose twelve kilos: one per month. It was a goal I never achieved. Also that year, a boy in my class whom I had a crush on, Andrew Huynh, shouted the whole class icy-poles in a moment of generosity. As he handed them out to the line of children before him, he skipped over me, saying, 'You need to lose some weight first.'

I wasted hours, days, weeks, months, decades, wishing my healthy, beautiful little body away for a skinnier version – so much so that when I was hospitalised in India at the age of twelve for food poisoning, I rejoiced at having lost eight kilos over the ordeal. Still, my weight loss goal increased with each year: twelve kilos became twenty, then thirty, then forty.

My parents, aunties and uncles weren't much help, though they meant well and firmly believed they had the answers to questions I had not asked. They tried to motivate me to lose more weight faster, which only screwed with my body image even more. I was constantly confronted with comments like 'You'll look nicer if you lose weight,' or 'As a girl you should be more delicate,' or 'Look at Preeti, she looks nice in anything she wears – if you lose weight, you can do the same.'

If we were at a party and I went to the buffet to grab more 'fatty' foods than Ma deemed necessary, she'd reach out and smack my hand. It didn't matter who was watching or how embarrassed I felt. If she was sitting on the couch with a bunch of aunties and from a distance, saw me help myself to snacks, she'd shout across the room, 'RUHI! CONTROL YOURSELF!' At the same time, her antidote for bad days was always good food – especially on days when Pa unleashed his bottled-up anger on me.

'I'm making your favourite food for dinner. You'll feel better when you eat,' she'd say in consolation.

Aunties and uncles jokingly referred to my sister as Timon, and me as Pumbaa. When I complained about the teasing, I was told to lighten up, it was just a joke and anyway, I should have taken the comments in the 'right' spirit and turned them into motivation to lose weight. They talked about how I would grow up to be the smart one and Maya would be the tall, thin, pretty one. Then, one auspicious day, I received the nickname *Pailwaan,* partly due to my strength, but mostly because of my body shape. When they called me this word, which translates to *wrestler,* it wasn't an aspirational title. My relatives said it was an affectionate pet name, but I knew it was a humiliating reference to beefed-up, oiled-up Indian men who brandished clubs and wore nothing but red loincloths to wrestle. For a boy, this would have been a compliment. But to me, it was a taunt designed to ridicule me as a young woman for being more like a pailwaan than a dainty flower.

***

School didn't do my self-esteem any favours either. There, I was, a 'fatso' with 'poo-coloured skin', according to the most-observant and least-tactful arseholes in the playground. At our Catholic school mass, I couldn't recite the right responses by heart like most of my peers could, so I mimed gibberish. My parents didn't let me talk to boys and carefully vetoed nearly every party of the handful I'd been honoured enough to receive an invitation to.

Even my clothes looked different because my parents opted to buy the generic uniform available at 'general' uniform shops. Not only was it a few shades darker than the yellow and blue of the official uniform, but it was also missing the school emblem. The rip-off uniform was a constant visual reminder of my unbelonging. I knew Ma and Pa were trying to save money, but it didn't make me feel any better at the time. No matter how much I tried to fit in, my Indianness always seeped through, just as black shoe polish could never quite conceal the brown leather of my school shoes, which Ma had found on sale. I wished she'd just paid a bit more to buy me a pair of proper *black* shoes that year, as the school dress code required.

And just as at home, the hurtful comments often came back to food – but for different reasons. The chapatis and palle I ate at lunchtime were messier to eat than sandwiches, so I would have to walk away from the group I was playing with to wash my hands, instead of just getting up to play tiggy when I was done. Also, I was informed by other children that my food was smelly and that I was smelly, like my food. Nevermind that I secretly thought Ma's cooking was delicious. I lacked the confidence and the self-esteem to tell my peers that I liked my Indian food and that if they had a problem with it, they didn't have to stand there and watch me eat. I could have even offered to share some of the full-flavoured food I had the privilege of growing up eating. But that wasn't the direction of the current. I was a behind-child who had to catch up to 'Australian' culture and 'Australian' playground cuisine.

There was a brief moment in Year 3 when I temporarily caught up. It happened when the kindest teacher, Mrs Egan (also the first person in the world to call me 'talented'), opened a book called *The Witches* to read out to the class. I was sure that someone had misspelled the author's name on the cover; it was supposed to be *Dhal,* named after the lentil dish we ate every night. My mistaken belief that an Indian man had written a book that every Year 3 class was about to read somehow granted me permission to take up space at school. In Year 3 we also happened to spend a whole term learning about India, which required every student to produce a poster and presentation on the country. At the end of term, we had to participate in the cross-arts festival to entertain and educate parents about India through concert. One day, Ma was invited to talk to my group of eight- and nine-year-old classmates about Indian culture. We got to pass around Ma's bangles and bindis, and once Ma had finished her saree-draping demonstration, several curious students approached me with a question: 'Is your mum a punk?' When I asked why they thought that, they said they wished their mums were cool enough to wear nose rings too. Of course, when the term was over, the forced interest in my native country and my brief sheen wore off. I went back to playing catch-up and trying to leave my Indianness at home.

When other kids asked where I was from, I'd tell them I was 'just Australian'.

'No you're not!' they'd spit back. Sometimes they asked if I was Italian or Greek, to which I'd reply, 'That's an interesting guess,' neither confirming nor denying their speculation. I even lied at times and claimed that I was Mauritian like my group of friends. In our school, it was a compliment to look Mauritian, but somehow looking Indian was neither as sophisticated, nor as exotic. Some teachers even gushed over my Mauritian friends' ability to speak French – while no one cared in the slightest about my fluent Kannada or my broken Hindi. Having noticeably undesirable traits was worse than not being noticed at all, and my ability to speak languages that required an Indian accent fell into this first category. The accent was so bloody hilarious to non-Indians, who were ready to demonstrate their Apu-mimicry at the drop of a hat, sideways nodding and all.

Far from feeling proud of my cultural identity, instead I carried guilt for being part of a diaspora that other Australians – 'real' Australians – seemed to believe was taking over. The irony of this belief, in light of Australia's colonial history, was entirely lost on me. At school, I was taught that Captain Cook 'discovered' Australia and the British 'settled' the country – and I accepted it. I didn't grasp the brutality Indigenous people had suffered at the hands of British invaders. I hadn't yet learned that these trespassers could have come peacefully – like traders had done before and many immigrants would again in the following century – instead of wreaking havoc with firearms and white-supremacist beliefs. I wish I'd had the knowledge to see the hypocrisy of white Australians calling Asian immigrants inferior and likening us to a spreading disease. I wish I'd been able to reflect on my own sense of entitlement to land that, although my parents purchased it, had not been anybody's to sell other than its First Nations custodians.

Still years away from such insights, as I grew older I coped with rejection by unwittingly hopping aboard the racist bandwagon myself. I adopted a 'black' identity in an attempt to gain acceptance, because according to schoolyard lore at the time, black people were considered cool and brown people were not. I lived and breathed hip-hop, or I acted like I did. I knew nothing of African American history, their ongoing plight or the origins of hip-hop culture. I knew nothing of how disrespectful it was to appropriate black culture for my social gains. Hell, as an Indian kid I knew nothing of *India's* history, except for a vague interpretation of events in which some dude called Gandhi got everyone to starve and made the British leave. I knew nothing of the Harrapans, the empires and groups of people who existed in India before 1600, the rise of the East India Company, the humanitarian atrocities in India that took place on the watch of the British empire, the systematic looting of India's immense wealth by the British or the horrors of Partition that followed, and so on. And as for Mohandas Gandhi, I didn't know that for all his genius and his service to the country, he was a racist and creepy misogynist too. I knew *nothing*.

Little me was preoccupied with other first-world, third-culture problems. For example, I was so embarrassed by my Indian accent that I reserved it for use at home only, switching it on and off as I walked through the front door. Yet I was too shy to use my Australian accent at home. It would have seemed unnatural to my parents, aunties and uncles. But to me, neither accent was more genuine than the other. I couldn't speak English until I was five years old, so when I learned it at school, I learned it with an Australian accent. Though my parents were fluent English-speakers, they only conversed in Kannada for the first five years of my life so that I wouldn't forget my native language – a wise decision in hindsight. But it was traumatic when, at the start of kinder, the only people I could understand and communicate with deposited me into a colony of English-speaking children. Add onto that all the ways I was teased for my Indianness, and even for my South Indianness by some North Indians who contemptuously referred to us as 'oolloo-goolloo' speakers for all the consonants we rolled, and it explains why I ruthlessly shed my Kannadiga skin. I couldn't fathom a future where I would enjoy speaking Kannada, so I purged myself of my mother tongue and lost an important skill. I decided that the best I could offer my parents when they spoke to me in Kannada were English responses with an Indian accent.

'RUHI!' Ma would shout from the other end of the house when I had a friend over.

'I think your mum wants you.'

'Yeah, I know. I'll go in a bit,' I'd say, continuing with whatever game we were playing.

'RUHIIII! EH! NING ESHT SALA KARIBEKA? HOW MANY TIMES I HAVE TO CALL YOU?!'

'Okay, I'll be back,' I'd say to my friend. 'Just stay here, okay?'

I tried to keep my friends and parents physically far from one another so that neither party would hear me speak in the accent they weren't used to. I never invited my peers to Indian functions for the same reason, but also so they wouldn't see me in the traditional clothes my parents forced me to wear. On such occasions, I was made to dress in a way that only the disco ball could rival for sparkle and mortifying conspicuousness.

Only one friend was an exception to the rule: Aurelie. Nobody else in the world existed when Aurelie and I played at each other's homes. We had the greatest fun inventing games and we laughed until our tummies ached and words gave way to snorts, farts and consequently more laughter. The stinky cycle was glorious. Aurelie embraced my family's food and our music, and she still hung out with me even when she saw how harshly and frequently my parents scolded me. She saw my little face crackle with annoyance when I was forced to wear prickly ghagras or chudidhars to Indian functions.

But where Aurelie embraced me and my Indianness, too many others didn't, and my parents just didn't seem to get it.

Whenever I came home from a rough day at school, which was most days, there was no opening for me to talk about my feelings. It was uncommon for anyone in our community to divulge their inner worlds. Even within immediate families, if someone noticed a shift in our demeanour and asked what was wrong, more often than not, we sought to keep the boat steady by lying.

'Yes, yes, I'm fine! Nothing is wrong!' was the standard reply. How dared any of us disturb the peace and happiness of the household to indulge in a cry or a whinge?

On occasions my parents summoned enough goodwill to lend the injured an ear, they would promptly offer logical solutions along with a pat on the back and an 'encouraging' remark about how these things *just happened,* and it was time to move on and prepare dinner.

The first time school bullying became too overwhelming for me, I decided I had no choice but to open up to Ma and Pa about it. Though they were enraged at the perpetrators, their immediate response was to offer actionable advice, which wasn't particularly useful to me, a young and nervous pacifist.

'Tell your teacher,' Pa said.

'Kick them one! Then see if they trouble you again! Otherwise show me which kid and I will show them what happens if they ever come near my daughter,' Ma threatened.

The first option would have provoked the bullies to come down on me harder for being a dibby-dobber. The second just sounded like a line out of *The Godfather* or something a Gulshan Grover character might say.

I was already such an outlier at school so I hesitated to take any steps that would isolate me further. I had to come up with a more subtle plan: Ruhi 2.0 – Australian edition.

***

Part of my assimilation project involved a change in diet. I complained to my parents one day, begging them for 'normal' food. Pa agreed to pick up some bread and Vegemite on his next shopping trip. I was relieved and optimistic that this new strategy would help me to better fit in. *My friends will ask what I have in my sandwich, and I'll say, 'Vegemite.' End of story,* I thought. *No need to explain what the 'gooey stuff' is anymore.* So while Pa went grocery shopping with a new item on his list, I stayed in the kitchen peeling vegetables for Ma. We were both drenched in the aroma of onions, chillies, cumin, cardamom and poppy seeds frying in oil. It was the smell of home and I enjoyed it – as long as none of my 'friends' were around. When Pa returned, he placed the shopping bags on the dining table and pulled out a jar of Promite.

'What?!' Suddenly I was standing in front of an insurmountable wall, purpose-built to block me from becoming the new-and-improved Ruhi – a Ruhi who was more acceptable to her Aussie peers. My eyes welled up with tears of hopelessness.

'Why did you do that, Pa? Why couldn't you just get Vegemite like I asked?'

'Because it's cheaper, Ruhi. Why pay $1.50 more for the same thing?'

'Because!'

'Because what, ma?' My poor father was at a loss.

'It's *not* the same thing! You don't get it!' The grizzly volcano in my stomach bubbled over. Over time, I came to know this feeling well – though it would be a long while before I could name it.

'Is it because your friends have Vegemite?' he asked.

'*Yes! Everyone* eats Vegemite! *Everyone* eats *normal* food. Except for me! You won't buy me ham and cheese. So I asked for Vegemite and you couldn't even get me that!'

'You can pretend this is Vegemite. It's the same thing, ma.'

I gave up on the conversation with Pa, and resigned myself to a more productive one with myself. This became a habit. *When I'm bigger and I have money, I am going to eat anything I want. And no one will stop me! I will do my own grocery shopping and I'll buy chips every week!*

I couldn't comprehend why my parents, especially Pa, were so obsessed with being frugal. At the time, I thought it was their Indianness; that was the only obvious difference between them and other parents who bought their kids the 'real' brands like Stringers, Roll-ups, Yogo and actual Vegemite. I didn't understand at the time that something inside Pa violently recoiled at the idea of debt and that every single dollar mattered so much to him. I also couldn't see that my parents were trying to steer us away from processed foods and toward fresh produce. Immature and ungrateful at the time, all I knew was that Pa's saving habits were bulldozing the social capital I'd built up over my primary school career.

But I wasn't allowed to complain. Throughout Pa's own schooling he only had one pair of thongs and one pair of canvas shoes at any given time. If either pair broke, he repaired them, as his family couldn't afford another. He told me this to guilt me but also because it was the truth. I needed to know how privileged I was so that I'd grow up appreciating what people in our position often took for granted. This knowledge made me feel wedged between shame, for being different, and guilt, for trying to fit in. So I spent most of my childhood stuck in the middle, waiting to be rescued by marriage.

***

By the time I was pregnant, I'd grown to appreciate my brown skin and my muscular physique. And although I wasn't guaranteed to be over my size issues in the long-term, pregnancy caused me to shift my focus from weight loss to strength gain. I kept working out at the gym at least three times a week, as I had done for the past two years in an effort to maintain fitness during the pregnancy.

Unfortunately, this change in perspective wasn't going to be shared by my parents. This was another reason I dreaded the prospect of telling my parents about their grandchild on the way. They'd noticed my weight loss since training with Jenn and told me they were proud of me. I resented that pride; it insinuated that my body wasn't acceptable when I was heavier and that if I were ever to put those kilos back on, say, *after having a baby,* I would once again occupy a body they considered disappointing and inferior.

Bench presses, hammer curls and deadlifts helped me hold onto my sense of sanity before and during the pregnancy. It calmed me to breathe deeply while I lifted during the hectic weeks of work, family dinners, catch-ups with friends, home-improvement projects, first trimester nausea and fatigue, as well as brainstorming answers to the looming question: *How on earth am I going to pull myself together to raise a daughter?*

I imagined that having a boy might have allowed me to leave some of my emotional baggage unpacked – at least for a while. My absurd plan was as follows: Jake would be the primary role model and I could just tag along being the lovely and loving and lovable little old mum. As time passed, I would slowly work through my issues whilst remaining emotionally available to my son.

But a daughter...

From the get-go, she was going to watch and possibly emulate my every step, my every sneaky mouthful of mindless snacking, my every frown in the mirror, my every eye roll over the phone to my parents, my every growl when I hung up, and my every quarterly nervous breakdown. I knew I didn't need to be perfect, but these behaviours stemmed from greater anxieties, and that troubled me. How might they impact her?

After gym, Jake and I would head straight home for a shower and dinner. I attempted to cook a South Indian meal once every fortnight and still relied on Ma and Pa to help me channel my South Indian ancestors' abilities to zhoosh up veggies like nobody else. Sometimes we ordered takeaway from the local Nepali and North Indian restaurant. When it arrived, childhood memories of Friday nights in the Stone Fruit House resurfaced and I pictured Pa pushing sideways through the aluminium security door, holding bundles of our aromatic North Indian takeaway in orange plastic bags. Maya and I would race to the kitchen to serve up with a fervour that we failed to muster on other nights when Ma asked for help setting the table.

'Naan, malai kofta, dhal makhani, palak paneer, get in our mouths!' we'd chant.

'Look at these girls! They act like we never feed them!' Ma would say.

After I moved out of home, I'd sometimes end up in tears when I tried to cook South Indian dinners and failed to achieve the same consistency or balance of spices as Ma could. Despite our fraught history of cooking lessons, she was a constant guide over the phone.

'Why is it so loose and watery, Ma?' I once asked, not sure anymore of whether I was talking about the meal or my face.

'Add some tomato paste or grind up some cashews and add the powder to the sauce. Call me later and tell me how it is.'

'No, wait. Can you please stay on the phone while I do it?'

'Ya, ya, okay!' she shouted over a Hindi TV drama blaring in the background. I did as she said.

'Oh yeah, it's working. And it tastes better too. Thanks, Ma.'

'See? Your Ma knows.'

5

Pseudoscience

It was late on a Sunday morning when we told Jake's parents we were expecting a baby. They were delighted in their own mellow way: we exchanged kisses and hugs. An hour later, Ma and Pa arrived at our front door for their turn to hear the news.

Jake offered them a seat on the daybed then I handed them a children's board book and asked them to read it. We'd done the same earlier with my in-laws and I'd sat opposite them on a chair. This time, I gave my parents the book and retreated to the farthest corner of the room where I curled up into a ball on the floor. I didn't think about what I was doing; it was a visceral instinct to distance myself from the impact. I was certain they'd be thrilled, in the same way they were over the moon every time I came home with an A-plus on an exam. But it made me cringe to think that I mightn't be able to distinguish their levels of excitement over a mere school test from that around my baby news. So I palmed off the book and promptly disengaged.

I lacked the self-awareness to see how counterproductive it was for me to insist on behaving like a 'normal' family, then keep cutting myself off emotionally in my parents' presence. I was a good Indian daughter; at least, becoming her was the hill I was going to die on. To this end, I was intent on planning the baby announcement in a way that would be memorable and exciting for the grandparents-to-be. After at least twenty years of pretending I was a member of a functional family (allowing for my first six years of life before my disenchantment set in) it seemed only natural to celebrate in this way. Even if, when I thought about it, it was a charade on my part.

Ma and Pa took turns reading each page. At the end, they found an envelope at the back of the book. I was grinding my teeth by that point. Pa opened the envelope and took out the card. They were still oblivious, even after seeing the rattle on its front. Pa squinted at the words inside.

'Oh. We didn't bring our reading glasses today. But I'll do my best,' he said. 'Okay, so it says ... Dear ... Ajji and Ajja...'

'Huh?' Ma was still puzzled.

Pa continued, 'I hope you will ... read this ... book ... to me when I am ... older. From ... your grandchild?'

Ma gasped. It had clicked.

'What is this?!' she cried out. 'What is this picture here?!' She lifted a paper flap on the opposite page to reveal an ultrasound photo.

'AYO! ARE YOU HAVING A BABY?!' she shouted. A smile formed on Pa's face.

I avoided eye contact, instead looking at Ma's golden anklets, hoping she'd direct her questions at Jake instead of me.

'YOU'RE HAVING A BABY?!' Ma kept yelling. She smacked Pa on the thigh. 'THEY'RE HAVING A BABY. AYO!'

Okay, so they were more pumped about this than my past A-plusses. Ma ran over to me in the corner and crouched down to hug and kiss me. I recoiled, trying not to make it too obvious. Then I extended one hand and gave her a light pat on the shoulder. Physical affection was not abundant in my childhood, so it was inevitably awkward when it came my way as an adult – except for the obligatory hello-and-goodbye pats on backs that resembled hugs.

Ma then rushed over to Jake. 'Congratulations, Jake! You're going to be a father!'

'Well done, guys. Congratulations.' Pa shook our hands and hugged us.

Then, it began.

'AYO, RUHI! GET OFF THE FLOOR! Don't sit like that! Come be comfortable here! Sit here!' Ma exclaimed, forcefully offering her seat to me. Never mind that I was comfortable where I was.

In an instant, I became a porcelain doll. Now that *she* knew I was pregnant, I was breakable. I was reminded of my straightjacketed childhood. Ironically, the news of a grandchild reverted me into my parents' incompetent minor, in need of training and fussing. Now that I was carrying the newest version of their pride and joy, I was suddenly too fragile to sit on my own wooden floors.

***

Over the next few months, Ma admonished me constantly.

'Eh! Don't lift your arms above your head!'

'You mustn't go to the gym when you are pregnant.'

'You should eat more of this.'

'Don't touch that.'

'Stop crouching.'

And so on.

Of course, there were dumbbells in my hands when I lifted them over my head for shoulder presses at the gym three times a week and I ate spicy food whenever I felt like it. It made no difference to Ma that I'd done my research, I'd had a comprehensive discussion with my trainer and cleared everything with my doctor.

It reminded me of all those times my parents received an email forwarded from a relative or a group text message with the next (clearly dodgy) panacea to every health problem. Maya and I, lucky things, always ended up with front-row tickets to the two-person TED Talk that would ensue in our lounge room. My parents were as passionate as their theories were obscure: if you're standing still with nothing to do, rub your fingertips together to stimulate your nerve endings and boost your overall health and wellbeing. Take a teaspoon of honey with cinnamon every morning to reduce cholesterol. Eating ghee will make you smarter. To cure all physical ailments, eat a whole bulb of roasted garlic every day. 'I did that and my knee pains are fully gone!' If you want to get rid of the flu more quickly, drink hot water to kill all the germs.

'None of this is proven to help!' I'd argue.

'Ruhi, there are some things scientists and doctors don't know. Books don't tell you everything!'

Yeah okay. So why the fuck was I forced to study three sciences in Year 10 in the hopes that I'd pursue medicine, if the authority on healthy lifestyle choices was going to be Jagdish Uncle in America, who chopped off his fingers using heavy machinery at work?

Any further counter arguments I usually presented at this point were simply met with a long, deep 'Nooooo' in a tone insinuating that I was the unreasonable one.

***

When I was fourteen we moved from the Stone Fruit House to a new build I shall call the Echo Chamber, which works as both a literal and metaphorical descriptor. It was about fifteen minutes from our previous home and didn't have carpet protectors inside. Thank goodness. Instead, we had white tiles that amplified Ma's voice and carried it across the ground floor and up the spiral stairs, where it was absorbed by the pistachio-green carpets. Ma had first discovered green carpets a few years earlier at a family friend's house-warming party. That night, when we got home, Ma declared her undying love for 'Sushila's pistha green carpet' and 'Sushila's swags and tails'. She specified to the builder that she wanted green carpets for the top floor of our new house and later that year, she returned from her trip to India with several boxes of velvet swags: maroon for downstairs and deep olive green for upstairs. At first, our new home looked like a hospital, with its sterile white walls and tiles. Once the curtains were hung, it was as if the house had decided to reinvent itself as the inside of a genie's bottle, but then got tired and gave up halfway through.

'RUHIIII,' Ma screamed from the kitchen one day, her voice travelling farther than I would have liked it to. 'EH! RUHIIII!'

'Yes, Ma?' I apathetically responded from a whopping one metre away, pure Daria Morgendorffer.

'Go get me some onions from the garage! Lagoo!' she yelled over the percussion of aluminium and steel dishes and utensils smashing together as she cooked.

I walked to the garage at my usual pace. Yes, the garage: that's where we stored our ten-kilo bags of onions after we dried them out in the sun. Living with a compulsive shopper like Ma meant there was no room in our maximalist house for unsightly, maximal onion bags. As I returned through the back door, the phone rang. I watched Ma answer and as expected, she spoke as though Michael Jackson had suddenly possessed her.

'Hello? Yes?' the subdued spirit murmured. When she hung up, I made the mistake of asking for the umpteenth time, 'Ma, why do you yell at us when we're right here?'

'IT'S MY NATURAL VOICE! THIS IS HOW I SPEAK!'

'No, it's not! You are so soft when you answer the phone or speak to your colleagues.'

'EH, HOGA!'

A few weeks later, when Ma and Pa were at work and Maya and I had the day off school, I decided to end the problem of Ma's constant shouting once and for all. Of course, I roped Maya in. We wrote an anonymous letter to Ma and left it in our mailbox, ready for her to collect on her way back in. At the end of the day, we perched ourselves at the top of the stairs – a clear vantage point from which to watch her come inside. When we heard her car in the drive, we held our faces in our hands and willed every sphincter in our bodies shut in order to hold in our giggles. The door opened. Ma scrambled through with her handbag, her shopping and the mail. She put down her bags and flicked through the envelopes, leaving the bills by the entrance for Pa to handle. Then, she opened the envelope with *To the householder* scribbled on it, probably expecting an invitation to a local garage sale. She froze as she read.

Dear neighbour,

We hope this letter finds you well.

We tried to come speak to you the other day but you were not at home, hence this note. We hear the voice of a woman shouting on a daily basis. Could we request that you kindly try to keep the noise levels down? It's not something that would normally bother us but our young daughter has been staying up at night, unable to fall back asleep after her nightmares. When we ask her about them, she says that she can hear the woman next door screaming in her dreams. Hopefully this does not offend you. There are no hard feelings, **nor is there reason to apologise.** *If you* *could simply speak more softly, our family would greatly appreciate it. Especially our innocent young daughter.*

Kind regards,
Your neighbours.

Ma looked straight ahead, her hand on her mouth. She glanced past the staircase. Maya and I flinched and immediately rolled back, muffling our laughter. I felt the slightest bit sorry for Ma – but not really, if it meant she would keep it down in future. We peeped back downstairs. Ma was now staring at the note again, still in consternation. Then we heard her shout, in spite of the letter she had *just* read, 'RUHI! MAYA! I'M GOING NEXT DOOR FOR TWO SECONDS. I'LL BE BACK!' My sister's eyes widened. 'We can't let her go! She'll embarrass herself.'

'Yeah, we can! It'll be funny!' I replied. 'They'll just say it wasn't them and Ma will conclude that it could be anyone in a nearby house.'

'That's so mean! I'm telling her!'

'No, don't!' I said with a laugh. 'Plus, she's already gone.'

Maya bolted down the stairs, flung the door open and ran outside. 'Ma! Ma! Come back!'

I walked over to the balcony and watched them below. Ma had already reached the neighbours' front porch. Maya was grabbing her by the arm, ushering her back to our house and telling her about our master plan.

The door slammed downstairs and my mum almost ripped a hole in her lungs. 'RUUHIIIIIII!'

Crap. 'Yes, ma?'

'COME HERE! NOW!'

I staggered down the stairs, falling apart giggling and snorting. Ma looked at me, trying to be angry but then burst out laughing as well. Ma was a pretty good sport that way; she was always the queen of April Fool's Day and enjoyed having a chuckle at the expense of others. She conceded that it was a pretty good prank. The only downside of the whole episode was that we now knew we had tried everything we could to get her to quieten down and we had failed; she was never going to stop yelling at us.

***

Another way the Echo Chamber distinguished itself from the Stone Fruit House – on top of its (annoyingly) excellent acoustics and vast family of custom-made swags – was its great, empty walls, calling out to Ma, begging for decoration. Ma hung glamour portraits of herself all over the place, so that you felt like you were being watched in every room as you moved through the house. Though she'd paid hundreds of dollars for the photos, most of them had been hidden away in storage at our old house. Now that they were on display in all their gilt-framed glory, the Echo Chamber felt like a shrine built in Ma's honour. In one portrait, Ma was wrapped in a maroon satin shroud. In another, she wore a grand silk saree. There was a particularly regal one mounted upstairs in which she faithfully stood by both of her daughters, all of us dressed in traditional outfits she had chosen. It looked like a portrait of the Raichand family in the film *Kabhi Khushi Kabhie*

Gham.[2] Other family portraits were scattered around the house, including some with our reluctant father, whose own treasured pictures had gone missing.

In every house we'd lived in before, Pa had set up a pooja shrine where he prayed every morning. It would feature his incense, weeboothi, kumkum, fresh flowers and three pictures he carried from house to house: of Lord Shiva, Lord Ganesha and Raghavendra Swami. When we packed up our belongings in the Stone Fruit House, Ma hid those pictures and claimed that they must have gone missing during the move. For a while, she was unsure of what to do with them: on one hand, they were important to Pa; but on the other, she cared too much for his soul to give back these artefacts of hell.

---

[2] I know that there are bigger problems to tackle around the world but has anyone else wondered why there is an 'e' after the second Kabhi when there is none for the first or has this massive typo just flown under all of India's radar like it did mine for the past two decades?

When Pa wasn't home, she'd point to Lord Shiva and say, 'Look at that. Chi! How can this blue man with snakes around his neck be a god?'

He looked nothing like the white-skinned, smiley, haloed, beer-bellied, blue-eyed, blue-caped, blondish, gold-framed picture of Jesus that Ma had hung up on their bedroom wall. The longer Pa kept worshipping these idols, the more impossible it seemed to Ma that he would join her on the 'right' side of eternity.

After a few weeks, she consulted me on the matter. At the peak of my teenage Christian self-righteousness, I supported her decision to throw them out and allow Pa to think they were lost. It was for his own good. Ajji would have approved too. For years, we'd prayed for Pa's salvation, convinced that not only did he require Jesus's permission to enter heaven, but he also needed Jesus's inner peace to settle his anger issues. *We* needed him to need Jesus because the angry outbursts were usually directed at Ma and me. We didn't comprehend that, like all people, Pa was a product of his past trauma.

Unjustifiable as his outbursts were, we failed to validate the genuine hurt our actions often caused him. Instead we concluded that his anger and frequent inability to control it, came from the devil. It was up to us to help him see the evil of his belief system, starting with his pictures. Hiding them was the nudge toward Christ he needed. It didn't matter that we lied, deceived and behaved nothing like Christ to get him there; what mattered was that we did it in 'love'.

I had been on the receiving end of Pa's hell-sent anger issues for years. Around the time I turned eleven, and we were still living in the Stone Fruit House, I spent most weeknights mystified by maths books that no amount of brain-racking, leg-twitching or teeth-grinding helped me decipher. *Elementary Algebra,* which Pa had sourced from a bargain-book kiosk at the local shopping centre, was beyond me. Not only was the content ahead of my school curriculum, but the mathematical symbols and sample workings also followed American convention. My textbook collection included Shakuntala Devi's annoyingly enduring book too, aptly named *Puzzles to Puzzle You* and first published in 1979. It proved to be ten times harder than *Elementary Algebra.* I wasn't even sure that children my age were the target audience. Devi might have been a mathematical legend and pioneering woman, but that book was a punishment to me. But Pa wanted me to advance ahead of my year level to prepare for entrance exams to Victoria's prestigious, select-entry secondary schools, so I stuck with it.

One evening, I copied an equation into my exercise book and stared at it, unable to progress. Pa had instructed Ma not to let me set foot out of my room until I'd finished all of the homework he'd set for me, plus touch-typing exercises in addition to actual schoolwork. So I languished at my desk. I knew what would happen, but there was nothing I could do. I bowed my head so the thin grooves in the wooden desk made an imprint on my brow, and I waited for Pa's station wagon to pull up in the driveway of the Stone Fruit House.

Eventually, I heard the ratcheting of the handbrake followed by the rumble of the engine dying down. The car door opened. The car door shut. Keys clinked. As the aluminium security front door unlocked and squeaked open, a malaise spread across my chest and arms. Then came footsteps. I was attuned to the rhythm of each family member's footsteps. Maya's flat feet slapped enthusiastically against the floorboards that Pa and I installed together after we'd lived at the Stone Fruit House a while. Ma's footsteps were not as fast but they were lighter. Pa's were heavy and measured. When he was angry, each baleful step almost made me wish I was deaf.

My bedroom door opened. Our customary small talk ensued; meaningful, edifying conversation between my parents and me was scarce.

'Hi, how was your day?' he'd begin.

'Good. How was yours?'

'Yes, good. Have you finished the work I gave you?'

'No.'

'Why not?'

'I didn't understand a lot of it.'

Somehow, after all the days, weeks and months of me not understanding, he still expected the penny to miraculously drop one day. In the meantime, my answer to that question never cut it.

'You don't understand or you don't *want* to understand?' The point of no return arrived on the back of that question.

'I *don't* understand.'

'Then I'll *make* you understand!'

And the beating session would commence. Pa was a toolmaker. His hands were rough. The only thing more painful than his hands landing on my flesh was a rolling pin or wooden spoon – whichever he or Ma had within reach. Much like a baseball player gives the bat a bit of a shake to re-establish their grip, Pa shook whichever utensil he was using at the time for greater impact. One smack never sufficed. He usually kept going until he felt satisfied with my outpour of remorse, all the while taunting me with my own words.

'You don't *understand?* You don't *understand,* huh?'

He shouted rhetorical questions and accusations.

'Do you understand *now?* Want to see what happens when you don't *obey?* You don't want to *apply* yourself! *That's* the *problem!*' He would hit me on every word that he emphasised. I slowly backed into a corner while the beating continued.

'*Stop* crying! Stop crying *now* or I'll keep smacking until you stop!'

Ma would eventually pull me away or stand in Pa's way when she felt it went too far.

Between such eruptions, Pa was a gentle, incredibly sweet-natured man – the kind whom children flocked to and felt comfortable around at family gatherings. He was the same dad who bought me a VLine train set with his meagre income for one of my earliest birthdays in Australia and patiently set it up with me. He clocked up hours and probably entire weekends playing card games, Cluedo and Monopoly with his daughters. He held onto the seat of my bicycle as I learned to pedal, ran up and down the street after me as I gained my balance then clapped with glee when he finally released his grasp and I rode ahead without him. He was the kind of dad whose hearty laugh made everything in the world seem right. We loved him when we weren't afraid of him. And it was this fierce and complex love that drove Ma and me to throw out his pictures, in the hope we could guide Pa toward a better life and afterlife. We did not yet understand that love, in its purest, most altruistic form, was given freely without expectation that the recipient shed pieces of their identity. Instead, each of us allowed our expectations to stunt the familial love we shared, its fullness only presenting itself in snatches.

Though Pa had undergone baptism before his 'love marriage' to Ma, he continued practising his Lingayat faith in Melbourne. It seemed to me he did so partially out of obligation and partially from a need to hold onto something from life as he used to know it. Though Ma was disappointed to see him return to his old religion, Pa approached his morning devotions with such quietude and modesty that it seemed benign enough. As long as Ma kept praying for him, she believed he would come around to Christianity one day. She also didn't have the heart to ask him to stop, knowing that he accepted her choice to take us kids to church since birth. When we arrived in Australia, Pa told Ma that he didn't mind which religion the kids were brought up with, as long as we only followed one. He didn't want to 'confuse' us by exposing us to both. Ma felt more strongly about her faith than Pa did his, so she had us baptised and brought us up as Sunday churchgoers.

When we moved to the Echo Chamber, we left our traditional Anglican church behind and joined a Pentecostal church nearby, which happened to be an echo chamber of its own. Under its influence, and dealing with Pa's ongoing angry outbursts (even though they died down in frequency), that's when Ma and I decided to take a more aggressive approach to the games that Satan was playing with my dad. The leaders of the church would never have condoned our actions regarding Pa's pictures but Ma and I decided we knew better.

***

> Date: *19/3/2017*
> Name: *R.L.*
> Address: -
> Phone number: -
> Email address: -
> Prayer Needs: *A safe pregnancy + wisdom on what to do about my job + relationship with parents. Thanks.*
> Would you like to be contacted by someone from the prayer team? *No.*

I popped the prayer slip into a snazzy little bucket in the foyer and opened the dark auditorium's glass doors to slink into a seat at the back with Jake. The service had already started. It was the fifth church we'd tried in the few years since I'd left the Echo Chamber Church of my youth, which I had attended for over a decade until I started asking questions and didn't receive answers. When I became a uni student and began learning to think more critically, I started to feel like something was off. So I got curious: 'Why isn't there any transparency about the finances of this church?' I wondered. 'Why, with such a multicultural congregation, do we only see white people preaching on the stage, except for maybe twice a year at best?' and 'Why are all the board members of this church (a) chosen by the husband-and-wife senior pastors and not democratically elected by the congregation and (b) middle-aged white men, except for the female senior pastor?'

The atmosphere in this new church wasn't all that different with its glossy, contemporary decor, flashing multi-coloured lights and booming Christian rock, with people jumping up and down during fast songs and slowly waving their arms in the air for the mellower ones. The songs were followed by a formal welcome and an offering message to 'encourage people in their giving'. Then a pastor introduced their *gorgeous, amazing, wonderful* husband or wife who was about to get up and give *an awesome sermon that will change your lives and you are going to leave this place different to the way you were when you came in! Ayemeyn!* I noticed it was in fashion for quite a few Australian pastors to sound

American when they said *Amen* – as well as to punctuate their sermons with a barrage of *Ayemeyns* and *Halleluyehs*.

Jake and I struggled with these absurdities – the rhyming platitudes, the vapid catch-phrases, the shouty preachers who loved alliteration a bit too much. But we kept going back. Partially out of obligation and partially from a need to hold onto something from life as we used to know it. Another reason we kept showing up was that, from time to time, there were speakers who seemed a little less solipsistic and brought a cogent, worthwhile argument to the table. Also, I found calm in some of the slow songs. Swaying, I'd place my hands on my protruding belly and sing them to our baby, hoping to counteract the cortisol I imagined her sloshing around in, on weekdays.

As the service went on, I found myself thinking back to when Ma first took Maya and me to the Echo Chamber Church. She was excited to see its vibrant kids' ministry and youth group, which our previous, more traditional church had lacked – probably due to its ageing congregation. I was immediately suspicious of the Echo Chamber Church. A lot of what I saw seemed like an attractive facade for a movement without real substance. But soon, we were sucked in by all the charismatic extraverts and vibey youth events.

Thinking of my unborn daughter, as I serenaded her with songs of peace and love, I wondered how much longer the church was going to need to pull up its premium cashmere socks. The rounder my belly got, the sharper my bullshit radar got. Every church we went to seemed to be filled with courteous, compassionate people, some of whom seemed conditioned through the shoddy use of scripture *not* to hold their leaders to account. I imagined that those who did know better were praying for a holy revelation to dawn upon their pastors when it came to the churches' cultural issues, rather than speaking up themselves. I knew because this group had once included me. I also knew those who *did* raise their voices were discreetly nudged out the back door quietly or made to feel that they had no other choice but to leave 'of their own accord'. I'd seen it happen over and over.

I wondered if I would have to wait until my daughter was twenty-seven and possibly pregnant with her own child before we saw some diversity on church boards and leadership teams – before women, queer people, black and indigenous people and people of colour were seen as equally valuable contributors and decision-makers within the church. How long would we have to wait before churches stopped whitewashing Christianity and actively engaged in its decolonisation? Before churches became more transparent about their finances? Before churches started carrying out their God-given obligation to care for the environment, or creation if you will? Before church leaders started to face facts about global warming, even if they *did* believe it was all part of the end times? Surely that detail didn't diminish their responsibility toward the planet and to those in the global south who would suffer most in the face of extreme weather events and rising sea levels.

That said, it was obvious that churches were making a positive impact on many lives. I could see that many churches and other types of religious institutions served as incubators for creativity and safe places for people like me who were running from past trauma (not ignoring the fact that people in these same churches were often responsible for causing new traumas or playing off that which was existing for their own gains). Still, I believed that churches had their place. Going to church, even the Echo Chamber Church, changed my life in wonderful ways before the experience soured for me – which is why Pa was gobsmacked when I told him I was leaving a couple of years before my pregnancy.

'But how can you leave? Those people are like family for you.'

Pa was referring to the youth and young adult community whom Jake and I hung out with and prayed with on a weekly basis; to the pastors who proudly and lovingly officiated at our wedding ceremony; to the various volunteering teams I served on and built friendships within; to the prayer and bible study groups I'd passionately led over the years; to the leaders I looked up to and cared deeply about before they themselves grew disenchanted and left.

'I'll still be in touch with the people I was close to.'

'But how can you stop going to that church? Being in that youth group changed your life. You were going off the rails and I saw a huge change, a *good* change in you after you joined that church.'

Clearly, he was pleased with the ways in which the church had subdued the rebel in me and ignited a spiritual fire in me instead. Becoming a good Christian girl wasn't that different to becoming a good Indian girl. Both involved honouring one's parents, one's pastors, one's husband, one's government, one's 'Heavenly Father'. Submission to one patriarchy primed me for submission to others and this naturally worked well for Pa.

'Okay, firstly, I wasn't *going off the rails,* Pa. And secondly, I've seen and been through some things that don't sit well with me. I tried raising my concerns but they fell on mostly deaf ears. So I'm not going to continue attending and keep putting my money into that place.'

'Ruhi, you do this everywhere you go. You expect every workplace, every church, every group you join to be perfect. And when it falls short of your expectations, you leave. I am telling you, *no* place with humans will ever be perfect!'

'I know, Pa! But these places need to have standards around fairness. And when those standards are breached, a code of conduct needs to be followed. This church used to have a HR department and they got rid of it. What does that tell you?'

'Okay ma but this place, these people, have done so much good for you, can't you give it another chance?'

'I have, Pa. Time and time again. It's been ten years now. Besides, why are you so bothered about it? You only attend when Maya sings on stage, but apart from that you don't even go to church, or the temple anymore.'

'That's different. We're talking about you here.'

'Okay, well now we're talking about you.'

But we didn't talk about him.

***

Since Maya and I had moved out – me when I got married in my early twenties and Maya when she secured a far-away job in her mid-twenties (reasons other than marriage and work would never suffice) – Pa attended church with Ma almost every weekend. They watched online sermons by American megachurch pastors almost daily. One Saturday night, Ma called me after the evening service to tell me the big news. When I picked up she was whispering – or attempting to.

'Ayo, Ruhi! You won't believe what just happened!'

'What? And why are you talking like that?'

'I took your pa to church tonight and ayo, I've been praying *sooo much* for him. You know how much we have prayed over the years?!'

'Yeah,' I replied.

She paused between words for dramatic effect before surrendering to the excitement and gushing out the rest: 'You know that part ... at the end when ... they ask us to bow our heads and close our eyes and tell people to raisetheirhandsiftheyw anttoaskJesus – inhale – tocomeintotheirlives?'

'Yeah.'

'Your Pa raised his hand!'

'Oh.'

If she'd told me this news five years before, I would have been equally elated. But now, I was more concerned with where Pa's head and heart were. If this change was spiritually refreshing for him, if he had found new meaning, I was happy for him. But if it was because he and Ma had become empty-nesters and he'd succumbed to the pressure to keep his wife happy, then I couldn't celebrate. It was no secret that she wanted him to be a Christian. Either way, it was Pa's choice and I wasn't about to interfere.

When I was little, I'd ask Pa why he didn't come to church with us. He'd say, 'All Gods are one. The God you worship at church is the same God I pray to in the temple or during pooja. And I pray for you every day.'

We used to talk about religion and politics when we were both in a good mood. It started with him explaining ideas to me and as I got older, we debated them. I briefly envisioned having these discussions with my dad after my daughter was born. Just the three of us, together, walking to the park near my parents' house where I used to take Maya when we first moved to the Echo Chamber. On those imagined walks with Pa, I always hit a roadblock in the conversation – much like in real life. Unless we were telling jokes or recounting a funny story, our discussions tended to lead to either a barricade, cordoning off territory that required him to be vulnerable, or a stop sign that I erected in haste because I sensed judgement on its way. For example, the time I told Pa I was leaving the Echo Chamber Church, I explained that it was only after I stepped out of the church's bubble that I understood how enduring and expansive God's love could be. He just shrugged.

That particular church had turned me into someone I wasn't. I entered the fray as the talented 14-year-old chameleon I'd become, having worked so hard to fit in at school. Once I was invested in the church, I would change my colours in any way I needed to climb the church leadership ladder. There was definitely a hierarchy and I was drawn in by the pull of popularity, offering myself to God in servitude and 'humbly' asserting my spiritual authority over those who joined my prayer and bible study group, giving out free advice and praying for those 'under' my care. I threw out my hip-hop collection along with any other music containing expletives. I stopped nurturing old connections to 'worldly' school friends who I knew were out drinking, clubbing and desecrating their bodies through premarital sex. Like Ma had done with Pa, I signalled to Jake (still just my boyfriend at the time) that I wanted him to act like a 'godly' man, even though he'd told his mother a year before that he was no longer going to attend her Catholic church every Sunday like he used to. Seeing how important church was to me at the time, he came along to young adult nights with me and was sucked in almost as thoroughly as I had been.

Other than my dream to become a pastor one day, my aspirations were wholly rooted in preparing myself to be a 'godly' wife and mother, whenever the God-ordained time came. Though Jake wouldn't change who he was, he started to view the world differently, like I did: all black and white, everything *us* and *them*. *They* were always the ones who needed saving. *We* held the keys to the truth that the rest of the world was seeking. I was never any good at dealing with my anger but it got worse after I learned at church that we weren't supposed to let the sun go down with our anger. So I suppressed it altogether instead.

At the same time, joining the Echo Chamber Church had given me a new lease on life. For a couple of years I'd been having nightmares where demons haunted and punished me. It may have been sparked by a profound dissatisfaction with myself, a helpless certainty that I'd end up in hell for my sins – that I wouldn't make it through the narrow gate. But I couldn't really say. Once I joined the church, my nightmares stopped. I learned to look beyond myself and I found great pleasure from volunteering. I met people who taught me how to live with gratitude and show genuine concern and love for others, even when it was difficult. Though there were aspects of church life that made me cringe when I looked back, I appreciated growing up with the sense of a divine presence I could draw on in search of joy, belonging, creativity and hope in hardship. I was sincerely grateful for this. Even if by the time my dad tried to talk me into going back to the old church, my imagined version of God existed on a venn diagram, at the intersection between Christianity, Judaism, Hinduism, Buddhism, Animism and the Force. For all his and Ma's efforts to provide me with a stable religious foundation, I ended up confused anyway.

A couple of weeks after Ma told me about Pa raising his hand at church, I lay in bed one morning, staring at the ceiling. I reached for my phone and sent Ma a text: *Did you ever end up* telling Pa what happened to his pictures of Shiva, Ganesha and the Swami?

I hadn't realised she had an early acupuncture appointment that morning. She replied after the session on her way home: *I had needles in my hand when you messaged. So Pa read it. Then I told him that I threw them in the bin.*

Oh dear. How did he react? I typed back.

He was okay. He probably realises now that there was nothing in those pictures. Had he not known Jesus, it would have been a big issue. But all good. Also, I cooked sabasgi palle and chapatis since you said you were under the pump and busy with work. Thought it would help you. Not sure how the taste is. Let me know.

6

Not that kind of Indian

When I finished uni (after eight long years), I landed a job in HR and recruitment for a global organisation. My parents were chuffed about the 'global' bit. They tried their best to be happy about the 'HR' part. It was a compromise.

The role grew on me over my year there but I never fully settled in. The thought constantly gnawed at me that I would not have been there had I studied a course more aligned with my interests, like a bachelor's degree in French, music, psychology or philosophy, if not bible college. Now, thanks to that underlying restlessness, paired with my new physical reality of being almost four months pregnant, I sensed I looked like one of the worn stray dogs I'd seen on the streets of Dharwad (minus the rabies).

'Morning' sickness had extended into the afternoons and evenings. Being in the office felt like being out at sea; the general nausea was amplified at both ends of the day, on the train to and from work. I'd never known exhaustion in my life like first-trimester fatigue. Walking around the office was like wading through concrete. Scrolling through my emails was enough to make me queasy. On days that I worked in the suburban office instead of the CBD, I used my lunch breaks to slink away to the underground car park for some shut-eye in the backseat of my car.

My days in the city office were the most testing, despite the iconic views from our skyscraper on Collins Street, just a block from picturesque walks along the Yarra River. Each morning, I braced myself, knowing that I wouldn't be able to fit a nap in. My team was headed up by a considerate, approachable manager who gave up their entitlement of a private office to be more accessible to the team in our open-plan set up. The downside was that I couldn't ask to sleep in their cupboard or in the corner behind their desk at lunchtime.

I was left with no choice but to go to the bathroom, put the toilet lid down, sit and close my eyes for five minutes every hour just to survive the afternoon. As I walked back to my desk, I would hear the voices of perky, energised colleagues on their phones around me, bending over backwards for their clients. At that stage of my pregnancy, *any* enthusiasm irritated me. So did the fluorescent lights overhead – I could have torn those bloody tubes out of the ceiling with my bare hands. If only I could reach.

One morning, I pressed the dial button on my headset to call a client. As I paced up and down the aisle through the middle of our workspace, I focused on the carpet's tessellated shapes to ensure I walked in a straight line. The pattern kept me from veering about like a rogue hatchback. *Ah, voicemail.* I conjured a friendly-ish voice message and hung up as I battled my unsuitably tall wheelie chair to sit back down at my desk.

A few minutes passed before a colleague interrupted my hard-won concentration. As she strode past my desk, she muttered something about the last 'typical, boring Indian candidate' she'd just interviewed for a job. She accidentally made eye contact with me and I saw the horror on her face when she realised I was sitting right there! *At my own desk.*

Panic-stricken, she rummaged through a stupid but useful compartment in her brain labelled, I imagine, *Ways to Turn Racist Remarks into Compliments.* You'd be surprised by how many people save brain space for such things. I can only assume they are forced to consult it quite often, each time someone like me wildly misconstrues their irony/wit/banter as that yucky word, *racism.* My colleague affected a look of innocent confusion. A nervous smile formed and the way she – perhaps unconsciously – shifted her gaze two millimetres to look past me, rather than into my eyes, told me that she'd found what she was looking for. 'Sorry, I don't mean *your* kind of

Indian. You're different. You know that! You know what I mean!'

I resisted the urge to pick up my computer monitor and throw it at her white, smiling face. It wasn't the first time someone on my team had made an insulting remark about Indian job-hunters. No genuine apologies would ever follow; instead, someone would simply 'check in' with an excuse and assure me that they weren't talking about *me*. Astonishingly, even team members of Indian descent were supine in the face of this racism. Sometimes, they joined in, as though their common heritage granted them permission to be racist.

On the one hand, my colleagues were being unprofessional and racist. One highlight over my short tenure at the company was the time I received 'a helpful tip that will save time' from a senior: skip all of the long, 'foreign-looking' names on the applicant list and only call people with 'white names', as they were guaranteed to be 'well-spoken' in their interviews. Firstly, they were not foreign names to me. Secondly, that technique required zero skills as a HR professional. Thirdly, fuck off.

On the other hand, I wasn't sure I could blame my colleagues for observing that a good portion of the Indian migrants they interviewed weren't exactly buzzing with excitement. I knew what it was like to lack vitality when looking ahead, powerless, at the career path set before you by your parents or your community, knowing that you could be in it for life. Several Indian candidates I met seemed to me like passive onlookers at their own interviews. Within seconds, I smelled the difference between a candidate who sat before me with a passion for the job and a candidate who was pushed down onto the chair by the sheer thought of their parents' disappointment if they didn't. Maybe my candidates smelled it on me too.

***

'Okay, let's be honest here,' Pa began after a sip of his Saturday morning coffee, seated opposite me at the dining table. 'It would be nice if you became a doctor but we know that's not going to happen.'

'Eh, hoga! She'll faint when she sees blood!' Ma chimed in from the kitchen. I was in Year 12 and it was time to start applying for university courses for the following year.

'So, I think your next best options are accounting or software engineering,' Pa continued. His meeshee – as we called his moustache in Kannada – sat like a crown atop his upper lip, each word that left his mouth infused with all the authority of the household monarch. Even when Pa's mates who emigrated from India before and after us shaved their meeshees, he kept his. I was glad he did. Not only did it mean that he was proud of his appearance and wasn't going to change it to fit in, but it also offered me a focal point when I felt too resentful toward him to look into his eyes. As he commandeered the discussion about my future, he talked about job security, room for progression and the level of prestige attached to a job title. No one could blame him for wanting those things for me, given that his own childhood was coloured by poverty and broken dreams. But while job satisfaction was not even a consideration for him, it was a biggie for me.

'Pa, I don't want to do accounting or software engineering.'

'Then what do you want to do?'

'I've already told you. Like, French or music or something.' I had just returned from a school trip to New Caledonia where we spent a week flexing our French muscles, having studied it for the past six years of high school. And I'd enjoyed taking piano and violin lessons when I was younger. I couldn't yet envision where music or French would take me career wise but they were a couple of the only disciplines that stood out to me in university handbooks.

'And how will you make money?'

'I'll get a job related to one of those fields.'

'Ruhi. Listen to me. I've told you before. There is no future in those areas. You don't like computers? You don't want to work in IT? Okay. Fine. Then become an accountant. I'm telling you, you'll be minting money like anything. Then with that money, you can go do French or music or whatever you want on the side. Look at your friend Melinda. She has started work as an accountant now and in her first year she is already making $60k annually.'

It was a dead-end conversation – one we'd had several times before. But at that stage, we were nearing the due date for uni applications. So I had something up my sleeve. When Jake – whom I was hiding from my parents and who was also in Year 12 at the time – told me that his mate was going to do a commerce and arts double degree, it was a light-bulb moment for me. Not because it interested me but because it signified a backdoor through which I could escape my parents' blueprint of my future.

'Well, what if I did a Bachelor of Commerce, majoring in accounting?' I suggested to Pa.

'Why? Why can't you just do a Bachelor of Accounting?'

'Because it will make me a more well-rounded candidate when I'm done. I'll have knowledge in other areas like marketing, management, *economics* and *business law,*' I said, hoping those last two subjects would win him over. My secret plan: after a year and a half of completing the compulsory core units, I planned to move over to a major in management or HR management and away from accounting without my parents noticing.

'Okay. Write it down. Bachelor of Commerce majoring in Accounting,' he said.

'Well actually, it's just a Bachelor of Commerce and you choose your major after you've been at uni for a year and a half,' I clarified. 'Also, I was hoping to do a double degree with a Bachelor of Arts. At least, that'll be my first preference,' I added – a detail I strategically slipped in toward the end of our discussion. I went in strong by making what was really a question sound like a statement.

'ARTS?! WHY ARTS?!' Ma exclaimed over the crackle of puris deep-frying in the kitchen.

'Because I know that if I find accounting dry, at least I'll have arts to enjoy.'

'Ruhi, you should just focus on accounting. If you stick to that, you will finish in three years. Why unnecessarily add on an extra year for an arts degree?' Pa retorted. He cared about this a great deal, just not in a way that enabled me to thrive beyond the moulds he kept putting me into. I was his ice sculpture, forever melting away.

'You can't fault me for wanting to study *more,* can you? And for an extra year, I'll have a whole other degree to show for it.' Neither Pa nor his meeshee looked convinced. '*Pa.* I'm going to *hate* uni if I only study things I dislike.'

'Okay, it's more work but if that's your decision then so be it,' said Pa, as if I was actually in charge of my own life.

'Ya, okay,' Ma agreed.

I walked upstairs to my bedroom and penned my future on the Victorian Tertiary Admissions Centre form – my first educational decision that did not require my parents' signatures. It may as well have. I filled out 'my' preferences, with the Bachelor of Commerce/Arts at the top, teaching at the bottom ('because teachers don't get paid well, Ruhi') and French, music or anything else I was interested in nowhere on the form. I paused to look up at the poster spread across my wardrobe: a black-and-white shot of a woman running through a cobblestone Parisian alley. The only colour in the picture was the bright red of her coat. *It's going to be a long time before I can be like her,* I thought.

When I was alone, I tried to push Pa and Ma out of my mind and let my imagination run wild. I daydreamed about another dimension in which I could study whatever I wanted, or not study at all until I found something I cared enough to learn about. *Who will I become? What will I be doing?* I built castles in the sky, only to remember I could never live in them. I was too far-gone into my micromanaged life.

I knew that if I rescinded from our verbal agreement and studied a course completely of my own choosing, if I told my parents to shove it, I might never overcome the regret. For starters, I was certain that Ma and Pa would continue to fight about me and end up getting a divorce. Among their confrontations around money, general personality clashes and one having issues with the way the other behaved at the last party – they fought about me. Ma thought Pa was too hard on me, while he believed she was a negative influence on me with her make-up, perfumes, hair products and impulsive spending. *Chemical woman,* he would call her, forever on a mission to disabuse her of her preoccupation with outward appearance. In truth, they were both interested in keeping up appearances. She did it with her clothes and jewellery; he did it by insisting his children be as close to his idea of perfect as possible.

Of course, Ma joined in at parties. 'Ya, ya, I am a happy mother! Ruhi finished her exams and she got a final score of 95,' she said to the aunties.

'It was 94.95,' I kept correcting her. I'd pleaded with her to keep it to herself, but who was I kidding? Pa was happy to share the news at first but soon grew reluctant when he heard that some of his friends' kids had scored 98.3 or 99.95. Then he told me that I could have and should have obtained a higher score. Either way, if I deviated from the promising career they envisioned for me, I couldn't see them recovering from the shame of it. They would blame each other for my shortcomings and eventually call it, citing irreconcilable differences. Divorce was not on the cards, I decided; my little sister was too young for me to let that happen.

My future had me trapped and my mood sank. I thought that by appeasing my family I was warding off my parents' depression and possibly even suicide. Poor mental health ran through both parents' sides of the family but its effects were more visible on Pa's side. One of my dad's younger sisters poisoned herself and died in her twenties, but not before going through an arranged marriage and childbirth. Her daughter, my cousin, passed away several years after her mother's death. She was fifteen years old. They told us it was a head injury but I wasn't so sure that's all there was to it. Another one of my aunties suffered a mental illness that Pa didn't talk about. I eavesdropped on his calls to India at the time and from what I could gather it sounded like something along the lines of depression and psychosis. Pa's brother also struggled with depression and I was sure that Pa had depression. His sense of duty to his family kept his arms and legs moving. When I asked him about it a long time ago, he cast the thought away and, of course, there was no chance in hell of him agreeing to see a doctor about it.

As I grew up, I became hypervigilant to his tone of voice, the pace of his footsteps and other non-verbal cues. Any inconsistencies were alarm bells signalling he was reaching a tipping point. As for Ma, her heart was like a transparent helium balloon hovering over her at all times; it was easy to detect her emotional state. Although she seemed like a happy-go-lucky person most of the time, when the balloon did pop, it was a frightening spectacle and the task of reinflation was onerous for everyone.

Back then, if anyone was going to suicide for the sake of the family, I'd rather it have been me.

***

At the beginning of 2008, I received a letter from a local university offering me a place in the Bachelor of Commerce/Bachelor of Arts double degree. I accepted, but not without a struggle.

Focus on what's in front of you, I kept telling myself. *This too shall pass. You'll be out of here in a few years. For now, there's peace at home.* So I focused. Or, tried to. I found small bursts of energy to devote to my studies. But mostly, life as a uni student was foggy. So I received my second letter from the university.

13 Aug 2008
EARLY WARNING LETTER
Dear Ruhi,

Your academic progress record, to date, shows that you have failed one or more units in your enrolment in semester one 2008. This letter is being sent to you as an early warning that you may be at risk of breaching the Faculty's academic progress rules at the end of the year. Poor academic results may lead to exclusion from all courses in the Faculty of Business and Economics for at least one year.

Phew. Just an early warning. I hid it from my parents. If I was able to pick up my game in semester two, they'd be none the wiser. University was unlike school in that I didn't have any teachers cheering me on. Our school teachers had warned us about this, saying that we wouldn't be wrapped in cotton wool forever, so we needed to learn how to hold ourselves accountable and to develop an inner drive to study hard. Easier said than done. My motivation was wholly extrinsic; I was trying to avert another explosion in our house, this time with higher stakes.

The small part of uni life I did enjoy was volunteering. I threw myself into charity work with wholehearted commitment, which is much more than I could say for my academic assessments. At least I was consistent; I'd regularly hand in essays late – that is, if I finished them at all. I just couldn't bring myself to write essays until the last minute. My tutors pitied me. More than one tutor told me I wrote high-quality essays that deserved a much better grade than they had earned, thanks to late-submissions penalties. But the complacency didn't stem from laziness, as my parents thought. I was having what I didn't know at the time were panic attacks – struggling to breathe and needing to lean on something to catch my breath again; feeling light-headed and dizzy; muscles tensing up – and my anxiety went through the roof every time I set out to do research for my essays.

On a few occasions, I handed in assessments so far past the due date that I obtained a big fat zero. But submission was a hurdle requirement; in other words, not handing it in at all meant an automatic fail for the subject. Handing it in with nil marks gave me a chance to pass the unit, at least. If I got a high enough score on the other assessments, I'd be okay. One year I achieved a whopping score of twelve for the Principles of Accounting unit, out of a total of one hundred. The next year I had to repeat the unit and this time I outdid myself with a grand score of five.

Everything was starting to blur when I looked at my textbooks. Sometimes it was because nothing made sense. Other times it was because my eyes were filled with tears as I strained to absorb information my preoccupied brain had no room for. I was unable to synthesise the words that I was reading. They were just ants crawling across the pages and over my eyes. The next letter I received from the University was more forthcoming than the last.

11 Dec 2008

UNSATISFACTORY ACADEMIC PROGRESS – 2008

Notice of referral and hearing

Dear Ruhi,

The faculty has referred your case to the Academic Progress Committee (APC) for review and hearing. You are required to show cause why you should not be excluded from your course and faculty.

I started to see a counsellor on campus – not because I thought it would help, but because I needed to demonstrate to the APC that I had reasons for my poor performance and evidence that I was doing something about it. Plus, with a letter from the counsellor I could apply for special consideration and hand in my assignments after the due date. I thought I was cheating the system – taking advantage of the counselling services just so I could have an excuse for my academic tardiness and generally being a slacker. Ma and Pa didn't know about the letters yet, but they demanded to see my scores at the end of each semester. They could see that I was failing. Pa often said, 'If you really want something, you'll apply yourself. The problem is you don't want it.'

That conversation always ended in me reassuring Pa. 'Of course I want it and of course I'll work harder!'

But I didn't want it, and I felt guilty for not wanting it: 'it' being what *he* wanted. I didn't know that I didn't have to wait for someone else to give me permission to say, 'You're right! I don't want it.' I was too afraid to walk away from his dreams. I was neck-deep in depression. In seeking out a counsellor, I was just trying to tick a box to mitigate the sentence I'd get from the APC. As it turned out, I *needed* to see a counsellor. I *needed* special consideration.

I needed to tell my parents about the letter. If there was a chance that the hearing would see me kicked out of uni, my parents were going to crack it even harder if they found out I had concealed the warning letters.

When I told them, they were angry and disappointed, as expected. What I didn't expect was how these feelings manifested in my father. His normal response would have been to become aggressive and to shame me. Instead, perhaps for the first time, he shook his head and said, 'Well, what can I do, Ruhi? I've tried forcing you. I've tried everything. If this is your fate, I can't help you. I wash my hands. Go do what you want.'

He sounded like Pontius Pilate, effectively sentencing Jesus to death without actually doing it. I felt like a disgrace, hollowed and dripping in my parents' disapproval having smashed their *izzat* and stolen their *maryade*. Almost being kicked out of an educational institution for poor performance was unheard of in my family. I'd hit a new low. *Even my dad* was tired of me. It was an excellent opportunity to walk away from it all. I should have snatched up the moment with glee, ditched my course and swapped over to something else I knew I'd enjoy. But I had been pulled so far away from what I wanted that I had no idea how to walk through the open door in front of me.

Instead, the next door I walked through led to my hearing with the APC. It was held in a long, narrow room with a table stretching across the breadth of the room. I wondered if it was all designed to make students feel smaller. A slight, unspeaking woman sat at the end, taking minutes. She glanced at me with a *there, there* look. Six jurors sat on the panel opposite me. One man in particular stood out. His imposing stature made the jumbo table look small and he had a shark's dorsal fin for a nose. I estimated he was in his sixties. He wore a beige suit and a menacing expression on his severe, craggy face, ready to rip me to shreds.

A voice came from the other end of the table: 'Take a seat, Ruhi.' It was the chair of the committee. This guy knew how to power pose even when he sat. In contrast, I sat there with my shoulders curled: a timid, brown hazelnut. Before I could become the Nutella on their lunchtime sandwiches, I did my best to hold it together in that hearing. My heart palpitated under sweaty skin and my eyes burned as they rubbed against their sockets, sandpapery after a few sleepless nights. My hair was dishevelled and gave away how fragile and exposed I felt.

Back then, I seldom cried. I had become numb from years of cohabiting with parents who used physical punishment as their main method of discipline, and then threatened to hit harder if I cried. Whenever I felt like crying, I sucked it in and with gritted teeth and sent my tears up into a rain cloud for storage. The cloud grew over the years until it became mammoth, dark grey and foreboding.

Shark Man spoke. He asked almost rhetorically, 'Why should we let you continue to study here?'

The cloud had reached capacity and the thunderstorm arrived. *Boom. Crack.* Tears. It started to pour and pour and pour. I don't remember how I answered that question but I remember that the straight face I was struggling to maintain shattered like a mirror. I was ugly-crying in front of the six jurors and the minutes-taker. None of them cared about why I was there, or so it seemed. Their job was to separate the wheat from the chaff – the students who were worth a second chance and the students who weren't. They were hoping to ascertain whether I'd be worth the university's resources into the future. They had no idea that I wasn't there to build a future for myself, to learn and contribute ideas. I was there because I had no other choice. My parents were going to lose face if I didn't pull through. And the ripple effect of that was too dangerous to risk.

I was excused from the meeting to have a moment to myself. As I stood outside the room, sobbing, my thoughts went straight to the troubling idea that my dad was going to hurt himself if I didn't live up to his tertiary-education dream. I didn't have the luxury of taking my parents' mental wellbeing for granted. I couldn't just think, *Pa's upset now but he'll get over it!* Plus, I knew that not all girls were valued highly enough to receive an education. But Pa's absolute devotion to our learning meant that every time I stuffed up at school or university, I sent another wrecking ball hurtling toward his heart. The way I saw it, either his heartbreak was going to manifest naturally as a cardiac arrest, or unnaturally when it became too much and he chose to end the pain himself – pain that was mainly caused by me. The guilt was overwhelming.

I recalled the deaths of some of my uncles. There was Sybil Aunty's husband, who died from liver failure; he was a sweet man before he became an abusive alcoholic. There was Tony Uncle in Sydney, whose wife found his body in their garage, hanging from one of her sarees. The idea of my dad giving up on me and on life felt like a very possible reality. A vague sense of resolve started to take shape in the smog of my mind. I went back into the room and pleaded with Shark Man, Power Poser and the rest of the panel to keep me there. I made promises to work harder and do better, all the while holding a lump the shape of Pa's heart in my throat.

It continued to rain. A few weeks later, I received another letter in the mail.

13 Feb 2009
FACULTY ACADEMIC PROGRESS COMMITTEE
Notice of Decision
Dear Ruhi,
Under the provisions of Statute 6.2 – Exclusion for unsatisfactory progress or inability to progress, the decision of the Committee is to allow you to continue your studies in 2009...

The committee included stipulations: I needed to attend workshops to help improve my study skills, reduce my full-time load to a maximum of two units per semester, rather than four, and continue seeing a counsellor. That was the part my parents couldn't comprehend. Why on earth would anyone talk about their problems to a complete stranger?

7

Feeling myself

One good thing to come out of my job in the city on Collins Street was meeting my counsellor, Ivana. Around the time I started working there, just before Jake and I decided to train together at the gym, I was crying to my best friend, Zam, over the phone about how tired I was of overeating and being ashamed of my body. Zam and I met in high school fifteen years earlier and by now, had known each other for half of our lives. She was almost like a twin separated from me at birth and somewhat like an adopted daughter to my parents. My parents told me to be more like her: an insanely hard-working med student turned successful doctor. And her parents, who were also South Asian, wanted her to be more like me: 'settled down' and married. Of course, there was nothing 'settled' about me; I'd become increasingly unsettled about my job, my relationship with my parents and now, my weight. Though we'd been friends for so long, it was only in recent months that I'd brought up my dissatisfaction with my body. When I said I wanted to do something about it, she recommended I see a counsellor and maybe consider a personal trainer to help me achieve my fitness goals. It was important to her that I was doing this for my own health and wellbeing and not because of anyone else's opinions about my appearance. Like every other suggestion of Zam's, I took it to heart. After a bit of online research, I found Ivana, a clinical psychologist experienced in assisting with eating disorders. Her practice was just on Little Collins Street, very close to my office, so on a lunch break the following week I had my first session with her.

Her room was an oasis in the heart of Melbourne, floating above the bustling streets about fifty storeys below. It was a fancy building decked out with mirrored lifts, marble pillars and golden railings, but the practice itself was modest. That first day, I sat on a cobalt blue couch, behind which a large window showcased views of the city and sky. I began with the expectation that Ivana would cure me of my unnaturally strong proclivity for eating and help me lose weight so I would be light enough to open that window on the day of my last session and fly right out without succumbing to gravity.

'What brings you here today, Ruhi?' Ivana asked in her mixed Australian and Eastern European accent.

'Well, I'm overweight and I'm trying to get healthier. But I can't shake my cravings or stop myself from satisfying them, so I'm wondering if you can help me find ways to deal with the cravings when they come along. I saw on your website that you've helped people with eating disorders?'

I prepared a blank sheet of paper in my mind, ready to jot down her tips. Instead, Ivana handed me a torch and an oxygen mask and walked me to a dark cave with a blurry, illegible sign above the entrance. It was only down the track that I could look back and read it with more clarity: *Ugly/Uncomfortable/Traumatic parts of Ruhi's Childhood.*

We spent a good two years fossicking around in there during which time painful memories from Dharwad and south-east Melbourne were projected onto the cave's tenebrous walls. These were often memories from the Stone Fruit House and the Echo Chamber, but there was also a deeper, darker memory from my last visit to Dharwad – one that I had been struggling to confront. Sometimes, if I hacked away at a section long enough, I ended up finding precious stones. Other times, I walked into an elaborate collection of cobwebs and needed Ivana's help to untangle myself.

One significant discovery was that many of my eating patterns arose from anxiety. It may have seemed obvious to someone else but I had no idea that I was comfort-eating all that time. *All those years!* I didn't know anxiety was *a thing.* I knew about depression from seeing the counsellor at university, but I thought I was well and truly over it. I was completely unaware of how it might have been connected to the persisting anxiety.

Ivana taught me that the more I talked about my feelings and unloaded in a healthy setting, the sooner I'd be able to process them and experience greater freedom. Any time I opened up about an incident I had not fully recovered from, Ivana asked me how that situation made me feel. I often began by telling her what I *thought* of it. She patiently encouraged me to talk less about my thoughts and more about how something or someone made me *feel*. It was a struggle at first because I wasn't used to talking about my feelings. When I was finally able to identify the emotion – for example, sadness or anger – she asked me where I felt it.

'What do you mean *where?*' I asked. 'Like where I was when I felt that way? In my house I guess.'

'No. Where in your body do you feel it?'

'Sorry, what? Can you give me an example?'

'Sure. Okay, I'm noticing that as you're telling me about what happened, you're sitting on the edge of your seat and your leg is twitching.'

'Oh that's just something I normally do.'

'That can be a sign of anxiety. You're also fidgeting with your fingers and from time to time you're rubbing your fingers along your eyebrows. Does your head hurt?' she asked.

'Yeah.'

'So, you're feeling some of the stress around your forehead. And what about your chest or your stomach?'

I looked at the clock on the wall. 'No, no, nothing.'

'Just take a minute.' She slowed me down. 'Listen to your body. There's no hurry.'

I sat still for more a few moments while Ivana held space for me. I had never been this conscious of the goings-on within my body, especially as a response to emotion. I only ever paid attention to my physical reactions when I stubbed a toe or accidentally got my boob caught behind a wall while hastily turning a corner in my house. I looked down at the indigo carpets and pulled a troubled face.

'I think I do feel a churning sensation in my stomach,' I offered.

Ivana smiled at my progress and returned to the significance of my posture. She pointed out that when I had begun the session, I had been in a relaxed position on the couch, but for a while now, I'd been teetering on the edge, as though I was getting ready to leave. We continued the body scans during my sessions. Over time, I learned how to identify different emotions and process them through language. I practised with Jake, Maya and Zam whenever I felt something, which, once I became pregnant, was all the time. It felt like such an achievement just to be able to say, 'I feel sad.'

By the time I was midway through my pregnancy, I wasn't yet finding the spare time to tackle the pile of parenting books on my shelf. Instead, I listened to podcasts by Clare Crew, Justin Coulson and Janet Lansbury on the train to and from work. The parenting advice touched on empathy, validating children's feelings and helping them feel heard, all of which reinforced the lessons I'd learned from Ivana about sitting with my emotions. It all made sense.

But it also meant that on many evenings, I came home to Jake saying, 'I feel sad.'

'Why?'

'All this great parenting advice is going to help us with our child, but it hurts to know that none of this stuff mattered when I was younger. That no one asked me how I was feeling.'

***

'What does counselling have to do with your studies? What are you going to talk to the counsellor about?' Pa asked after I'd outlined to him and Ma the uni's conditions for me to stay.

'My problems, I guess?' I replied.

'What problems do you have?'

'Probably family issues more than anything else...'

'What? How can you even *think* about discussing family matters with outsiders?'

This precedent was set when, in primary school, I called the Kids Helpline number on the back of a cereal box. I was trying to run away from home (again – I'd tried a few times but could never follow through) and wanted someone to tell me where I could go. Every time the phone bill arrived in the mail, Pa trawled through with a pen and circled the phone numbers he didn't recognise. Then he would grill Ma and me about them. When Pa saw the Kids Helpline number on the phone bill and looked it up, I was in trouble.

'You must never discuss family affairs with outsiders again, do you understand?! And what problems do you have anyway?!' Pa asked and then, not waiting for an answer, continued, 'There are people who face *real* suffering. No food. No house. You've seen those beggars in India without arms and legs! What do you have to complain about?'

His lecture ended with a reminder that my parents had sacrificed everything to come to Australia for us kids – which I took as a warning that I must always seem happy and without complaint, or else be chastised for being an ungrateful little shit.

He was right in some ways. Physically, medically, educationally, I was catered for, however, when Pa belittled my pain like that, it revealed his disregard for emotional and mental health. Perhaps that was ironic, considering the clear mental health struggles threaded through my family, but such indifference was common in our culture. I'd noticed that in our Indian communities, both in Melbourne and India, mental-health issues were more often than not ignored for several reasons. As in many other cultures, until very recently, people were generally uneducated on mental health and therefore unable to recognise the symptoms. In our circle, superstition also played a part. I sometimes overheard stories of distant relatives who were labelled 'demon-possessed', where there was clearly mental illness involved. Ma once told me the story of her aunt, who 'went mad' and spent the rest of her life locked up in a room in her son's house.

Where illness manifested in a tangible, physical disability, people in our communities generally accepted it. But when it was 'invisible', as with learning disabilities, chronic fatigue or depression, for example, it either went undiagnosed or the diagnosis was ignored; these weren't considered *legitimate* problems. Instead, those who struggled were blamed. Parents, especially, often put it down to weakness of character, which could easily be fixed if the child simply tried harder – and there was no grace period for trying harder. Results needed to be instantaneous; the family reputation was at stake. If those grades didn't improve by the next report, parents would come down on you even harder. Basically, you were screwed. Plus, you got to carry a heap of guilt around for disappointing them.

'Next time I have to yell at you for [insert behaviour], I'll have a heart attack. Then you will feel bad for disobeying your mother – but I won't be here anymore!' was a common phrase Ma used to guilt and manipulate me. Or the classic: 'Hai Bhagwan, oh God, please kill me and take me up to heaven. I cannot bear this child anymore.'

My parents weren't the only ones dramatic enough to flippantly throw around death-talk in unfavourable situations. I was around to hear aunties, uncles and the parents of my South Asian friends say the same things to their kids. Parents in Bollywood movies also used similar sayings. In our household, it led us all to become desensitised to actual cries for help, direct or indirect. And whenever something troubled me in my teen years, I rarely thought it significant enough to share with my parents who agonised over every perceived character flaw.

Instead of empathising with me, I knew they would only ever try to fix me. Which is exactly what happened when they read the note from the counsellor I saw after the APC hearing, who'd written a letter in support of my next special consideration application. This time I'd applied well in advance, knowing I was going through a rough patch, and not as an afterthought. Upon reading it, Ma and Pa scoffed at her comments about me suffering from depression.

'There is no such thing as depression,' Pa said. 'These white people have fancy names for every little thing.

Everyone feels down from time to time but you just have to move on with life.'

'If you believe in Jesus, nothing like depression can come near you, Ruhi. Just believe and give all your problems to God,' said Ma.

'It's all in your head. Don't be weak. Be strong. If you keep telling yourself that you're depressed, then you will stay depressed,' Pa continued.

It was beyond frustrating that they refused to accept the name of what I was feeling while trying to pull me out of it. Their fear of legitimising my 'weakness' meant they couldn't recognise my mental illness as reality – as a chronic condition and not a momentary lapse. I gave up on starting new conversations with my parents and quickly retreated from those they initiated. To be in their presence was a constant discomfort. *They don't get it. They won't get it,* I kept reminding myself. Their refusal to accept what I was going through felt like they were rejecting the real me when I wasn't or couldn't be the model daughter.

Interestingly, Pa and Ma didn't seem to consciously link any of what they read in the counsellor's letter to the cases of suicide in our own family. Perhaps it was too far-fetched a conclusion for them; they didn't know that I'd already been having suicidal thoughts by that point. After considering the comments in the letter from the counsellor, Ma and Pa said that if I was going to see a therapist, it had to be Dr Anita Anand. She was a distant relative and a psychiatrist. Best to keep things in the family, they said, though it seemed counter-productive to me. *If you don't want anyone close to you knowing, wouldn't you rather I saw an 'outsider'?* I thought.

I booked a few appointments with Anita Aunty. She was a good listener and judging by the fees she reduced for me, which others were willing to pay, she was good at her job too. But I didn't continue with her for long. She prescribed some medication to help with my depression, which I treated with suspicion. I'd inherited Pa's aversion to meds and would even forgo paracetamol for headaches and I didn't want to be a chemical woman. Also, it was awkward having my parents pay for something that they didn't actually support and wouldn't have allowed me to do if it wasn't required by the APC. I gave up on my appointments with Anita Aunty after completing the required number of sessions.

I persevered at uni for eight years in total and earned my double degree. Still desperate for Pa's approval, I wanted to show him that I could do it. *How could he just 'wash his hands' of me?* I wanted him to take me back into his hands and pat me on the head like a dog. *Good girl.* Also, he and Ma had successfully convinced me of the desolation that surely lay ahead if I were to move into adult life without a degree. However, there were upsides of following this advice: I learned how to write essays, form arguments and question everything – the latter two of which annoyed the crap out of my parents. (Even though, when Maya and I were growing up, Pa constantly encouraged us to ask 'why'. 'Question everything. Never stop asking if there is a better way to do things.' We just weren't allowed to ask 'why' when it came to our parents' actions.)

My parents had told me that life would be a hard slog without that piece of paper. I wasn't experienced enough to know that *anything* worth pursuing was going to be a hard slog anyway – or that if I was going to break my balls at work every day just to keep my parents happy, the endeavour wasn't going to last long.

***

At the end of the working day, I often reflected on my interviews and the candidates I'd met. I couldn't help but think that a fair chunk of the newly migrated South Asian women and men I'd interviewed were seeking jobs that, like mine, were a natural progression from qualifications they'd been forced to acquire, and not necessarily ones that might make them feel curious and alive. I was despondent because I knew that many of them wouldn't be ideal candidates in the eyes of our clients' hiring managers. On many occasions, I presented some of these capable people to hiring managers for roles I knew they could carry out with their eyes closed. More often than not, they were turned down, and the feedback I got was that they were looking for people who would be 'a better team fit', which I took to mean people with the 'right' accent, who seemed willing to assimilate to 'Australian' culture – white culture. A colleague of mine once worked with a client from one of the Big Four banks. The hiring manager was of South Asian descent and yet, he specifically stated – off the record of course – that my colleague was strictly not to send through the CVs of any candidates with an Indian accent.

Around the time I told my boss about the pregnancy, the workplace racism began to fatigue me to another level beyond regular gestational exhaustion. It got to the point where even kindness from my colleagues left me cold. People at work started to congratulate me when news of our baby became public knowledge. Those with children said things like, 'You and Jake must be so excited,' and 'Enjoy this special time, you won't get it back again.' I imagined that those sorts of sentiments made other pregnant women feel flowers bloom on their hearts, but

I just felt morose and bereft of any maternal excitement.

'Do you feel like you're not enjoying the pregnancy?' Jake asked over dinner one night.

'I don't know. It's not like I'm having a bad time. I mean, it hasn't been easy but I was prepared for that, you know? The sickness is supposed to ease up soon so that'll be good. But I'm not sure that's the main reason I'm feeling so down.'

'What do you reckon it is?'

'Maybe it's because people are certain that I'm treasuring this time and it makes me feel like a rubbish mum because I haven't thought much about our baby. I know she's in there,' I said, patting my belly. 'And I'm conscious of making healthy choices, like moving away when I pass someone smoking on the street, eating well, exercising ... you know.'

'Mm hmm.'

'But I feel disconnected from the whole experience. Everything is so busy and it takes all my energy just to do what's already expected of me. Work is all-consuming. And I'm not enjoying it as much as I used to. I'm sick of all the racism. I don't want my pregnancy to fly by while I'm focused on all of this shit!' I put my cutlery down and started to cry.

Jake wrapped his arm around me. 'Yeah. And it doesn't make it easier that you leave at 7am and get back after 7pm most days. Maybe you need to be stricter about finishing at 5.30?'

'But that just means I'll be bringing work home, which I don't want. And it doesn't solve the problem of me disliking work. I'm putting all this effort into doing something I don't even want to stick with long-term. But *this!*' I pointed to my belly, 'I'm nurturing another human being in my body and I'm hardly noticing her. Plus, I'm terrified of messing her up with my parenting. Where am I supposed to find time to do the research I want to do on how to be a freaking parent when all I can manage in the evenings is to collapse on the daybed, too depleted to move? I've got all these books to read and still haven't opened them!'

'So what do you want to do?'

I knew my answer was going to sound ridiculous, so I let it out slowly. Like a clown pulling a chain of handkerchiefs out of her sleeve.

'I think ... I need ... to quit.'

'Okay ... Do you feel that maternity leave is too far away?'

I cleared my throat. 'Yes, I do. And what am I going to do after mat leave? Go back? And what am I supposed to tell our kid when she hears me telling her to follow her dreams and asks me why I haven't?' It was the first time that thought occurred to me and I was surprised by how much sense it made.

'Yeah, good point.'

'So what do you think?' I asked nervously.

'I don't want you to keep feeling this way. I want to support your choice but we do have to look at the budget.'

So we did. At first I was panic-stricken that our financial situation might require me to keep working. But after a great deal of discussion and some lifestyle adjustments that would allow us to live off Jake's income (funnily, he'd ended up working in academic governance at the same university I was almost kicked out of) we made it happen. It helped that we'd been watching TV shows about tiny houses and minimalism. We'd also been educating ourselves about conscious consumerism and the environmental impact of accumulating material possessions. Jake and I didn't feel a strong need to continue the kind of lifestyle we had led; it wasn't lavish but it was cushy. We sold and donated some belongings and I decided to stop spending money on manicures, pedicures and clothes. Our priorities changed. We wanted less instead of more. There was a thrill to our new approach and knowing that once I wrapped up at work, I could finally start reading those parenting books on my shelf.

The following week, I informed my manager of my decision to leave. Once I'd served out my notice period, I was no longer a pawn on my parents' chessboard. I still didn't know what I wanted to do career-wise, but I was going to be free! I could finally divorce myself from my old, unsatisfying life trajectory and start from scratch. For the first time, I realised that I mattered in my own life. *I* mattered.

So, as the leaves on the plane trees started to caramelise, I walked out of my workplace in the Rialto Towers on Collins Street for the last time, ready to shed the yoke of my parents' professional aspirations.

Next item on the agenda: tell Ma and Pa I quit my job.

Fuck.

8

Thanks for the panic attacks. Here's a heart attack in return.

Weeks later, as we neared the five-month mark of my pregnancy, Melbourne was changing gears. People began to move slower – even those who weren't pregnant. Autumn took us out of the oven and put us into the fridge where we congealed into our darker wintery selves. Former colleagues from overseas had told me that Melburnians were known around the world for our obsession with wearing black. When I looked around, I was shocked to agree with them, having never noticed. I liked it. What a sexy reputation, I thought. If my first winter as a pregnant woman meant more black, more blankets, warm puddings, mulled wine (or at least the smell of it) and cuddles on the daybed, *Bring. It. On.*

Daylight savings had ended and the sun was setting at around five o'clock in the evenings. The calm sea breeze that had floated up our street all summer long now seemed hostile in its pursuit of warmth to snuff out. Red-nosed, rugged-up people nodded as they passed Panda and me on our daily walks.

'Hello.'

'Morning.'

'Bloody cold, isn't it? Bloody Melbourne weather.'

It seemed that no amount of time spent living in Melbourne disqualified its residents from feeling surprised by the weather or complaining about it. I'd sensed this most acutely back at the Echo Chamber Church where, during prayer meetings, members praised God for 'his perfect ways' and 'wonderful creation', and immediately after saying 'amen', moaned about the 'miserable' weather as they greeted one another. Like every new generation of parents, Jake and I identified many things we wanted to 'do differently' when our kid came along, including the discouragement of weather-related bitching.

Now that I was a free woman, having thrown off the shackles of my ill-suited career, I had time to read those parenting books that taunted me daily. The more I read, the more I wanted to do differently. The more I wanted to do differently, the more I stressed about my parents undermining me. The more I stressed about my parents undermining me, the more I grieved that they didn't do differently enough with me, which led me back to what I wanted to change when it came to my daughter. I read when I woke up in the morning and again in the afternoon when I'd finished cooking and cleaning. Then I'd hit the books again before bedtime. The cycle of stress-grief-resolve-stress-grief was relentless.

It became increasingly difficult to get up twice, sometimes thrice, in the middle of the night to relieve my easily burdened bladder. When I returned to bed, I often struggled to fall back asleep because of my rising anxiety. I grew nervous that I would fail at my attempts to break the cycle of abusive parenting. I was tense about our finances now that we were living off only one income and concerned about the pressure it might put on Jake. I worried about worrying, fearful that the rising cortisol in my body would hurt our baby. Jake told me that I was grinding my teeth in my sleep again, which I hadn't done for a long time.

During an afternoon waddle to a local café, I talked about how I was feeling with my sister-in-law, Sarah, who was also pregnant. She was four months ahead of me and grappling with similar grief about her own childhood. We shared notes on books and podcasts.

'We're going to be hippie mums,' she once said to me, sensing early on that our chosen styles of parenting contrasted with what seemed 'normal' among our families and friends. But we got to be peculiar together.

'Have I told you about Viv before?' I asked.

'I don't think so.'

'She's this incredible woman I used to know at my old church. I recently remembered something she said a while ago that I thought you'd love.' I told Sarah about Viv, an early childhood educator who went on a study tour to Italy for professional development. The organisation there specialised in the Reggio Emilia approach and worked on the belief that children's opinions were as valuable as the teachers'. There she'd learned that the word 'education' was a derivative of the Latin, 'educare' which meant 'to bring forth' or 'to draw out'. This emphasised the idea that children were already enough, and so the role of the teacher or the parents wasn't to make them better but to help them access their own innate abilities.

'Viv said that after this trip, her thinking shifted hugely around who children were. When she went back to work, she did a whole lot less talking in class and a whole lot more listening and asking questions.'

Sarah sighed. 'I wish more people saw it that way.'

'Me too. In my family, we were always taught to respect our elders but it never flowed the other way.'

Sarah let out a tired laugh in agreement. Though necessary, it was exhausting to reflect back on our upbringings.

I continued, 'I never want to forget this when I have our daughter.'

Sarah was one of a handful of people who knew that Jake and I were expecting a girl. She and her partner had decided not to find out the sex of their baby, keeping it a surprise until birth. Even though Jake and I found out as soon as we could, we kept it a secret from most people, hoping to circumvent the ineluctable onslaught of pink, frilly gifts. When I first told Sarah, her response was, 'Aww, that's wonderful! I can just imagine my brother being a fantastic dad to his daughter. There's something about a little girl that makes her dad's heart sing, isn't there?'

'Ha! Maybe with Jake and our daughter. And for you with your dad. But for me, the phrase, "There's something about a little girl that makes her dad have heart attacks," would be more fitting,' I snorted.

'You can't hold yourself responsible for his heart attack.'

'Um, yeah I can.'

***

Pa beat me one too many times during one of Ajji's visits to Melbourne. I was still in primary school and still lived in the Stone Fruit House. Ajji couldn't bear to keep watching her son-in-law repeatedly strike her young granddaughter, even though she had done the same to her own children as they grew up.

One night, she threw herself between us and yelled at Pa, her voice cracking, 'If you treat your daughter like this, she will leave you and go!'

She then hurried me into another room, shut the door and held me tight, drawing ovals with broad strokes across my back with her open palm, as though she was grouting broken tiles together in a mosaic. She shushed and cooed over the heavy sobs I let out between restricted intakes of breath. I sounded like a beeping alarm clock: 'I – don't – want – to – live – here – an – ny – more – Aj – ji.' Thank God for Ajji; that particular evening, Pa's anger was more terrifying than usual. But Ajji and Ma weren't always around. If I happened to get in trouble for something later at night, after Ma had gone to bed, I had no choice but to endure for as long as it lasted. Sometimes, if it was loud enough to wake her up, she would intervene. Other times, I was not so lucky to be saved. Crying and rocking myself to sleep was normal. Too normal.

Around this time, still during Ajji's stay, Maya struggled to fall asleep one night. She pleaded with Pa to stay with her in our room and Pa acquiesced. He laid down in her single bed with her while I was across the room in mine. I had been in trouble earlier that evening. What for, I couldn't tell you. But I was nervous about Pa staying with us that night. The room was dark and a short while in, I got up, opened the door and turned on the hallway light, making my way to the loo for a wee. Then I returned to bed. Not long after, I went again. And again. And again. And again. After about five trips to the toilet, Pa was furious. 'Why are you going to the toilet so much?!' I wasn't even sure what he was suspicious of. But for some reason, my recurrent visits to the bathroom were not acceptable.

He warned me through gritted teeth. 'If you go to the toilet *one more time, just wait and see what I will do to you!*'

I couldn't recall how much water I'd drunk. But this was strange even for my well-hydrated self. So when the next urge to wee came on, I stayed in bed, petrified of his injunction. The decision process of what to do next was a mental obstacle course with only two pathways, neither of which ended well. Wet the bed or wet my underwear, not both. Instinct hinted that it was more shameful to wet one's underwear, so I swiftly pulled them off, sat up and relieved myself in bed. Pa heard the trickle in the dark. He arose promptly, turned on the bedroom light and I saw his face. Beneath his bushy eyebrows, his eyes bulged out of his head, as they did when there was about to be a reckoning for my misdeeds. He strode across the room toward me, seething with anger and whatever followed became a suppressed, irretrievable memory that I've scratched at but haven't been able to open.

The mornings that followed my beatings were unpredictable. Sometimes, Pa gave me the cold shoulder for days, the total length depending on the severity of my transgression. Other mornings, his behaviour was pleasant, as though nothing had happened. I learned the following pattern: afternoons, evenings and nights were for the stripping of my dignity, and mornings were for the reinstatement of it. On days that face-washing and moisturising did nothing for my swollen face and eyes, I walked around with my head bowed. When Pa happened to notice, he put his hand under my chin and tenderly lifted my face. This almost always moved him to make his speech of reassurance.

'I don't like smacking you, Ruhi. You think I enjoy hitting my daughter? You think I enjoy making my daughter cry? I smack you out of love. If it was some other child, why would I care? When I did something wrong, my parents smacked me also. If parents don't punish kids, they won't learn right from wrong, and as your father I am responsible for teaching you. Henceforth, please obey me straight away so we don't have to go through this.'

'But can't you just tell me?'

'I try, Ruhi. I try. I tell you once, twice, even thrice! When you don't listen, that's when you get into trouble. One day, when you have children, you will do the same and you will come back and thank me. Trust me.'

Never, I quietly promised my unborn children.

Pa was on a die-hard mission to ensure I was 'ahead' in every way that mattered to him. But he was so sincere in the mornings, I was often brought to tears by how well-intentioned his actions were and how earnestly he wanted the best for me. Punishment was the way he knew to steer our tight ship. Still, I knew one thing for sure: all of the beating, shouting and shaming wasn't just about discipline. If it was, he might have had a clearer idea of when to stop. I could see it even though he couldn't: this was about unleashing pent-up anger.

It was around this time that I experienced my first panic attacks. I'd always found it difficult to describe a panic attack. Thankfully, as an adult I came across the perfect description in Amy Poehler's book, *Yes Please.*

'The best way I can explain a panic attack is that it's the feeling of someone inside my body stacking it with books. The books continue to pile up and they make me feel like I can't breathe.'

As an antidote, she offered, 'Meditation helps a lot. Sex does too. Calling someone equally as anxious on the phone makes you feel less alone.'

Seeing as I was clueless about meditation and sex, calling someone was the only option left. Or it might have been if my parents didn't monitor my calls at the time.

***

When I was in Year 8, a friend of a cousin of a friend called Mason, who attended a nearby boys' school, used to catch the afternoon bus with my friends and me. Despite Pa's hope for me to go to one of the top-tier private schools, I'd ended up attending a girls' school a few suburbs away. All the work put into preparing for selective school entrance exams was for naught because Ma won the argument with Pa about whether or not the hour-long train commutes to the elite schools were worth it – 'No! That's too much time! And who knows what kind of boys are there?'

My parents believed that I only ever sat with girls from school on the bus, which was true to begin with. I decided it was best if they didn't know about the boys we made friends with later on. Had I told them, they would have banned me from taking public transport to and from school altogether. Worse, they would have found out about Mason, who happened to fancy me. At the time, I thought, *Woah, someone likes me? Me?!* Given that I was raised to be modest, attention from any Tom, Dick or Harry was welcome attention, for the most part. Even when it was Dick and I didn't think terribly highly of him.

When Mason called our landline, he may as well have shaved off Pa's meeshee. Pa picked up the phone and put it on speaker – a common practice in our household, because ... radiation poisoning.

'Hello?'

'Hi. Can I talk to Ruhi?'

'Who is this?'

'It's a friend. My name's Mason.'

'Ruhi is *not here*. What do you want to tell her?'

'Can you get her to call me back please?'

'I'll let her know, bye.'

I was in the same room as Pa, close enough to hear him lie about my whereabouts but too far to hear the voice in the phone. He looked at me with his golf-ball eyes, demanding answers.

'Which boys are you talking to?'

'What? Who was that?' I asked.

'Some Mason. How does he know you?!'

'He's my friend's cousin and sometimes he catches the same bus as us.' *Lies.* He *always* caught the bus with us. Also, you'll recall he was *a friend of a cousin of a friend;* I knew that if I portrayed the relationship as familial rather than friendly, Pa would be less severe about it. In our vehemently heteronormative culture, friendship between boys and girls was dangerous and forbidden territory, in case they ended up smitten with each other. But if they were family, they would steer clear, one hoped, of anything too intimate or shameful. Though my friends and I found this rule irrational, when we considered our parents' backgrounds it seemed fair enough. That was until we learned that Hindu and Muslim family friends of ours had married their relatives. Moreover, my cousin's wedding to our uncle (her mother's and my father's younger brother) had recently been confirmed, which was both fascinating and terrifying to me (marrying my uncle and being cousins with my own kid? – no thanks). So really, all boys, related or not, were off-limits. It was just that our parents didn't perceive relatives as much of a threat; if a boy related to my friend was on the bus, it was safe for my parents to assume that he sat on the bus with us because he had to, not necessarily because he wanted to. The volume and speed of Pa's questioning escalated: 'WHY is this Mason calling you?'

'I don't know!' *Another lie.*

'HOW did he get our phone number? DID. YOU. GIVE. HIM. OUR. PHONE. NUMBER?'

'No! I don't know how he got it! Maybe from one of my school friends?' *True, for the record.*

'You are NEVER to speak to him or any other boy again, DO you understand?'

'But why? He just wanted to talk. It's not like I was going to his house or something.' Even suggesting it was scandalous.

'DON'T ask questions. If he calls again, put the phone down straight away. And if he calls while your Ma and I are not home, I WILL find out. Never give your phone number to boys and tell your friends not to as well. DO YOU UNDERSTAND?'

'Yes, Pa.' *Lying again.* I did not, in fact, understand.

A few days later Mason called again. This time Ma picked up the phone. I was surprised when she handed it to me instead of hanging up on him. But it made sense when she walked into the next room and picked up the cordless handset to listen in.

'Hey, how are you?' Mason asked.

'Yeah, good thanks. My mum said that you want one of your books back but I don't have any of your books?'

'Yeah I just said that so she'd give the phone to you.' *Oh no.* I saw Ma's eyes widen. 'I wanted to talk to you,' he said. I could hear him smiling at the other end of the line.

'Oh. Um...'

Ma lunged toward me, motioning for me to hang up.

'Tell him not to call again!' she said in a terse, growling whisper. I obeyed and we didn't hear from Mason again – a relief, mind you.

***

Lacking the privacy I needed for honest conversations with my friends over the phone, or the ability to have honest conversations at all, combined with my knowledge deficit in the departments of sex and meditation, I couldn't have taken Amy Poehler's advice if it had been available to me back then.

As I got older, the panic attacks continued. They were guaranteed in scenarios where I struggled to get my head around a concept. Even after I'd overcome the crippling shyness of my childhood, which had prevented me from ever raising my hand to ask questions or verbally engage in my classes. By this point, I'd developed enough confidence to ask as many clarifying questions as necessary, but I still suffered panic attacks when comprehension eluded me.

Years later, after marrying Jake, my panic attacks became more sporadic. Therapy helped and I was sure the sex did wonders too, but nothing proved as good for my mental health as the simplicity of companionship and the promise of love without performance in the safe space that Jake and I called home.

While I rejoiced in my mental health improvements, I still worried for Pa's wellbeing. I still suspected that he suffered from undiagnosed depression, possibly among other things, and like me, did a marvellous job of disguising it with a bubbly personality and seemingly positive attitude to life.

When my phone rang late one night, I wasn't shocked like the rest of our family and family friends were. Its trill was a death knell – the only way a ringing phone can sound at midnight. Pa had suffered a heart attack and was in the emergency ward at hospital.

Jake and I visited the following morning. We tracked down Ma in the cardiac ward. She'd become a one-woman call centre, fielding local and international enquiries about Pa's health. In a matter of hours, his room was crammed with aunties and uncles. They overflowed out to the corridor. News spread quickly, as it always did in our Indian community, that Pa's life was suddenly threatened by heart disease. Only, it wasn't sudden. His lifelong partiality to white rice, sweets and deep-fried snacks, mingled with his angst over many things – but mostly over my mother and me – all became too much for his heart to handle.

I showed up to offer my support but also to have another crack at connecting with my moribund father. The positive prognosis from the doctors stood at odds with my tendency to catastrophise. Death was always around the corner. I was sure of it. Both of my grandfathers had minor episodes – small anomalies in their heart waves before the big kahuna came with one final, fatal chomp. No warning. No chance to say goodbye.

Far from being able to share a heartfelt conversation with Maya or me, Pa could hardly get a few words in at all, since one-third of Karnataka had shown up to block the arteries of the cardiac ward. I scowled at Ma for tactlessly channelling visitors straight to Pa's sickbed after his heart attack. Expectations needed to be managed. Appointments needed to be organised. The word 'no' needed to be employed. I was furious. But I could also understand that with her husband in this state, I couldn't expect Ma to suddenly become less of a typhoon after a lifetime spent whirling from one situation to the next.

So I called my sister aside to discuss how we were going to deal with our human spinning top. Maya's charity and preternatural knack for soothing our parents – where I tended to rile them up – was the only well to draw from in this situation.

'I know,' Maya said. 'This is not cool. He's just had a heart attack for goodness sake! He needs to rest.'

'Yeah. I think we need to have a word with her. It's not fair on him, her, us or the hospital staff. And what the hell were all these people thinking? I know they came out of respect, but did no one stop for a minute to think, *Oh, maybe we should give him a moment to recover from his heart attack before we barge in there?*'

'I know right?!'

'Plus, you know Ma. All of this attention is making her feel better, even if it's at the expense of Pa recovering in peace.'

Maya sighed. When things quietened down and there were only two families lingering, I asked Ma how she was feeling.

'Ya, fine.'

'How do you know you're fine when you haven't stopped to think about how you feel? You haven't slowed down to eat or breathe, with all these people around.'

'I'm fine! I told you. It's good to have the whole jingbang[3] here,' she said, chuckling. 'What else will we do anyway, sitting here alone, bored?'

'Yeah, I understand, Ma, but I think you need to consider how many people it's appropriate to have here at any given time. And you need to factor in breaks for both you and Pa.'

'Ya, ya, I know. But they all wanted to see him. I couldn't say no,' Ma said, resisting surrender to encroaching tears.

'Yes, you can, Ma. And if you're not confident with saying "no", you can say "later" instead. It'll be better, not just for you guys but also other people in this ward who might be processing sad news. You never know. It's insensitive to have everyone in here like this. And it doesn't matter that I've told them a million times to keep it down. None of them know how to whisper! The nurses

---

[3] This is Ma's own version of cockney. Jingbang just meant 'gang'.

and admin staff have come over twice already now, telling people to be quiet.'

'Ya, you're right. I know. I know,' said Ma, her voice withering. As we talked, Maya nicked Ma's phone and set it to airplane mode before slipping it back in her bag.

'Also, Ma, there's no one here that you need to be strong for. We're all grown up. It's okay to cry. You're tired and it's been a huge day. Please take some time to yourself to process.'

'No, no, I'm fine.'

'Alright, well, it's okay not to be.' I walked away.

Later, after everyone had left, Jake was talking to Pa in his room. Meanwhile, Maya and I sat with Ma and her cousin, Sunil Uncle, in the waiting room. Ma paced the room, finally plonked down and managed two or three breaths before her grief tumbled out in uneven bouts. Maya and I exchanged a knowing glance. Maya got up, took a couple of steps over and stood next to Ma, rubbing her back. Her displays of sympathy toward Ma and Pa were not circumscribed – unlike mine. Among my closest friends, I was known as a warm person ready to provide a hug when needed. In the presence of my parents, however, I erected a bulwark that only words could permeate. Maya's relationship with our parents was of another nature entirely, involving hugs, kisses and gentle touches on forearms.

Once, during a backyard after-party-pity-party, which my uncles often indulged in, I heard Pa say of me, beer in hand, 'I smacked her. I scolded her. I shouted. I did everything. But it didn't work. There's no point doing all that with your kids.'

As we got older, this was the advice he would give his peers with children younger than Maya and me. While it was unfortunate that I had to be the first dud draft in his parenting project, his new philosophy was a welcome change and a relief. With Maya, he used reasoning instead of punishment. Their relationship wasn't without friction but Pa's newfound ability to *agree to disagree* and *let some things go* allowed Maya to successfully steer her own boat with Pa onboard and Ma wakeboarding behind them. In contrast, I was the shipwreck child.

When we were little, I was jealous of the 'special treatment' she received. But as I matured and got over the petulance of, 'Hey! Maya did something naughty. How come I get in trouble and she doesn't?', I recognised that Pa had set a different tone for his relationship with Maya, not out of spite for me, but because he was smart enough to change tack when it became clear that his approach with me was ineffectual. Somehow, Maya never became a spoiled brat. Instead, she stuck up for me.

Often, some of our friends who had turbulent relationships with their siblings asked Maya and me how we got along so well. I could put it down to three things. First, Maya was the closest thing to a real-life angel fluttering around with flowers in her hair. I think she was just born like that, but she also did the hard inner work to stay that way – someone who is quick to forgive and even quicker to extend love and kindness without judgement. Secondly, we both took our faith seriously as kids, growing up on shared values of compassion and acceptance we learned in Sunday School. So when one of us had the chance to be a bitch to the other, we sometimes gave in but mostly didn't. And lastly, my best friend in primary school, Aurelie, was charming, playful and affectionate with Maya whenever she came over. When I told Maya to piss off – 'You're so annoying. This is *my* friend!' – Aurelie invited her to play. There's nothing like the jealousy of an older sibling when she notices that her little sister starts to prefer Aurelie over her own flesh and blood. So I decided to get my shit together, limit Maya's contact with Aurelie and reinvent myself as the lovely big sister I became known as. And you'll be glad to know that the Aurelie ban was lifted after I'd had a few months to win my sister back.

Since then, we've always had each other's backs and grabbed the baton when the other was about to drop it. So when Maya saw Ma crumple up into a blubbering mess, she stepped in because she knew I had nothing genuine to give.

***

The next day, I returned to the hospital. Pa was tired but overall, he was feeling better. A stent had been inserted into his heart. He was told that from then on he needed to change his diet and have regular check-ups with a cardiologist.

I brought a hamper of healthy snacks, fruit and wholemeal sandwiches from home, knowing that Ma and Pa found hospital meals too bland. Later that day, I was incensed at the sight of the unopened food bag. Although the hordes of visitors were better managed on day two, they were still there. Any success we'd had from putting Ma's phone on airplane mode the day before was cancelled out when people started calling Pa's phone instead. Still, it could have been worse.

And that afternoon, it did get worse.

I was on the outer edge of a conversation between Pa and some members of our extended family, when I looked up and saw the last thing I wanted to see at that moment – or *ever*. Maya looked up at the same time, stricken. It was *him*.

What the fuck is he doing here?! Oh, of course! Of course Ma invited him this morning when she turned her phone back on. What the hell was she thinking?! Oh, that's right – she wasn't.

I was suddenly overcome with the fury of a raging bull – not toward the unwanted visitor, who was still far down the other end of the corridor, but at my mother. If her husband hadn't been lying in a hospital bed at that moment, I would have had no problem raising my voice over everyone present and giving her a piece of my mind for her absolute insensitivity. I had told her the night before that she didn't need to be strong for us. But she *did* need to be *responsible*. She needed to be my *mum*.

Maya went into rapid-response mode. She did a hurried sweep of the room, corralled my belongings and shoved them into my hands. I hastily said goodbye to everyone.

'Where are you going ma?' Pa asked.

'Home. Glad you're feeling better. Bye.'

'Okay but ... okay, okay, no problem, you're in a hurry. Thank you for coming ma. See you next time,' he said.

'Bye. Bye everyone!' I hugged Pa and waved at my aunties and uncles instead of giving them a kiss or a hug like I normally did. Then I rushed out with Maya, not knowing it would be one of the last few times I'd see my relatives all together like that.

I brushed past the individual, shields up and holding fire, not for his sake or for Ma's, but for my sick dad lying in the room I'd dashed out of. I drew on my customer-service training from my teenage years working as a concierge, where we were taught not to bring our feelings to work. My sangfroid in the workplace, regardless of any inner turmoil, was legendary. I could disarm others with ease in a heated moment. I could de-escalate situations with my deep, certain voice. I could probably negotiate with terrorists if I had to. But in that moment in the hospital, when *that* person held out his hand to shake mine midway down the corridor, all I wanted to do was spit on his face.

I didn't.

Because, no matter how I felt about them, I was required to show respect to my parents' guests.

9

Rite of passage

Reverence for guests, elders (especially older men) and for the family unit was often upheld at the expense of self-respect. This was especially obvious in the Bollywood movies we watched, which also became my primary source of information regarding sexuality and intimacy in the absence of dinner-table conversation about these topics in my childhood home. The lessons I gleaned from these films might not have been quite so woefully inadequate had an adult thought to explain some of the recurring themes – for example, good touch versus bad touch, consent and respect. It would have been helpful if someone older and wiser had highlighted the repetitive message that men were in charge of sex and romance, and told Maya and me that, in real life, women were allowed to say 'no'. If our 'no' wasn't heeded, it was perfectly reasonable to shout, scream, punch, kick, scratch, or do whatever we needed to defend ourselves.

In the movies, it was almost always male protagonists instigating choreographed foreplay – shoulder- and neck-kissing, saree-unwrapping, jewellery-removing and so on – while the coy object of his affection closed her eyes and turned her face away to hide her inescapable pleasure. Realistically, none of the adults in my extended family was going to teach Maya and me that women were also sexual beings who desired and initiated sex; but they *could* have taught us that it was actually not okay for men to stalk and harass women with their all-male posse, professing their so-called love, like they did in the movies.

Constructive discussions about respectful, consensual sex were forbidden even among adults. No one in my family spoke of the three-letter S-word, except for Roberto Uncle, who had a new catalogue of 'dirty' jokes for every party. The few times I did hear anything about sex, it was from the mouths of drunken uncles at parties we should have left hours earlier, according to Pa.

Public displays of affection were also off the table. My parents never held hands or kissed in front of us, let alone when they were out and about. An occasional side-hug or pat on the shoulder was the extent of the physical affection we saw.

From where I was sitting, Indian culture seemed allergic to intimacy – the two philosophically incompatible. Growing up, several South Asian friends of mine hid their romantic relationships from their parents. I watched aunties and uncles behave more like colleagues than couples. Babysitters were only ever employed when absolutely unavoidable, such as during work hours. As far as I knew, none of the couples, my parents included, ever hired a carer so they could enjoy date nights or time alone together. I was incredulous when I finally learned about the Kamasutra and that it originated in what is now known as India.

Therefore, I expected my mother's bewilderment over the phone whenever her invitations to weekend family events were met with, 'Sorry, Ma, Jake and I have plans,' in the years leading up to my pregnancy.

'What plans?!'

Oh, the shock. Every time. The thought of my husband and I wanting to spend time alone together was nonsensical to my parents, who hoped to see the family together most if not all the time. It would have been unfathomable to them if I said, 'Jake and I are hanging out, just the two of us,' much less, 'Our plans are to have sex this arvo.' I'd never been that honest with her, nor did I plan to be, but on the occasions she did coax it out of me that we were just spending time together at home, her unchanging response was, 'EH! You can sit at home with Jake anytime! Come here now and eat yummy rice and dhal I made. It's your favourite dhal with the big big tomatoes!' Nothing was ever big or small to Ma. Everything was 'big big' or 'small small' – a direct translation from the Hindi terms bade-bade or chote-chote, or in Kannada, dhod-dhod and sann-sann.

Speaking of big and small things, my parents never ended up having 'the talk' with Maya or me in our adolescence, other than to say, 'Don't do anything before marriage!' Still, I always had a sense that they knew something cheeky that we didn't, because whenever we moved house, they ensured there was a lock on their bedroom door. The lock was never discreet. It didn't have to be; we kids were clueless.

After Maya and I both moved out of the Echo Chamber House, she would return to stay with my parents on weekends. Maya discovered that my parents had taken to locking their bedroom door at night when she was over, and if she ever had to wait a moment after knocking on their door, this was Pa's explanation: the lock held the door shut, stopping it from banging due to the draft from their window. When Maya told me this, I believed Pa. But I wasn't sure that was the only banging that went on.

Good for them!

***

'Any time I've spoken to an aunty lately, every single one has commented on how they can't believe I'm pregnant ... that it seemed like only yesterday that I was small enough to sit on their laps ... blah blah blah, you know...'

'Ya, even for me it feels like that. Ayo, how fast the time has gone!' Ma said between sips of her mango smoothie, the closest thing to a mango lassi at our local shopping centre.

'Then I change the subject and tell them how you and Pa conceived me because neither of you had self-control.'

'YOU WHAT?!' She stopped dead in her tracks opposite the noisy food court.

'Ha! I tell them about that time when I was a kid learning about the reproductive system. Remember that? I asked you how long you were pregnant with me for. You were so proud of yourself when you said, "Exactly nine months and nine days! You were perfectly on time!" So I got an old calendar...'

'Ayo yawa! Chi! You holas hudugi! Dirty girl!'

'I counted nine months and nine days backwards from my birthday and what did I find? Your wedding night!'

'SHEH! What's WRONG with you?! And you're wrong about the dates!'

I had to cross my legs to stop myself from weeing as I fell apart at her reaction. My pregnant belly, which was nicely rounded like the rest of me by then, jiggled up and down. As much as Ma wanted to throw me into a naughty corner, she couldn't stop herself from laughing with me. At least we were able to talk about sex by then, however indirect it was. I supposed getting pregnant really took the guesswork out of it for my parents in terms of what I knew or didn't know about it all.

Once we calmed down from our squeaking and giggling, we resumed our mission to the maternity boutique. We each glided alongside elegant clothes rails, pretending to check sizes as we eyed price tags under shimmering molecules of glass orbs shining extra light into the room. As expected, the prices reflected the high quality of these fetching, functional, mostly striped garments – with an extra sixty bucks chucked on top to cover costs of keeping those contemporary chandeliers running all day, every day.

'I got paid today, so I want you to choose a dress you like and I will buy for you,' Ma spoke into my shoulder with the hushed voice she used in public.

'Aw. Thanks, Ma. That's so nice of you but you don't have to do that,' I said, pretending I'd rather pay for it myself.

'Please. Don't argue with me. I am your mother. I want to do this. You never let me buy things for you and I'm tired of seeing you wear the same harrak, worn out clothes all the time.'

'They're not *harrak*. I just don't want to wear a brand new outfit every three days like you.'

'*Summa kundher!* If you don't want, then think of it as a gift to my grandchild.'

'Fine. Thank you.'

She pushed me into the change rooms, which made me sweaty and nervous. I hated trying before buying and loathed shopping in general, for two reasons: buying lots of things went against my newfound anti-consumerist values, and being at the shops gave me an unstoppable urge to defecate. For the longest time, I put it down to a weird psychosomatic quirk, the cause of which I could never figure out. According to Ivana, however, this was a visceral high-anxiety response to decision-making in particular settings – for me, this was often at the shops.

When Maya and I were little, at least once or twice a week after school Ma dragged us on impromptu shopping trips, where we wasted hours moaning about our tired legs and hungry-for-chips bellies. Earlier than that, in Maya's infancy, Ma took us to Target and Big W where she frequently charged me with the responsibility of standing guard over the baby in the pram, surrounded by a cloud of white shopping bags full of her purchases.

'Ma ... hurry up...' I called out repeatedly, sighing and groaning as she scurried between clothes racks in the women's department. Then we moved to the make-up and fragrance area where I was stationed in another corner with our precious cargo. The same happened when we shuffled over to shoes and accessories. When it finally came time to head home, we'd rehearse our 'what to say to Pa' routine, which covered where we went, what we did, whether we spent any money and so on. I wasn't to give him the *real* answers to those questions, of course. I was lying for the greater good: to maintain peace in our family.

'You know how Pa is; we don't want to make him angry,' Ma would say. More often than not, we arrived home in the nick of time before Pa's car pulled up in the driveway. My role was to grab the bags, bolt into the house and shove them into the back of Ma's wardrobe, behind her not-new clothes. There weren't any gaps between clothes through which anyone could spot the bags – so vast was her existing collection. I then had to swiftly change out of my uniform to give the impression that we'd been at home all along.

Every couple of months, she would integrate these new wardrobe additions in a stealth operation that would take place when Pa was busy with longer chores such as lawn mowing, vacuuming or doing the laundry. She sat, cross-legged, in front of her wardrobe, removing, folding, checking to see if the coast was clear, removing, folding. Sometimes she took a few older items of clothing out and threw them in a donation bag. But mostly, she just untagged her new clothes and incorporated them with the rest of her wardrobe. Later, when Pa asked if the outfit she was wearing was new, she'd say, 'Eh! No! I bought it months ago. Didn't you see it sitting in my cupboard all this time?'

Until I hit my late teens, I didn't have a problem with Ma training me as her co-conspirator. I lied for her because I felt sorry for her; she was trying to fill a void with rampant spending. She should have been allowed to spend her salary however she wanted, but she was under Pa's domineering thumb. Sooner or later, he would see her cash withdrawals on the bank statement and an explosion would ensue. Threats to leave could be heard from the other end of the house. Ma knew this would happen but, like any addict, she couldn't help herself. The pity I felt for her led me to help her in other ways.

For some time in the Stone Fruit House, before Pa went to work each day, he would disconnect the TV and VCR. He had returned home too many times to find that dinner wasn't underway, the house was still untidy and we kids were disorganised – and Ma was to blame. He would only reconnect everything for Ma once when the chores had been completed, dinner had been eaten and Maya and I had showered, ready to commence homework. But Ma knew that I'd figured out how the wires worked. Every day, she got me to turn on everything after school so she could watch *The Days of our Lives* and *The Bold and the Beautiful*. At a quarter to six, I'd rip the cables out again. When Pa asked Ma if she'd watched TV, the answer was always, 'No! I was working! You can ask Ruhi!' I'd nod in agreement.

My sympathies shifted as I got older. I began to see how frustrating it was for Pa to be deceived and gaslighted on an almost daily basis and how maddening it was to try to work toward financial security with an uncooperative partner. It went against every post-poverty value he held dear to see his partner burn through their joint income in a matter of hours after payday.

Ma sometimes blackmailed him into going shopping on a Friday night. Her father had bought her everything she asked for and more, even though it drove him into debt. We told Pa that if he *really* loved his wife and the kids, he would get over himself and come to the shopping centre or the cinemas with us. Sometimes, these outings were harmonious. Other times, it ended with Pa angrily loitering outside the shops, seething as he leaned over the upper-floor balcony, waiting for Ma's ever-stretching 'five minutes' to end. Maya and I would part ways, one of us going with Pa and the other staying with Ma so that neither of them felt alone or unfavoured by the children. Eventually, Pa took to threatening to leave without the other half of the family. Once or twice, he did, only to come back at Ma's relentless summoning hours later.

But even when I started to reassess my loyalty to Ma, she kept covering for me. She couldn't bear to see my spirit downtrodden (at least at the hands of somebody other than her). At times, if it wasn't for her support, I felt I would have lost all reason to live, as Pa ensured that academia took centre stage in my life while the delete button was pushed on my hobbies and interests.

'After all that practice, Pa said I'm not allowed to dance at the Indian function this year,' I'd cry as my years of Bollywood dance performances at festivals came to an end. 'He said I'm getting too old for it and need to focus on my studies.'

'You keep practising. I'll talk to your Pa,' Ma said.

Another time I asked, 'How come my music teacher sees how passionate I am but Pa can't? She even said that she'd organise private violin lessons during lunchtime once a week, instead of during periods like other students, and I wouldn't have to have to pay for violin hire or classes.'

'Listen, I will sign the permission form. We won't tell your pa. If he asks about the violin you are bringing home, we will both tell him it's part of your compulsory music periods. He doesn't have to find out about the extra classes,' Ma said.

Yet another time, I'd complained, 'Pa constantly tells me to lose weight and he won't even support me when I ask for money to go to boot camp at gym.'

'When is it? Monday, Wednesday, Friday at five o'clock in the morning? Don't worry, I will drive you there and I will pay for it. How much is it? Six hundred? Okay. Good – you are doing something for your health. I will help you. Don't worry about Pa, I will talk to him.'

As a pregnant adult, I was relieved to be able to go shopping with Ma and not have to worry about the aftermath between her and Pa. After trying on a couple of dresses in the maternity boutique's change rooms, I was done. Ma reluctantly returned her next five suggestions to the racks from where she'd plucked them.

'So? You like any?'

'This navy one is nice.' I held up a maxi with a breastfeeding flap tastefully labelled *Curved extra layer for nursing access.*

'Okay. I'm happy you found one you like. You're so fussy. And you're a big stubborn-head! Like your Pa!'

'What's he doing?'

'Who knows? Enjoying time home alone.' In recent years, Ma and Pa had taken their claws out of each other's throats, adopting more of a live-and-let-live attitude – with exceptions of course. It helped that they'd achieved financial freedom, paid off their mortgages and didn't have to support mine and Maya's education anymore. Ma's wardrobe had since expanded from her bedroom's walk-in-robe to the double-door storage cupboard above the stairs, as well as the wardrobes in the two vacated bedrooms. She no longer hid her new purchases from Pa or forced him to go shopping. They'd also made peace with the fact that, once their daughters left, they only had each other in their Echo Chamber House. With too much cultural pride and rectitude at stake, divorce was never an option. It seemed they'd mutually decided that shaking their heads and rolling their eyes was as good a coping mechanism as any at their age.

'I want to buy dinner for you at the food court. Come.'

'Thanks, Ma.'

'Hoga! Stop thanking me. I am your mother. If I don't do all this, who will do for you? Come. Tell me what Jake likes and I will buy for you to take home for him.'

***

Growing up, the only shopping experience *both* of our parents enjoyed, much to mine and Maya's displeasure, was our Saturday trip to Dandenong Market. During our first decade in Melbourne, it was the only public place where my family could camouflage – among chaos.

'Gingahhhh. Dollarbag-dollarbag-dollarbag-dollar-Gingahhhh,' a man chanted in the same spot every week, leaning against a pillar and holding tiny bags of ginger in each hand. His customers were scarce, which led me to believe the return on his investment mustn't have been high. When someone did approach him, once in a blue moon, he only got one dollar for hours of droning.

'FRESH TOMADOES! GET YOUR FRESH TOMADOES OVER HERE!' boomed another stall owner. The floors were covered in onion skins and disintegrating bananas. Maya and I held tightly to our parents as we ploughed through the crowds. Pa believed this market trumped local greengrocers and supermarkets everytime when it came to fresh produce and value for money. For Ma, the side of the market that sold clothes, accessories and household goods, was the most fun. I was too snooty to appreciate how multicultural the place was and how much it benefited the diverse community. Immigrants from all over the world made their way to Dandy Market on Saturday morning. It was a hub of entrepreneurship and a place where my parents could feel a little bit more at home.

'Please, can we go home now?!' I'd whine.

Maya helped. 'My legs hurt! There's nowhere to sit down! I'm so hungry!'

Ma would buy us bánh mì from the Vietnamese food truck to quieten us down for a while. Also, she knew how much we loved those crispy, tangy baguettes.

One Saturday when I was about fifteen, Maya accompanied Ma to the quieter, cleaner side of the market with homewares and apparel, while Pa and I went into a fruit stall, bustling with bulk-buyers. Pa asked me to look for a box of as many unspoiled mangoes as possible. We stood on opposite sides of the same large table, surveying a small hill of slanted mango trays, a dozen in each. People rubbed shoulders with me and bumped into each other constantly.

Then I felt a warm body, taller than mine, press against me. I assumed someone was leaning over me to grab a crate. But they stayed there for a good thirty seconds or so. *Maybe they are still choosing?*

I felt something shaped like a banana against my backside, moving from from side to side and forward and back. It was weird and I felt ill, unsure as to why.

Is someone doing something wrong? Have I done something wrong? Is the person behind me actually confused about which mangoes they want? Or ... are they rubbing against me for another reason? Could that be ... a dick? Surely not. Why would someone rub a dick against me? Is this something people do?

I'd only ever seen the miniature, flaccid penises of my baby cousins during nappy changes. I had some sense that as a boy grew, so did his private parts, but I had no idea how much. Even though I'd studied sex-ed at school, I hadn't understood what an erection was. I was clueless about arousal, dry sex and certainly about desperate creeps who walked around crowded places rubbing their feral cocks against young girls. I never turned around to look at the man's face before he walked off. My dad hadn't noticed and I never said a word to him about it. I didn't have the language to describe the event or my feelings about it. When I realised what had happened, several years later, all I could hope was that the stupid fucker eventually got his dick chopped off by the old granny at the market who would fling her machete around as she split open pumpkins and coconuts.

Regrettably, that wasn't the only time I was assaulted. When I was at the bus stop a few years later on my way to uni, a bald, middle-aged man ambled over, pushing his bicycle along the footpath. At first, he stood in silence, staring at me. I watched him from the corner of my eye and turned my music off, keeping the earphones in. He slithered closer.

I prayed for the bus to hurry up. It was already thirteen minutes late. Every second that slid away tugged with it my sense of safety. As the man moved closer, I noticed his reddened face and bulging eyes. He was stout and hefty, like a vermilion bowling ball. He attempted conversation in a raspy voice and I gave vague responses, not saying anything of the closing distance between us for fear that I'd escalate the situation with no one around. There was a small clutch of shops nearby, but still about five hundred metres away. The road was like a mini freeway, long and straight. There was nowhere I could run or hide without him catching up on his bike.

I could breathe again when I saw the bus come over the crest. The Bowling Ball saw it too. He lunged toward me and grabbed my breasts. I pushed him back violently and raised my voice, my skull about to explode.

'Don't touch me! Don't you *dare* touch me again!' I shouted. He hesitated as the bus neared, then took another step toward me before retreating to his bicycle. The bus doors opened in front of me and, having witnessed our scuffle, the bus driver asked if I was okay. I said yes, but I wish I'd asked the bus driver to call the police right away. I was conditioned to avoid making a fuss about those sorts of things – even though I wasn't the one who caused trouble.

I sat shaking in my usual spot at the back of the bus, where I could keep an eye on everyone in front of me and no one could sneak up behind me. I called Jake. He picked me up from the bus stop at uni and I sobbed in his car, apologising for not holding it together. He held me and I was safe again.

I asked if he'd take me to church. My youth pastor cleared the next few hours of his afternoon. He prayed with us and urged me, if I felt comfortable, to go to the police. It occurred to me for the first time that if I stayed silent, I'd only be making it easier for the perpetrator to hurt another person. Who was I staying silent for? It wasn't for me.

That afternoon, Jake and I went to the police station to lodge a statement. I was later invited to the Victoria Police headquarters to describe the Bowling Ball to an illustrator. Two detectives were assigned to my case. They kept an eye on the area and questioned local shopkeepers. They asked if I'd ever seen him at that bus stop before. I told them I'd been catching that bus for over a year and I'd never seen him. I never saw him again. Nor did the detectives.

A week later, I told Ma and Pa about it. It hurt them that Jake, my pastor and the police all knew about it before they did. But there was no chance I'd have gone to them first, not after what Ma told me to do the last time I confided in her about something major. And certainly not after how it made me feel, years later, knowing that I'd listened, like a Good Indian Daughter was supposed to.

10

The Good Indian Daughter

The Good Indian Daughter, a paragon of virtue and repository of values was as much a part of my childhood as problematic depictions of sexuality. She graced the sets of almost every Hindi movie I watched during my childhood. Films with lead female characters became more popular as I got older, but more often than not, those heroines were still shrunken and demure in the face of various patriarchies. The Good Indian Daughter was *so* good – too good to take matters into her own hands. There were some exceptions, but even in those films where this woman acted in her own interests, she was either portrayed as a villain or as someone having undergone a psychological makeover – taking on new traits such as boldness, strength and newfound self-esteem – only made possible by a benevolent male saviour such as a lover, lawyer, father and so on.

While the Good Indian Daughter might look different from family to family – depending on class, caste, religion, location and other factors – one thing's for sure: on and off screen, the 'goodness' of this archetype is rivalled only by its longevity. Enduring decades, if not centuries, of grassroots (and more recently, national and global) pushes for gender equity, the mythology of the Good Indian Daughter is still alive, well and rigid AF.

In the films I watched growing up, this girl or woman *existed* for her family. She bade her lover farewell because her obstinate parents didn't approve of their relationship. She continued to cohabitate with her nasty in-laws until either her husband stood up for her, or his parents had a change of heart – or else the Good Indian Daughter died at the altar of self-sacrifice. She was expected to hold everything together on the home front. Her own identity faded into the background while she sang and danced for everyone else. Her vibrant sarees and exquisite jewellery were louder than her voice. Her raison d'être was her role as wife, sister, mother, daughter or daughter-in-law. Hardly anyone in these films cared about the work she did or wanted to do, her beliefs, her interests, her talents or her dreams; all of these revolved around male protagonists. And even when her dreams were entertained, they were only made possible by a male saviour. Predictably, these characters and their stories were mostly written by men. Sadly, women's real-life stories are also still being written by men.

Traditionally, Good Indian Daughters have borne the onus of preserving our family's honour. We carry it on our shoulders and in our genitals. As uterus-owners, we are the vessels of procreation; as vagina-owners, we are the duty-bound gatekeepers of sexual propriety. However you look at it, we are the biologically ordained fulcrums of morality.

Some years ago, prominent social scientist, poet and activist Kamla Bhasin went on Aamir Khan's talk show, *Satyamev Jayate.* Of the audience, she asked, 'Why did you place your community's honour in a woman's vagina?' In doing so, she forced the viewers to confront a disturbing truth: if an Indian woman is raped, society tells her that *she* is damaged; *she* has lost her honour, while those types of narratives are rarely applied to rapists. Her vagina, her crime.

If a girl or woman fails to meet social expectations – at home, school (if she has access to education) or work (if she is allowed to work), as a wife and as a mother – that 'failure' is not just hers; she has let down her family too. They can become shrouded in a shame so consuming it could even drive them to end her life in what's known as an honour killing. Google this term and click the *News* tab for a sobering glimpse at how rampant honour killings still are – and it's understood that many more cases never make it to the headlines.

Women pay with their lives for all kinds of 'offences': premarital sex; premarital pregnancy; falling in love with someone of the 'wrong' caste, religion or gender; rejecting a favourable proposal for arranged marriage; seeking divorce; dressing 'inappropriately'; or being raped, among others. The word 'honour' before 'killing' here feels oxymoronic; how can anything in that list be reason to murder someone in the name of honour? And *how* can the perpetrators of this misogynistic violence against one of their own expect to preserve *their* honour?

While honour killings are an extreme on a toxic spectrum, violence against women takes many other insidious, and more mundane, forms in Indian society. For example, some families make excuses for the rapists and pedophiles among them: fathers, uncles, brothers (not ignoring the relatively smaller number of women who commit acts of sexual violence). Sons disappoint parents, of course – a bad school report, a late night, refusing to do chores (if he is ever required to), premarital sex, impregnating a woman before marriage, disrespecting a woman, beating a woman, seeking divorce, or literal *rape* or sexual assault – but when (or if) he is pulled up on his behaviour, it's usually written off as youthful foolishness. If he's past his youth, he probably writes the rules himself.

In a 2018 study in *The Lancet,* clinical professor Rakhi Dandona and her colleagues point out that in 2016, almost 40 per cent of women around the world who suicided were Indian. Even though Indian women made up only 17.28 per cent of the global population of women that year. The same study shows that gendered discrimination, in its many forms, is a key indicator for increased suicide risk. Other factors included: arranged and early marriage for women, domestic violence, young motherhood, social status, economic dependence and risk of depression, among others.

When you look at suicide rates across India, my home state, Karnataka, is a grim frontrunner, alongside Tamil Nadu and Tripura. Drawing from my own experiences and the experiences of women in my family, I was all too familiar with some of the societal, cultural and familial dynamics that might lead a young woman to see suicide as the only solution. In that oppressive environment, problems could seem insurmountable, especially when we were discouraged from seeking support 'from outside'.

Though I was one of the luckier ones, valued by my family in many ways, it was abundantly clear to me, even as a young girl, that daughters were less desirable, less admirable, less able than our male counterparts.

As documented in the United Nations Population Fund's (UNFPA) State of World Population 2020 (SWOP) report, India recorded an average 461,500 'missing' female births every year between 2013 and 2017 due to prenatal sex selection (abortions), even though this practice is illegal. As journalist and author, Barkha Dutt, puts it, 'Missing was a polite euphemism for gender-driven genocide.' In 2011, the *Times of India* published an article headlined, '90% of 11 [million] Abandoned Kids are Girls'. When unwanted daughters in India are not aborted or abandoned, they are buried alive, poisoned, stoned, starved, suffocated with pillows or their illnesses are left untreated until they die.

Barkha Dutt goes into further detail in her book, *This Unquiet Land: Stories from India's Fault Lines:*

> 'In 2006 ... a girl was aborted or murdered every twelve seconds in India. If she wasn't murdered in the womb, sand or tobacco juice was forced down her nostrils when she opened her mouth to cry so that she would choke and die. Renuka Chowdhury, the then Minister for Women and Child Development in the UPA government at the centre, admitted that in the previous two decades alone, 10 million girl children in India had been killed by their parents. She called it a "national crisis".'

Another study in *The Lancet,* published in 2014 and researched by Alkema, Chao, You, Pedersen and Sawyer, revealed that India had the world's highest rate of excess female deaths, which is the difference between girls' estimated life expectancy – based on factors like families' financial and job security, access to food and drinking water, social class and religion, literacy, and urbanisation – and girls' real observed mortality rates. Biologically speaking, girls five years old and younger are actually less vulnerable to early mortality than boys, so excess female deaths in any measure is cause for concern. And yet, UNFPAs SWOP report suggests that in India, around one in nine girls who die before the age of five could have lost their lives due to postnatal sex selection (murder).

The discrepancy between boys and girls' postnatal survival rates has been documented in India from as early as the beginning of the twentieth century. In a 2003 article for the academic journal *Demography,* economist Rohini Pande quoted a 1901 census to highlight how Indian parents preferred boys, even then:

> 'There is no doubt that, as a rule, she [a girl] receives less attention than would be bestowed upon a son. She is less warmly clad ... she is probably not so well fed as a boy would be, and when ill, her parents are not likely to make the same strenuous efforts to ensure her recovery.'

Pande went on to outline discrimination between Indian boys and girls in more recent years: at the turn of the millennium, boys were still more likely than girls to be taken to a doctor when sick, boys had higher immunisation rates and boys were less likely to be malnourished.

Pande points out that so many of these differences stem from the idea that Indian boys are economic, social and religious assets; the idea that Indian boys are breadwinners and inheritors of property, while Indian girls are liabilities – especially due to dowries, which are now illegal but continue to be exchanged. When it comes to family ties, it's the sons who are expected to care for parents in their dotage, while daughters will be busy doing the same for their in-laws. Boys will carry on their family name, while girls will take their husband's – and so on. These phenomena aren't just characteristic of rural and lower-class families in India; they also apply to more affluent households and families that have emigrated.

In so many of our households, these dynamics are fed by the deep-seated belief that Indian women are the property of the men in their lives. Barring a relatively small number of women in progressive settings, a woman is rarely viewed as an individual unto herself, belonging to herself, in charge of her own decision-making and risk-taking, as well as her own safety. The elders in her family, usually men, call the shots on the extent to which she is allowed to enjoy these rights and freedoms. Please don't write to me saying, *Not all Indian families* – I know, but it must be acknowledged that it *is* typical for Indian girls to belong to their fathers, then for women to belong to their husbands later in life. Author and academic, Nivedita Menon summarises this dynamic well in her book *Seeing Like a Feminist:*

> 'This form of family [patriarchal, patrilineal, virilocal] is an inherently violent institution that is gendered to the core,' and involves '...a violent reshaping of the self of the woman getting married ... She leaves her home ... and goes to

her husband's home or to that of his parents. She changes her surname, in some communities even her first name, and her children bear their father's name; thus, her own name, even if she is one of the rare instances of retaining her name after marriage, is obliterated. Women have to learn to remake themselves completely, but even more significant is the fact that the entire period of their lives before this singular event of marriage, is spent in anticipating and preparing for this specific future, from choice of career and job options to learning to be adaptable from early girlhood.'

When women can't be palmed off onto husbands (consensually or not), they become the burden of brothers or other male family members. In many cases, women can also belong to their employers or governing bodies. At the worst of times, strangers wandering the streets without a moral compass as well as lecherous men within a woman's own community presume to claim that ownership. I've even heard a prominent religious leader in India declare to his multitudinous followers, as an argument for a man taking multiple wives, that it is better for a woman to become a second or third wife rather than the inevitable alternative: 'public property'.

According to Indian government statistics, on average, a woman was raped every fifteen minutes nationally in 2018, with more than 34,000 cases of rape reported for the year. Of course, countless incidents go unreported, and as Sudarshan Varadhan points out in the *Reuters* article, 'One woman reports a rape every 15 minutes in India', rapes that result in death are classified as murders, not rape cases. In 2019, the National Crime Records Bureau (NCRB) reported 405,861 cases of violent crimes against women for the year. Additionally, NRCB data cited in a *Scroll India* article, revealed that, of all rape victims each day, nearly ten are Dalit women, who are subjected to caste violence as well as gendered violence. To make matters worse, Dalit women receive little solidarity from upper-caste people, even self-proclaimed feminists. This attitude also permeates the legal system, which often treats cases involving lower-caste, lower-class female victims with poorly disguised apathy.

I talk to Indian people about these infuriating realities for women (and there are many other kinds of inequalities we have not touched on here). I've spoken to family members, friends, uncles (to my parents' disdain), acquaintances at gatherings and even Indian politicians at literature festivals. Some are horrified and speechless. Some, particularly older men, deny these problems even exist – for example, arguing that caste discrimination is illegal in India – so how can it possibly still play out, right? Even though these attitudes are alive, well and have followed Indians overseas.

These same Indians shake their heads when I bring up gendered violence, like I'm pulling the statistics out of my arse. Some ask what the point of talking about these problems are when 'there's nothing we can do about it'. Some say that the solution is to teach boys from a young age to respect women. Some believe sex education, including curriculum around consent and respect, is part of the solution.

While I was pregnant, I had a chat with my cousin, Danny, who lived in India and had recently finished high school. I'd been keen to ask him about the government's newly introduced Adolescent Studies initiative in schools.

'Didi,' – as he calls me – 'they don't teach us properly. Even if we want to ask questions, we cannot. It is very shameful to talk in class about it.' Danny told me that because class discussions on the topic were taboo, students were expected to just take notes on and memorise their teachers' dubious monologues. Unlike my experience of sex-ed in primary school, Danny and his peers were not given relevant homework to discuss with their mothers and fathers. Most parents, even in the most developed cities of India, disavow the responsibility of teaching their kids about sex. According to a 2015 study in the *Indian Journal of Psychiatry* by Ismail, Shajahan, Sathyanarayana Rao and Wylie, 88 per cent of the young men and 58 per cent of the young women across Mumbai colleges reported that their parents had taught them zilch about sex. Instead, those young adults turned to books, magazines, youth counsellors and, most of all, porn. Meanwhile, many Indian legislators and politicians regurgitate arguments that sex education for adolescents would corrupt them, and incite a generation of sluts to rise up against Indian values.

After my own rocky start to sex education in Year 6, the conversation continued at school but ended at home. I wish it hadn't. I wish I could have clarified concepts I didn't understand in the classroom, but I was too shy to ask my parents. I wish I'd had the confidence to name and talk about all of my body parts in their presence. I was going to need the language soon enough. Even if I was going to be told to adapt, to adjust, to excuse, to move on – all euphemisms for suffocate – anyway. Like many Good Indian Daughters are primed to do.

***

As I grew into a teenager, I became more and more disillusioned with our family trips to India. I'd wallowed for the duration of the flight from Melbourne to Singapore on the second-last trip I took, before I stopped going altogether. I was going to miss out on everything my friends had planned over the holidays: laser skirmishes, indoor ice-skating and sleepovers. Alliances were going to be strengthened over party pies and tomato sauce, while my own friendships would languish in my absence. I dreaded being on the periphery again when I got back.

When we arrived in Dharwad, these concerns dissolved as soon as I started playing with my cousins, making friends with students at Ajji's school, drawing pictures with them, maxing out Ma and Pa's camera reels and vegging out in front of Cartoon Network and Hindi MTV, while Ma cleared out the local shops and Pa did the rounds to his side of the family. I studied my late Ajja's gemstone and coin collections and went to Lakshmi Talkies with my family every week. I enjoyed my protected status in Dharwad, where Ajji and my aunties believed I could do no wrong. This superpower came in handy when my parents lost their cool with me; if anyone were to upset me, Ajji, Helen Aunty and Sybil Aunty would have torn them to shreds. At least, that's what I knew to be true at that point in time.

Then, one day an old man knocked on Ajji's front door. Pathravalli was his name. Ajji recognised him as a friend of Ajja's from the local Lions Club. Apparently, he had stopped by to see how everyone was going during their first trip back home together since Ajja had passed away a few years earlier. Given that Ma had returned from overseas, Helen and Sybil from interstate, it just so happened that none of their husbands were present. Perhaps my family was feeling particularly vulnerable that day; against their better judgement, the sisters opened up to this stranger about how their marital struggles and issues with their in-laws made them miss their father so much more. And guess who happened to have all of the solutions to their problems?

First, Pathravalli deduced that the evil eye had been cast upon our family. There was no doubt about it: all of

Ajji's daughters were more than photogenic. Judging by that fact combined with the impressive jewellery the three women adorned themselves in, even as they wore their cotton batik floor-length nighties at daytime in their own home, it was clear that they were cursed by the envy of outsiders. Pathravalli offered to perform dhrushti and remove the power of the evil eye that clung to their twenty-two- and twenty-four-carat-gold bangles, earrings, anklets and mangalsutras. Ma and her sisters obediently placed all of their jewellery into a steel bowl and Pathravalli hovered over them, whispering hostilities to the unwelcome spirits with a wave of his hands. For the problems involving their husbands and in-laws, he recommended the name of a swami for the three sisters to visit. None of this sat well with Ajji, but her daughters would not hear a word against this kind Samaritan. Even as a teenager, I could tell something was off about this guy; his beady eyes, his skillfulness in weaseling information out of the sisters and, most of all, the unwavering confidence with which he talked about his superstitious beliefs.

On this same trip, I learned about the multifarious uses of the humble lemon. I already knew that lemons did overtime compared to other fruit – flavouring, detoxing, cleaning – but in India, some people employed lemons as vessels for curses and blessings. Ma spoke of cursed lemons as black magic. When she and her sisters returned home from seeing the swami, they had lemons tied up in their saree pallus. These were for luck, I was told. The swami had consecrated and chanted over them, summoning each woman's greatest desire into reality. For Sybil Aunty, it was the assurance that her husband would start listening to her. For Helen Aunty, it was the guarantee that her relationship with her in-laws would improve. And for Ma, it was the promise of a third child: the baby boy she'd always wanted. None of these wishes came true, but the swami got to keep the money.

The following week, Pathravalli was back. He wanted to see how things were going since the swami had bestowed the sisters with lucky lemons. Not much time had passed – not enough for them to interact with their husbands and in-laws yet – but the women beamed and held to their high hopes. Pathravalli had one more suggestion to help them on their journeys, one more parting gift: now that he'd removed the evil eye from their jewellery, it was time to do the same to the women themselves.

Now, this had to be done properly. No cotton buds, broomstick straw, chilli or other props like Ma used when she removed ketta dhrushti from Maya and me back in Melbourne. Pathravalli wanted to use his bare hands. And in order to really get those bad spirits, he had to make contact with their bodies. I watched on from behind the curtain of the indoor courtyard as he commanded one of Ajji's servants to bring over a bowl of cold water. All three ample-breasted sisters lined up in Ajji's sunken lounge and Pathravalli placed the aluminium bowl next to Sybil Aunty on the far right. He started on the left with Ma and ran his hands down her body, starting with her head, then along her shoulders, breasts, and down her hips and legs. He ended by shaking his hands over the bowl and instructed Ma to observe the cloud of black dust in the water. There was the evil; could she see it? Like the emperor who approved of his grand new invisible robes, Ma nodded. Pathravalli moved onto Helen, then Sybil, each one nodding in recognition of the evil in the water, oblivious to the evil before them: an acquaintance of their father's molesting all three of his late friend's daughters in Ajja's immutable absence.

'What about the young girl there?' He pointed to me. I took note that he referred to me by the word for young girl – *hudugi* – and not by my name or as Ma's daughter – *nimma magalu* – as though I was a stray who could more easily belong to him than to myself or my mother. Despite my misgivings, I was ready to follow the old man's instructions because: (a) I didn't think I had any choice but to obey, as did my mum and my aunties and (b) they were convinced that he only had our best interests at heart and wanted nothing other than to buttress the cavity left by my Ajja; who the hell was I to stand in the way of such altruism? Moreover, from a young age, multiple family members – parents, siblings, aunties, uncles, grandparents – were allowed to touch my body, bathe me and massage my skin with coconut oil. And I was supposed to let them; I was used to other people who 'knew better' touching my body without requiring my permission.

'I think she needs dhrushti taken also.' He pointed his finger in my direction. 'It's important for young girls because they attract evil eyes a lot.'

I submitted and walked across the room toward this man I'd never met but referred to as 'Pathravalli Ajja' out of respect. Looking back, I couldn't remember if Ma and my aunties beckoned me over or if they simply didn't object when I answered his call. I was singled out from the three women who'd been cleansed before me; this fucker decided that, in my case, he would go *under* my clothes. He started from my head and rubbed me all the way down past my developing boobs and other private parts. Then he shook his fingers over the water bowl.

'See the black dots floating in the water?'

'Not really,' I said timidly, mustering a smile to compensate for my disagreement.

'You have to look harder,' he said, like a dodgy Rafiki. 'Anyway, it's there. I can see it.' He moved the bowl away.

At some point, beyond the limits of my memory, Ajji had a word with Pathravalli and forbade him from returning to her house. Ajji had been the one to invite him in for a cup of tea on his initial visit, but she'd resented his presence since he told her daughters to see a Hindu swami.

When Pathravalli left that morning, after the water-bowl cleansing, we all sat in silence for a while. After a few minutes, Helen Aunty stood up to get on with the day and the rest of us Good Indian Daughters followed suit into the bruised afternoon. For years, no one spoke of this incident again.

***

When my parents moved to Australia, they had a plan for Maya and me. They would see us through school then a tertiary education, all completed as swiftly as possible. Our qualifications would lead to full-time jobs and as soon as we were set up with long-term careers, my parents would promptly scout out potential suitors for us, marry us off (because sons got married while daughters got married off) and wait for grandchildren. The to-do list they had mapped out for the first three decades of my life was officially rendered obsolete just ahead of my best-before date, at twenty-seven years old.

Once I'd completed my degrees, which took eight years instead of four (strike one), and only occurred *after* Jake and I had got married (strike two), I quit my full-time job of *only* one year (strike three and out) to have a baby (oh, wait, you're back in!).

My parents were the last to hear about me quitting my job. When I did tell them, the silence in their living room was unnerving and so unlike the fracas generated by most of my previous life choices. Jake sat on one end of the couch next to where I stood while Ma and Pa sat together on the other end.

'Well, you've made your decision, haven't you?'

'Yes, Pa.'

'She's telling us now, after everything has happened. She didn't even bother asking us anything before her decision.' Ma turned to Pa in disbelief.

'Well, they both seem happy. Are you happy with this, Jake?' Pa asked.

'Yeah, of course. We'd talked a few years ago about one of us staying at home for a while once a baby was in the picture,' Jake said, reminding me that we had in fact discussed that at the start of our marriage; even then I'd known that if I didn't have a job that I felt passionate about, I'd be much more interested in caring for a baby full-time, and if Jake was the one with the less satisfying job, it would have been him. Hearing it again strengthened my resolve for going down this path.

'He's happy. She's happy. What can we do now? We can only wish them all the best.' Pa sighed.

I didn't explain our reasoning to my parents – never attempted to describe how my workplace's toxicity had become unbearable. I'd spent enough of my life pitching them my unmade decisions, only to cave to their we-know-what's-best-for-you arguments. If I'd had a healthier relationship with my parents, I might have sought their advice on major life decisions.

As it stood, my relationship with them was a paradox of unflappable faith and deep distrust. We had an enduring safety net in one another; no one in our family would ever be hungry or homeless and whenever one of us was sick, the others banded together to provide support. In a way, we trusted each other with our lives. Our steadfast commitment to one other would always trump our personal frustrations. But a desolate truth niggled at me, especially during my pregnancy: I'd lost all faith that my parents knew who I was when they weren't dictating my identity to me. I wondered if they'd even recognise me when I inevitably spilled out of the Good-Indian-Daughter mould they'd fashioned for me. Though they loved me, I wasn't sure if they'd *like* me as my most authentic self. I didn't trust them to back my decisions and in Ma's case, I was convinced that she could and would only prioritise my wellbeing or that of her future granddaughter until doing so conflicted with the urge to please someone else whom she esteemed more highly. Then again, wellbeing can be subjective; maybe when Pathravalli visited Ajji's house back then, Ma genuinely believed that I would benefit from what he was offering.

Several years later, she eventually decided that he was a mendacious middleman for the swami who gave out wishes like a medieval priest selling indulgences. This revelation arrived a little too late for my liking. In the meantime, I'd learned that the people who hurt me most in life were the men in my world – and the women who enabled them. Jake was the exception and Ma had subjected him to arbitrary curfews, rules and a generally frosty welcome when we started dating. Given it took Ma two days to trust Pathravalli and two years to trust Jake, I questioned her judgement of character. When I was pregnant and thought about whether or not I'd be comfortable ever leaving my daughter in her care, I decided it was a risk I wouldn't be willing to take.

When I *told* my parents I'd quit my job, instead of asking them for permission to do so, it was the first time I'd hinted to them that Jake and I – just us – were going to be responsible for decisions involving our daughter. It was time for my parents to take a step back.

Ma and Pa huddled on the far end of the couch, as though it was them against the world. Ma stared at the tiled floor, then out the window at our mostly concreted backyard. The familiar guilt tugged at me. I felt the urge to take it all back, tell them I was wrong and they were right and I needed them and of course they'd help me raise my daughter. I didn't want to break their hearts. But then I remembered Pa's heart attack and the Man in the

Hospital. I remembered Pathravalli and all the other ways I'd been hurt by their actions in Dharwad and in Melbourne. So I held myself back. There wasn't much left to say, so we left my parents in a palpable haze of disappointment.

The next time I was in Ivana's office, I described my progress with moist eyes. I wanted to celebrate the step I'd taken to live *my* life on my own terms, but I couldn't do it without hulking a sack of guilt behind me. I was also mourning my parents' freedom; as I saw it, they had drifted through life without really contemplating – let alone acting on – what they wanted to get out of it (apart from their marriage to one another). Tradition and cultural etiquette had informed their decision-making, which meant they'd rarely tuned into their own personal hopes, passions and desires. It was the curse of straddling two generations: for the most part, they'd lived by their parents' choices for them and when it was finally time to exercise their decision-making power with their own children, I had retched and gagged and swiped at the reins for the better part of almost thirty years.

Ivana pointed out that my guilt was unconstructive. Was feeling sorry for my parents going to change my mind about quitting my job? No. Was it going to stop me from breaking the cycle of parental abuse with my own daughter? No. Did it mean I was going to abolish the healthy boundaries I'd put up between my parents and me for self-preservation? No. In that case, was it helpful to feel guilt for my decisions? No ... I guess.

I left that session with clarity on two things. Firstly, it was okay to feel sad for my parents. After all, Ma and Pa were also subjugated to toxic, paternalistic social and cultural norms in their formative years. So, it wasn't surprising that they parented from a place of old and new traumas, first as children then as immigrants. It grieved me to imagine how they must have been punished for pushing boundaries as children.

I once asked Ma how she got the prominent scar on her head. She told me she was nicking some bella (jaggery) from the kitchen while Ajji was making sweets. Ajji warned her off, threatening to brand Ma with a chuchga (steel spatula) heated up on the stove fire. Ma went back for more bella one too many times, so Ajji chased her down with the chuchga. Desperate not to be caught, Ma ran through the house and outside, where she tripped and fell onto a large rock and sliced her head open. Of course, Ajji didn't mean for that to happen. Still, I heard that other times, the beatings and verbal abuse her kids endured at her hands were grievous, to say the least, before Ajja could rescue them.

Meanwhile, young Pa, his cheeky school-wagging older brother and their friends were stealing sugar cane from the fields next door when the plantation owner caught them red-handed and dobbed them in to my Pa's mum, my other Ajji. I had to admit, her methods of punishment were creative. This time, she tied her sons to a pillar so they couldn't escape and smoked chillies over a fire in front of them, making sure their eyes burned. This way, they would remember their mistake and never make it again.

Ma and Pa laughed when they recounted these stories. In hindsight, they appreciated their parents teaching them 'right from wrong'. They insisted that even though they were upset at the time, these kinds of torturous punishments didn't have a lasting impact on them. I begged to differ. As they did with their own childhoods, they looked back on mine with rose-coloured glasses too.

The second thing I was clear on as I left Ivana's room was that, while it didn't hurt anyone to commiserate with my parents, it wasn't helpful to anyone for me to assume responsibility for their feelings. Yes, I had hurt them many times. And I was free to apologise for where I'd gone wrong. But I could no longer be answerable for their feelings, the seedlings of my guilt. I wasn't going to change my tune to please them.

It's been said that when you grow up, you become your own parent(s). But I was determined not to fall into patterns of parenting I'd experienced growing up: not because my parents didn't have big hearts, not because they weren't excellent people in a thousand ways and not because I was ungrateful for them. But the parenting journey I'd begun was not a case of reflecting on the parenting I'd received and deciding for myself which parts I liked and which parts I didn't. I had to scrap the pre-existing foundation, because the oppression of women and children was at the heart of it. I say children because they are, more often than not, repositories for their parents' ambitions. My parents never woke up thinking, *How can we continue the cycle of oppression with our daughter today?* They were doing the best they could, to the best of their knowledge, to raise daughters who were equipped to cope with and live in the world as it was: a man's world.

I realised that as a mother I needed to prepare my daughter for that same world, but to also use my imagination to picture a world where women were equal to men, and to ready her for that kind of world too. After all, women who know they matter and live accordingly perpetually straddle those two worlds, don't they?

I realised that one of my greatest fears was inadvertently recreating expectations that my daughter be a Good Indian Daughter too. Or *good* at all; I'd developed the opinion that *good* was too often a euphemism for *convenient* when it came to children and their behaviour. I flinched when I heard people use the term good girl or good boy on children (I couldn't even say it to Panda anymore). Not only did I begin to see it as a lazy way to parent and think about other human beings, but I also knew how damaging it was to a young person's sense of identity. It's reductive and downright exhausting to conceive of yourself as a shapeshifter, ever oscillating between *good* and *bad* depending on what your parents think of you minute by minute.

In my experience, that kind of parenting raised children into adults who literally shat themselves in the supermarket over the moral quandary of choosing between protein-enriched peanut butter and the salt-reduced kind.

11

A baby shower fit for a queen who hates parties

As I entered my third trimester, Ma asked if she could host a Kubsa for me. A few weeks had passed and the tension between my parents and me had fizzled. The suggestion of a South Indian baby shower was Ma's take on an olive branch.

All of the Melbourne aunties would be invited, sarees would be worn, and like Ma, Ajji and all of our female forebears had done before me, I would receive symbolic gifts, placed into my lap by my aunties. Tradition dictated I'd be presented with: two coconuts heavy with water, believed to calm the fetus; glass bangles, so the baby could hear me pottering about; five betel leaves and betel nuts, for prosperity; five pieces of fruit, usually bananas and dates for good health; two turmeric roots for future generations' wellbeing; a brand-new saree blouse; two handfuls of rice; and flowers, a fragrant blessing for the mother and baby. Ma envisioned me wrapped in a silk saree – dark green to signify prosperity and fertility. She dreamed of bangles on my wrists and jasmine in my hair. It sounded wonderful, in theory, and I was sorry to take it away from her.

I didn't decline immediately because bad news needed to be drip-fed to Ma. She was still recovering from the shame of her eldest daughter having absconded from a promising career. I told her I would think about the baby shower and get back to her. In truth, my thinking was done. To me, a Kubsa meant an afternoon of nattering with women who were not involved in my life beyond the well wishes they passed on through my parents. I didn't think they actually cared beyond the opportunity to dress up, show up, then end up on the phone to one another afterward, judging the event and Ma's food, fashion and decoration choices. A Kubsa would mean following superstitious customs that didn't carry much meaning for me personally, and mingling with Gossip Gerties in a function of fake laughter and empty words, just like so many of the parties my parents had taken me to as a child. Of course, I did have aunties who were genuinely interested in my life, and I in theirs – aunties with whom I could have truthful conversations. But they were the minority.

I preferred one-on-one morning-tea catch-ups over parties any day. It was anomalous for Jake and I to plan anything more than a dinner, or really any event with more than four attendees. But then again, I've always seemed to be allergic to parties.

***

The first party I ever caused a commotion at was my own. It was my second birthday. Thanks to Ma, I was donning a pink, flouncy number complete with a white fascinator in my dark whorls of hair. To boot, my feet were adorned with frilly white socks in white patent leatherette sandals. As per Indian social convention at the time, the women huddled around the kitchen preparing food while the men gathered outside, beer in one hand and their appraisals of politics and cricket in the other.

When lunch was ready, the drill was for mothers to fetch their young children and form a circle together on the floor. What followed could be described as a spectacle of barbaric ways to fatten children. A couple of aunties tenderly offered their children spoonfuls of food, but they were the exception. The other aunties chattered as they shovelled rice and dhal into their kids' mouths – whether they were hungry or not. When this force-feeding ritual inevitably led to tears, the aunties would shush or reprimand the little diner who was making a fuss. Slightly older kids were cautioned by their mothers against going back out to play before they'd consumed every last crumb on their plates, lest they incite the wrath of their fathers, the police or, worse, the budda. (Not to be confused with Buddha, *budda* sometimes means *old man,* but in this context means *monster* – interesting double entendre.)

One particular aunty would hover an open safety pin in front of her toddler as he ate. He gobbled up each next morsel to avoid the prick but when he didn't want any more food, the screams began.

Naturally, Ma was an advocate for this very niche brand of torture and had a unique approach when it came to her own children's mealtimes. When Maya and I were toddlers, Ma would feed us in an upright, seated position. The minute we decided we were full and rejected the rest of our meals, she would lay us on the ground in front of her, face up, back down, pin down all four of our limbs under her outstretched legs and continue to stuff us with food. Our kicks and screams were futile; each time we opened our mouths to let out a cry, she swiftly moved in with another spoonful.

One time, I watched Maya choke, splutter and bawl her eyes out, shaking her head from side to side, trying and failing to inch away from the dreaded spoon. There wasn't much you could do when your parents reckoned they knew your body better than you did and Ma believed this method was necessary for her daughters to be healthy and well-fed. Crying under these circumstances was the sort of thing your parents called you a naatak company for – the literal translation being *theatre company*. The closest term in the English language is *drama queen*. How ironic that those of us who grew into 'overweight' teenagers got told off by our parents for having no self-control when it came to food.

Of course, nobody thought that far ahead on the day I turned two years old. Once the palles, chicken and lamb dishes (beef and pork were generally excluded as a courtesy to the Muslim and Brahmin aunties and uncles) had been warmed up and bissi-bissi chapatis were fresh off the tava, it was time to feed the children. Our mothers called out to us, but no one responded. Unable to find us in any of the bedrooms, one aunty went outside to ask her husband if he had seen their two sons. He said no. Another aunty came out asking after her daughter. Her husband was equally bewildered too. A pattern emerged. None of the children were accounted for. Panic set in.

According to Ma's recollection, the parents ran around hysterically calling out for their children and were met with silence. The fathers dispersed onto the streets, yelling out our names: *Nazia! Bhargav! Gowri! Dheeraj! Ruhi!* And so on. We were nowhere to be seen.

A few minutes later, an elderly woman approached them. 'I saw a line of children making their way to the shops,' she said. 'There was a little ringleader in a pink dress at the front.'

Desperate, our fathers bolted in the direction of the shopping centre. Lo and behold, they found their precious offspring being led toward grave danger under the command of a tiny Pied Piper. I had helpfully pressed the button at the pedestrian crossing for us. My dad and uncles caught up in a matter of seconds, before we braved the main road spanning six lanes. If ever the parents needed convincing of our collective ability to discern when our own stomachs were full, there was the proof: a bunch of toddlers and preschoolers executed a coordinated journey to a shopping centre, guided only by a two-year-old and her spatial memory from trips to the shops with her mum. Reciting this story made Ma beam with pride and shudder in equal measure.

***

Growing up in the care of a tribe can be a special experience for both children and adults. My aunties were like second mothers to me. In Kannada, the specific term used for an aunty or an uncle, if they are your parents' siblings, can be either Chikamma, Chikappa, Dhodamma or Dhodappa: respectively, Small-mum or Small-dad, if they are younger than your parents and Big-mum or Big-dad if they are older. Their authority, and the respect we were required to approach them with, was embedded in the language.

In Indian families, it was – and still is – common to be 'raised by a village' or within a joint family where these bigger or smaller parents co-existed with biological parents. Many families managed this dynamic successfully; children benefited from the physical proximity and hopefully, emotional closeness to their extended family. Likewise, the child enriched the lives of the aunties, uncles and grandparents around them. This set-up also meant tired parents could fall back on assistance in close quarters.

Of course, each family is different, and for some living in a joint family was not a viable option. Even best-case scenarios could become tricky if guardians sometimes took for granted that someone else was watching the young ones (unfortunately, as my South Asian peers and I got older, the grown-ups actually started to watch us *more* closely and *more* critically). In worst-case scenarios, there was the danger that *nobody* was watching – except for one twisted adult.

According to a 2007 study conducted by the Ministry of Women and Child Development, in 50 per cent of all *reported* child-sexual-abuse cases in India, the perpetrator was known to the child – usually someone in a position of trust and responsibility and often an uncle or neighbour. Similarly, 2014 data from India's NCRB confirmed that 86 per cent of all victims in *reported* rape cases knew their abusers. A later NCRB report stated that 39,827 children were sexually assaulted in 2018 and 21,605 child rapes were reported – roughly one every twenty-four minutes – and 99 per cent of victims were girls. It's important to remember that these sets of data have emerged in a culture that shies away from tackling such topics, so we can assume many more cases go unreported.

Also in 2018, Australian Bureau of Statistics (ABS) data revealed 7852 sexual assaults against children aged fourteen and younger were reported across Australia The number of victims of sexual assault aged 0 to 14 was 3.5 times higher for girls compared with boys. If you look at those recorded incidences of child sexual assault in both countries, proportionate to their respective total 2018 populations of 0 to 14 year olds, a child in Australia was roughly 15 times more likely to be sexually assaulted than a child in India that year. Although, it is worth keeping in mind that the definition of 'assault' might differ between countries and that there are bound to be errors in the reporting and recording processes in both countries.[4]

During my pregnancy, I started to think about who I could and couldn't trust with my baby. I knew from experience that, sometimes, the people I thought I could rely on couldn't be trusted. I could imagine Maya being an incredible Chikamma to my daughter and several of my cousins being dependable people in her life, but I struggled to see many of my other relatives in the same light, my parents included. It wasn't because I expected any of them to sexually abuse my baby – how can anyone anticipate it, really? – but because I knew a handful of them were okay with covering things up to protect the reputation of people who shouldn't have been protected.

As my pregnancy progressed, I began to have vivid nightmares. In them, I saw my parents babysitting and

---

[4] I have also assumed in my calculations that the sexually assaulted children referred to in the NCRB report are 0 to 14 year olds as this is unclear.

inviting the Man From the Hospital over to meet my baby in my absence. In one nightmare, they asked my little daughter to keep secrets or to lie to Jake and me about seemingly inconsequential things – in doing so teaching her how to manipulate others, like Ma had done with me. In another nightmare, Ma took photos and videos of my baby behind my back and sent them to relatives whom I didn't want in my daughter's life. In less intense dreams, my parents escorted extended family members over to the hospital or to our house unannounced after the baby's arrival. I dreamed about Ma showing up during my labour and expecting to steer as first mate, or waiting outside until it was all done and then joining in on those tender first moments with the baby – moments that I wanted to enjoy with Jake and our daughter only.

In real life, Ma was starting to say things like, 'Call me when you go into labour, ya?' To which I replied, 'I'll call you after the baby has arrived.' She'd wave me away, probably hoping I'd change my mind closer to the due date

– not that she knew what it was. When she asked, we fudged the truth, pointing to mid-to-late September though we knew it was earlier in the month. We didn't want any visitors until we were back at home and I had recovered from postpartum tiredness as much as possible. Neither Jake nor I was interested in putting on a happy face for guests when we were busy enough providing first-class, round-the-clock hospitality for a newborn. So we planned to limit our company to Maya, Zam and our parents until we hit the six-week mark and had established a rhythm. I outlined this request to Ma and asked her to relay it to any of my aunties and uncles who, instead of contacting me directly, would go straight to my parents to ask about when they could visit.

'That's very bad, Ruhi. You should not stop people from coming to visit the baby,' Ma said.

'Well, that's your opinion. Also, I am only stopping them for a short time, until we are comfortable having guests—'

'No, that's not right. People will want to bring gifts, see the baby and wish you well. You should not tell them not to come to the hospital.'

'I've explained my reasons to you. And you don't have to agree but it's not going to change my mind.'

'*Tsk-tsk.* This is wrong. This is not how we do.'

'If aunties and uncles want to visit us before we're ready and they contact you instead of me, are you going to relay what I've said to you now? That we won't be ready for visitors and we'll let them know when we are?' I interrogated.

'No. We can't say no to people like that. It's not our culture—'

'So, you don't have a problem saying no to your *daughter,* who's asking you not to invite visitors on her behalf, for reasons that are important to her,' I retorted. 'But you have a problem saying no to a bunch of people who you're not even that close with?'

She clenched her teeth.

'Okay, well, if you and Pa can't say no to people,' I continued, 'Can you at least tell people who call that they should get in touch with me or Jake to find out when they can visit, and we can talk to them instead?'

'Fine.'

Resolute as I was, I felt sorry for Ma. I knew it pained her when I veered off our cultural script like this, but I wished she could have been able to pause and contemplate why I chose to reject certain traditions.

Then again, maybe that was too big an ask. She often admitted to us herself that she loved being the centre of attention. I admired her self-confidence, but sometimes it was too much for me, the shy introvert she dragged along. For example – and don't get me started on my extended family's singular obsession with party themes and dress codes – she was the type of person who wore red to a party where the specified dress code was black-and-white; who wore grand sarees when invitations specified a western formal dress code, saying that the hosts were Indian and wouldn't mind; who wore white to a wedding (back when brides we knew consistently chose to wear white); whose fortnightly manicures ended with a thick coat of glitter almost every time, just to turn heads. Traditional parties and festivals provided her with another reason to glam up and another platform over which to glide in the limelight, attracting compliment after compliment. Moreover, I think she wanted to be seen as the kind of mother and wife who kept traditions going. She thrived on the attention of others. 'Ya, I love when people give me attention and appreciate how I look. What's wrong with that?' she'd say. *Absolutely nothing,* I'd think. *More power to you.* At least until her next round of plans for party domination involved me at the centre.

I still hadn't accepted Ma's offer to throw the Kubsa yet but I was still haunted by the memory of the last time we had a party in honour of my reproductive organs. It didn't go down too well for me.

***

One morning, soon after my tenth birthday, I went to the toilet. When I stood up to flush, I looked down and became light-headed at the sight of blood in the toilet bowl. Disconsolate, I shuffled over to the kitchen and broke the fatal news to my mother, whom I knew I would be survived by.

'Ma,' I croaked.

'Ya?'

I began to cry.

'Ayo, en aatha? What happened?'

'I think I'm dying,' I announced to a fairly unmoved Ma – this was nothing she hadn't heard before as a mother of two hypochondriacs.

'What?'

'I have bum cancer,' I mumbled through tears.

'Huh?!'

'I said I have bum cancer!'

'What is that? How can you think that?'

'All this blood came out of my bum when I went to the toilet! Okay?! I'm dying!' I sobbed.

'Let me see,' she pushed past me and went over to the toilet.

Her reaction was exactly like Indiana Jones' in *Raiders of the Lost Ark* when he finally discovers the location of the Ark in the Map Room. She turned to me, her face almost glowing, and with all the melodrama of Indiana's orchestral crescendo, she announced, 'YOU'RE A WOMAN NOW!'

'Huh?' I couldn't for the life of me figure out why she was so bloody elated.

'Come here!' She grabbed a bulging plastic bag out of the bathroom cupboard. I'd seen it before, but never stopped to wonder about its contents. She pulled out a packet and opened it to reveal a smaller packet inside. It was all so mysterious and reminded me of the introduction to the *Get Smart* series, but with packets instead of doors. She tore the smallest packet open to reveal what she called a *pad.* Then she showed me how to adhere it to my undies.

'Put it in your chuddie like this and make sure you change it every few hours. Then, put the old one in a bag before you throw in kachra,' Ma said. I was to follow this procedure every day, for around five days, every month, indefinitely, it seemed. She warned that it might hurt but that all women went through this and I was now part of the club.

Ma then zipped over to the phone and proceeded to call all of my aunties, one after another, launching into each phone call with, 'Ayo! Have you heard the good news?! My daughter became a woman today!'

Meanwhile, I was clueless, and a little pissed off. *A few days older than ten, and I'm now a woman? A woman with a hefty half-nappy in her chuddie? And why is Ma so overjoyed? Why do other people need to know about what's happening to my private parts? Is this something that people normally celebrate? Or is it just Ma being over the top again?*

Between her phone calls, I asked Ma what she meant when she told me I'd become a woman. I was informed that once I started bleeding, it meant I could have babies.

'But I don't want to have babies!'

'Eh! Not now! When you have grown up and got married! This is called a *period*. Now that you have it, your body knows how to have baby when you're older,' she said. None of it made sense. I received some clarification the following year when we did sex-ed at school, but for a long time menstruation remained a nebulous concept to me.

The next day, Raksha Aunty, my father's sister, came over. Because we didn't have any reasonably priced saree shops in Melbourne (all of the women in my family bought their sarees in India), she'd visited the local haberdashery on her way and purchased a five-metre length of floral, dark-green chiffon. Ma paired it with one of her own green-cotton saree blouses and wrapped me in it. But first, she made me strip down to my underwear, chuck on a towel and sit down on an old dining chair while she and Raksha Aunty rubbed haldi (sandalwood and turmeric paste) all over my body. I'd taken part in haldi ceremonies before, at Sybil Aunty's and Helen Aunty's weddings, never imagining that I'd find myself at home in Melbourne, a mere child, preparing for womanhood in the same way brides prepared for marriage. Ma must have missed her sisters, who were both still in India while she carried out the necessary rituals without them.

'Okay, go and have a head bath[5] now and come back quickly. Lagoo,' Ma said, once I was fully covered. I showered, washed my hair and put on my first pad without Ma. Then Ma wrapped me in the new saree, combed back my hair and placed a red bindi on my forehead. Raksha Aunty put some green glass bangles on both of my wrists and finally pulled my look together with a dab of red lipstick. Because no one was around to see it, thank the Lord, they took photos of me sitting in the lounge room of the Stone Fruit House, dressed head-to-toe in the colour of fertility.

Then, Ma performed her dhrushti ritual to remove the influence of evil eye. It was nothing like what Pathravalli had done to me in Dharwad. This was the kind of dhrushti that Maya and I were familiar with growing up. Ma normally did it when we'd come home from a place where people might have complimented us a lot, like a party, or

---

[5] In my family, 'body baths' were showers where we didn't wash our hair and 'head baths' were showers where we did.

a place where people might have even looked at us lustfully ... like a party. It was also performed on auspicious occasions, such as the day a girl had her first period.

Ma took a large cotton ball, shaped it into a doll and held it in front of my forehead, before sweeping it downward toward my toes. Following each sweep, she spat on the cotton ball. After the third and final sweep, she spat on it three times. Then she burned it on the stove. In a matter of seconds, it was subsumed by the fire, along with any lingering evil – or so she believed. Sometimes Ma used strands of straw from our Indian broom combined with salt, red chilli and mustard seeds instead of a cotton ball. There were several variations of props for this ritual, depending on what we had at home.

Every time dhrushti was removed, the house fell silent; we weren't permitted to speak during it. Before an outing, Ma would draw a black dot under our feet with kajal and then remove dhrushti afterward, believing she was protecting us from sickness and bad luck. When we did fall ill, we'd hear Ma lament that she forgot to take our dhrushti. It was one of the many Indian traditions that sat comfortably alongside Ma's Christian beliefs. To Ma and her ancestors, belief in Jesus didn't preclude belief in certain superstitions that pervaded many Indian cultures. Ajji performed the same rituals for her daughters, as did my great-grandmother.

A few nights after my first period, against my will and my father's advice, Ma threw me a Period Party – at least, that's what I called the celebration that unfolded. Ma laughed when I called it *Period Party* – but that's exactly what it was. In South India, no one would flinch when a boy's voice broke, his shoulders broadened or his balls dropped, but the first time a girl bled was apparently cause for the whole community to party. I swear, for people who didn't like to talk about sex, it felt like Indians celebrated fertility more than any other culture on Earth.

In line with customary requirements, I wore dark green again, this time in a knee-length, pleated velvet dress with flowers embroidered along the high, round neck. Ma had stitched it together in a matter of hours; sewing was one of her many talents, which also included threading, knitting and dancing. Though Ma's sewing skills were of a relatively high standard, unfortunately for me she used the same outdated frock patterns she'd followed when I was three years old.

Aunties, uncles, cousins and family friends started pouring through our front door. As I greeted them, I was suddenly hyperaware of having boobs and wished that someone would hook a cane around my neck and pull me offstage every time an uncle stiffly shook my hand to congratulate me – *on blood coming out of my vagina.*

If the term 'FML' existed in the year 2000, it would have been apt for my use at that exact point in time. I was envious of my female classmates who did not have to go through this spectacle. So few of them even *had* their period yet, and those who did seemed to know a fair deal about it. In the absence of motherly or sisterly counsel, I, on the other hand, turned to *The Puberty Book* by Kelsey Powell and Wendy Darvill for answers. I had a feeling that Vaani Aunty had guessed at my predicament, which is why she covertly passed on her daughter's used copy to me.

As embarrassing as the Period Party was, I had it pretty easy compared to other South Indian girls. According to Sybil Aunty, if I lived in Chennai, her new home, it wouldn't be abnormal for my parents to exhibit life-sized posters of me in our neighbourhood, declaring the wonderful onset of my womanhood. *Woohoo! She's not allowed to talk to boys but she can have their babies now!*

Having lived through the experience of walking around in what was essentially a wet nappy and realising Mohan Uncle didn't know how to talk to me anymore, I promised to never throw a Period Party for any future daughters I might have had, unless she wanted one.

***

'Ruhi, have you made a decision? I have to start planning your Kubsa now if we have it in a few weeks,' Ma asked hopefully over the phone.

'Yeah, Ma, I have. Jake and I have decided to host our own baby shower instead, at our place, on our new deck.' Jake and I had just had all the pebbles excavated from our courtyard and replaced with a deck surrounded by bamboo, perfect for hosting a cosy gathering.

'Okay...' She took her time. 'But why don't you do that and I can also host a Kubsa for you here at my place?'

'No, thank you, Ma. I don't want a Kubsa.'

'Why not?!'

'I already told you why not when you first asked me.'

Ma was lost for words. I thought this might have happened. She and Pa hadn't had the best time adjusting to mine and Jake's life choices when they were at odds with what my parents wanted. They were trying. After a long silence, we ended the call. I told Ma the following week that she was welcome to help prepare for the baby shower that Jake and I were planning, but by then she'd lost heart.

On a crisp day in the middle of winter, our parents, siblings, grandparents, only five of my aunties and a handful of our closest friends attended our low-key baby shower. I'd asked my parents to come early and help us set up – not because I needed their assistance, but to include them. An hour after the actual start time, they were still nowhere to be seen and the event was only planned to run for three hours. We were halfway through when my parents finally arrived with a casserole dish full of gulab jamuns. Ma blamed it on the time taken to make the jamuns and still failed to understand that I couldn't care less about all the things she wanted to *do* for me; I just wanted her to *be present.*

A cute set of *Advice for the New Parents* cards sat on the mail table for guests to fill out as they entered. These were people whose input genuinely mattered to me. Each guest also pencilled in their predictions for the usual specs of our soon-to-arrive baby: sex, weight, hair colour, name. Even though there weren't that many people – about twenty – our petite home was crowded. Toward the end of the afternoon, I lounged on the daybed with Zam and sister-in-law Sarah and my cousin Jia, while Maya read out the nuggets of advice and we all guessed who wrote what. There were some hearty laughs and a lot of *aww* sounds.

My brother-in-law and his partner wrote, *Keep calm, carry on and don't drop the baby.* A beloved mentor from my old church wrote, *Relax, breathe, laugh. Trust God in the moment for creative solutions. Ask for help from people you listen to for practical encouragement.* Ma wrote, *Don't let Panda babysit.* Everyone giggled. Helen Aunty, who by now had joined us in Melbourne, wrote, *Be cool, be calm and breathe. You don't need advice, time will teach you everything. Just pray.* One of my cousins wrote, *You should watch* Jane the Virgin *for all your parenting troubles.* Another cousin wrote, *It's your creation!*

'Thanks for that, mate!' I called out to him.

Yet another cousin wrote, *Dress them up in the coolest baby shoes. Make sure they understand the greatness of* Star Wars *and also musicals.* She also guessed the baby would be a male, and that we would name him Methuselah and call him 'Meth' for short. Sixteen out of our twenty-two guests predicted we'd have a boy, while only six guessed it would be a girl.

The icicle that had formed in my chest during our first ultrasound began to melt away as I warmed up to the thought of a baby girl. I was beginning to accept the idea that maybe my initial gender disappointment had less – actually nothing – to do with the baby being a girl and more to do with the lifelong shame I carried around for the kind of girl *I* was. I'd bought into the threadbare narrative that girls were more complex, more vulnerable and therefore more difficult to raise because, apparently, we required so much more of our parents than boys did.

I knew my parents didn't have it easy with me – and I was drugless, partnerless and spineless for most of my upbringing. I could recognise that the real problem lay in the societal and cultural ideals I grew up with, both

Australian and Indian. Both cultures upheld, in different ways, toxic and divisive ideas of masculinity and femininity. The problem lay in those societies' preservation of messed-up masculinities and misogyny; that boys weren't allowed to cry and that girls were overly emotional, for example. It lay in both cultures' tendency to blame girls and women for their misfortunes, rather than deal with entrenched power dynamics. It lay in the idea that boys become men by being manly according to popular standards – career-driven breadwinners, tough enough, of a certain height and shape, and so on – while girls were not only expected to be womanly – career-driven until marriage and motherhood, cordial enough, slim and elegant – we were also expected to be blemishless, undamaged, untouched.

    Sitting on the daybed surrounded by loved ones, I felt proud of myself for quitting my job (even though certain people thought of me as backward for the decision) and giving myself the time to read parenting books and to learn in preparation for our baby. I learned that every single baby – male, female or non-binary – needed eye contact, physical affection, food, safety and freedom to thrive. But also, they needed authentic, respectful, dependable guardians who were willing to grow, learn and approach their mistakes, biases and fears with humility. None of the nonsense I'd heard grown-ups say at parties every time another aunty announced her pregnancy: *Let's hope it's a boy – boys don't need much attention and they're happy with just food and toys; Will be good if it's a girl, na? Girls are quiet and they'll help you around the house; Boys are easy – with girls, you have to constantly worry about them being chased by boys or bringing one home; Hopefully this time you'll have a boy to finally carry on your family name.*

Leaning on Zam's shoulder, I looked up at the brown-paper bunting that hung along the longest wall of our lounge with *Spring Chicken* in golden lettering on the flags. Maya had lovingly put it together and hung it up.

When guests asked how I was going, I stuck to pleasant, generic responses, not divulging anything about my nightmares featuring my parents. My closest friends already knew about them, but I didn't want to have to explain to my aunties – Vaani, Helen, Tina, Malee and Raksha – that I was stressing out about my parents becoming grandparents.

I glanced over at Ma and Pa from time to time, to see if they were doing okay. Pa hung out with my father-in-law and Jake, moving between the deck and our lounge. They seemed to be enjoying themselves over a beer. Meanwhile, Ma was one-sixth of a huddle of aunties around the heater. She was putting on a brave face. I couldn't expect her and Pa to be having the time of their lives. A minimalist celebration with a handful of people was a far cry from what they'd had in mind when they had envisaged their daughter's Kubsa. After all, they had wanted to invite four hundred people to our wedding and we'd had to negotiate it down to three hundred for the ceremony and one hundred and sixty for the reception – literally one-tenth of the size of the last wedding we attended in India.

A week before the baby shower, Ma said to me, 'You know, it's hard for me when your aunties ask me why I am not doing Kubsa for you.'

'I understand. I didn't say no to hurt your feelings. I decided against it because it's just not right for me,' I replied.

'If I were you, I would sacrifice to keep my mother happy. What's the big deal with going through Kubsa for your mother's sake?'

Emotional blackmail was the currency of our familial relationships; Ajji dealt in it too, and she and Ma both wielded it within their immediate families. The fact that, when we pulled them up on it, they called it 'honesty' and not 'blackmail' only highlighted their capacity to manipulate. Their deceit was so subtle, so artful and so entrenched that, no matter how hard we tried, none of us could ever fully fathom, let alone change, this aspect of their wiring. You either lived with it or you didn't.

I sighed. 'Well, that would be your decision, Ma. We are different people with different priorities and I'm not going to feel bad about it just because you find it hard to respect my choices.'

***

Later that day, I called her about a recipe. 'Ma, I think I put too much masala in the pav bhaji – what do I do?'

'How much?' she asked.

'Like, half of the packet.'

'Have you added tomatoes?'

'Yep.'

'Put some sugar.'

'How much?'

'Maybe a few teaspoons.'

'Okay, can you please wait on the phone while I do it?'

'Ya.'

After mixing it through, I tasted some. 'Mmm, yeah, this is better, Ma. Thank you!'

'See?! Your mother knows.'

I thanked her again, then, just before hanging up I felt compelled to ask, 'Ma, do you ever feel like you ... failed as a mother?'

'Why? Are you worried about failing when the baby comes?'

'Yeah, sometimes. But did you ever feel like a failure after you had us? Obviously you *weren't* a failure, but did you ever feel that way, even just for short periods from time to time?'

She stopped to think about it for a minute – a rare exercise for my impulsive mother. Then she answered, 'No. I've never felt like a failure when it came to being your mum.'

Deep down I'd hoped she'd say yes.

12

Unsolicited advice

I met Jake's parents for the first time after we'd been dating for two years (since I had to hide Jake from my parents for two years, he decided not to tell his either). They began to invite me to family gatherings soon after. The first celebration I joined them for was eventful. It was the birthday party of one of his grandparents, and unlike birthday celebrations in my household, people weren't shouting to hear one another speak and guests were able to walk without the house resembling a dodgem-car track. There weren't any boisterous children being rounded up, and I was enjoying the new experience of being able to kick back at a family get-together sans squealing children running up and down stairs, and without having instructions shouted at me to keep an eye on them while serving appetisers to guests. I met some of Jake's lovely extended family and some of his parents' friends, but I spent most of the party catching up with Jake, his brother and sister in the family room, away from the open-plan lounge, kitchen and dining area. As we re-emerged into the main hub of the party, we passed a woman whom none of us recognised. She smiled politely at Jake's brother, then Sarah, then Jake, as they walked ahead of me. Then, as soon as she saw me, she shrieked and dropped her plate of food on the ground.

I bent over to help her pick it up but she held out her hand, which I took to mean that she didn't need my assistance. For a brief moment, I noticed the lack of music and missed the sound of kids high on sweets being chased by flustered parents. After the woman had slunk away, pink-faced and mumbling something to herself, the four of us exchanged confused looks.

'What the hell just happened?' I later asked.

'Maybe she just ... got a fright,' Jake replied.

'Yeah, but she seemed fine when she saw you guys walking ahead of me. She only lost her nut when she saw me...' I felt uneasy. *Surely not – surely, she wasn't startled by the way I look?* The more I thought about it, the more sense it made.

'Guys, I'm the only brown person here,' I continued. 'Do you think ... do you think she's like ... racist?' But no one could know for sure; the others didn't know this lady, after all.

I didn't think about it much after that, until eleven years later on my first Mother's Day with a baby on the way. We were at Jake's aunty's house in one of Melbourne's most affluent suburbs. She and her partner lived in a gorgeous heritage home with old wooden floors and trim, stained-glass windows and masses of foliage outside – an ideal setting for afternoon tea. I managed to chat to most of Jake's family before my feet grew sore and I plonked myself on the couch by the fireplace. Sweet Jake brought me a cup of tea, then returned to a conversation with his brother by the kitchen bench. Again, there wasn't any music playing. I was taking in the view of the garden through the floor-to-ceiling windows when one of Jake's aunties, a midwife, took a seat opposite me. We were soon joined by Jake's mum. My pregnant belly, of course, was the icebreaker.

'I can't tell you how many babies I've delivered in my lifetime,' Diane said. 'If you ever have any questions or concerns, you're always welcome to give me a call.'

'Thank you Diane. That's kind of you to offer.'

She and my mother-in-law then proceeded to speculate about who the baby would look like when he or she arrived. Most women acquaintances loved nothing more than to treat my belly as a round table for such discussions – *Wouldn't it be amazing if the baby had your tanned skin and Jake's blue eyes? Ohmygawd.*

'Well, Ruhi's genes are more dominant so the baby definitely won't be getting Jake's eyes,' my mother-in-law said, no trace of disappointment in her voice, to my relief.

'I've delivered a few Indian babies in my time. *Gawd,* they can be so *hairy,*' Diane chortled, patting me on the knee. 'One of them, I remember, had hair all over his back. Oh! And there was another Indian baby I delivered with hairy *ears!* The hair was so long you could almost plait it!' She dissolved into laughter.

To my surprise, my mother-in-law chuckled along. Perhaps she laughed along for the same reason I did. It was shocking to hear Diane's words and I didn't know how else to respond in that moment. I could feel anger rising within me but I was confused at the same time. I'd only met this woman once a year at Jake's family shindigs, and every encounter up until then had been superficial. Was it worth pulling her up on her microaggression? Later, on the drive back home, I kicked myself for letting it go. I wished I'd had the courage and clarity of mind to tell her how inappropriate her remarks were.

Sadly, my own aunties were no better. Yes, it was different because Diane was a white, blonde woman with little to no body hair who spoke of all Indian babies as a homogeneous group, and it didn't sound like she considered ample body hair to be a desirable trait.

But some of *my* aunties also made racist, uncouth comments.

'Ayo, you've been in the sun too long, *Karriawa!*' they'd say to me, my sister and my cousins, especially during Summer. If not 'Karriawa', they sometimes used the word 'Kappi': both were derogatory terms for someone with dark skin, the loose translation being 'blackie'.

'Rani Mukherjee is a good actress, but have you seen real-life pictures of her? She is very dark,' another would say with a *tsk tsk*.

'Ayo, Leila is dating a kala boy?'

No racist or colourist behaviour was acceptable, whether it came from Diane or any of my own aunties. I promised myself that when Maya had a baby, *if* she decided to have children, I'd do my best to take a more thoughtful and inquisitive approach to conversations with my nieces and/or nephews, instead of flinging my opinions and tasteless anecdotes around willy-nilly.

Some of my cousins and aunties talked about how wonderful it would be if my baby had the shape of my eyes but the colour of Jake's, or the colour of Jake's soft brown hair but the thick texture of mine, or his sharp nose and his dimples. Helen Aunty lamented the way her child had inherited her husband's dark skin instead of her own fair complexion and told me I was lucky to have married a 'foreigner' with whom I could bring a fair-skinned baby into the world.

Her comments took me back to when I'd visit India as a teenager. As soon as we'd all settled into the Dharwad-bound van in Mumbai, Helen Aunty and Sybil Aunty would begin the mandatory appearance analysis. I remember Helen Aunty kicking things off with the first nonchalant point of enquiry: 'You all have become fat. How come?'

'One day when you come to Melbourne, we will take you to McDonalds,' Ma replied. McDonalds was still non-existent in India at the time. 'We eat there every Friday. We should reduce. Actually, you all have put on weight also.'

'Ya, ya, we have. What to do?' was the reply. I was always lucky enough to be dragged into such riveting conversations.

'Ruhi,' Helen Aunty called from two rows behind me in the hire van. 'Where did all these pimples come from?'

Really?! It's called puberty! I wanted to say, but I didn't think it safe to say the P-word out loud at the time in front of either my extended or immediate family. It seemed to be as taboo as the three-letter S-word. Either way, it didn't matter because Helen Aunty had taken the next logical step and assumed my silence translated to *Please, tell me exactly what you think.*

'You mustn't have these hairs falling on your face, baby. I know you girls like to have a fringe and all nowadays, but if the hairs touch your skin like this, pimples will start coming on your face,' she said with confidence.

'But Aunty, I don't think that's the reason—'

'When you wake up in the morning, just take some saliva from your mouth, ya? And put that on your pimples. Otherwise, toothpaste will also help. Just a little bit like this, darling.' She showed me the tip of her index finger. In our culture, for all our secrecy around emotions and big-picture problems, people approached life's in-between bits with alarming directness. The truth needed to be told for the benefit of others – especially those younger than you – regardless of how it might make them feel in the moment.

In our family, there wasn't much of a distinction between truth and opinion. Although I understood my aunties' sense of duty to us, it still made me fume when even in our twenties Maya received links to videos on 'how to naturally brighten and lighten your skin', or I found weight-loss articles in my inbox from my mum or aunties.

The elders insisted our cultural habit of truth-bombing was a positive; it was good that people were so candid with one another and genuinely cared when family members became overweight.

'You're so lucky to have a family that cares enough to tell you,' my aunties, parents and grandparents would say. But I rebutted that it was a pointless exercise for three reasons:

1. My body was not public property or the willing subject of someone else's scrutiny
2. No one was interested in hearing about the books and articles I'd read on how inherently fatphobic the science on 'excess' weight and weight loss is; how inaccurate BMI and weight in general are, as measures of health; and how the task force delineating BMI standards was actually funded by the pharmaceutical companies that had the only weight-loss drugs on the market.
3. The people giving advice were hypocrites: none of them cared enough about *themselves* to work on their own legendary cholesterol levels, pluck out their sweet teeth or wind back their daily communion with white rice.

'Ya, but they are telling you because they love you and don't want you to repeat the same mistakes they made,' Ma would say.

'Has it helped, Ma? Have our bodies thinned and our skin lightened just because Prabha Aunty commented on it?' It was supposed to be a rhetorical question.

'Well, you didn't try her tips or suggestions, did you? Maybe if you tried you'd see a change.'

***

Just after my friend Aurelie gave birth to her first baby, she invited a very-pregnant me over to visit. I never needed directions to her house. When we were in primary school together, her family had lived a few streets away from ours. Then, when she got married, she and her husband chose to stay in the area and bought a property two doors down from the Stone Fruit House I grew up in.

As Aurelie warmed our creamy fettuccine, the fresh aroma of lemon and dill wafted into the lounge. I looked around at the spotless furniture, the blithesome wedding photos hanging on the wall, the vaporiser steaming away next to their plasma TV, and the immaculate floors.

'Your place is so tidy. I'm amazed at how you've managed to keep it so clean with a newborn!'

'Aw, thanks. Though I wouldn't get any of it done without my parents and in-laws helping me pretty much every day. They look after bub while I get all the chores done. Seriously, when you have your baby, you're going to need as much help as you can get. Just say yes to anyone who offers! Don't ever turn them down. It's a *full-on* time.' Aurelie's gaze became distant for a moment, as though she was still reeling at the thought of all the energy gobbled up by early motherhood.

'But I don't know that I *want* the help.' I placed my bowl of pasta down on the coffee table.

'You'll need it. *Trust* me!'

'I know I will need it, but having my parents around will be more stressful than if Jake and I did the work ourselves. Whenever I'm with my parents, my anxiety goes through the roof. They walk into my house and immediately begin to criticise. Just the other day, they came in and said that I need to paint our old buffet for what has to be the thirtieth time.'

Aurelie smacked her forehead and giggled.

'And every time, I give them the exact same response,' I continued. '*It's supposed to look distressed to go with our house's coastal theme.* My problem isn't just about the buffet, it's about the fact that they've always wanted me to change myself, and now my house, to adhere to their ideas of what's acceptable. I shouldn't have to keep justifying my decisions.' I was on a roll. 'And you know what I'm dreading? Their reaction when I refuse to explain my decisions about our baby once it's here. Even when I do try to help them understand my choices, they don't listen. Instead, they harass me about them over and over until I do things their way. *Paint your buffet, paint your buffet, paint your buffet. Lose some weight, lose some weight, lose some weight.* I can't stand the way they talk *at* me. We can't hold a human conversation of any depth because all they want to do is give me advice.'

'I know. My mum is the same. She's *so* annoying, constantly telling me how to raise my baby. Dad's great though. He just goes with the flow and does what I ask him to when he comes to look after bubba. But – *far out* – Mum drives me up the wall.' Aurelie rolled her eyes.

'Why do you ask her to come over that often if you don't like being around her?'

'Because you have to – you have to get their help or you'll go crazy! Plus, she loves being a grandma, so she benefits from her time here as well. But I have to remember to pick my battles. No point entering into an argument every time you disagree. Any time she gives me advice that I won't use, I just nod my head and say, "Yes, Mum." You just have to let it go in one ear and out the other.'

I sighed. I wasn't a huge fan of that approach. Instead, I just sidestepped relationships that grated on me – not that my way to cope was better than Aurelie's. It was a matter of preference. It sounded like having her mum around, though irritating, might have decreased Aurelie's mental load, helping her to be more present with her baby, which was of utmost importance to her anyway. In tolerating one another's foibles, it meant she and her mum could continue their relationship. Ma and I on the other hand seemed to be going down a different path.

'I've been craving my mum's cooking for a while now,' I admitted, 'but I haven't asked her to make me anything and I've turned down her offers to because I don't want to feel like I'm taking advantage of her. It'd be a different story if we enjoyed each other's company; then I could accept a favour without guilt. But at the moment, I think it's unfair of me to welcome her presence only when I want something, then shun her at all other times.'

'At the end of the day, as much as they bother us, our parents love us and they want to help us,' Aurelie said – not realising how this particularly insufferable cliché incensed me. I needed to leave. I didn't want to insult or overwhelm Aurelie by instigating a philosophical interrogation of that comment. She had enough on her plate. Though we were proud of having stayed in touch so long since primary school, we only got to meet once every year or every few years, so I didn't want to sour what little we had left. I thanked her for having me, blew her baby a kiss and lurched toward the door to the safety of my car.

I pulled out and as I passed the Stone Fruit House two doors down, I glanced at its yellowing grass and brittle paling fence. It was so arid, I felt thirsty just looking at it. Good riddance, I thought.

All the way home, the dreaded words Aurelie had said churned around my brain. *Why are people still saying things like this?* What about mothers and fathers who were abused by their own parents and didn't know how to sever the cycle? What about parents whose mental illness hindered their ability to show love in a way their child could receive it? What about parents who were narcissists, manipulators, gas-lighters? Or parents who just had poor people skills, especially with their kids? The widespread assumption that parents loved their children unconditionally was problematic to me. Especially when parents assumed it of themselves when, in reality, they'd put little effort into connecting with their children on a deeper level.

At the end of the street was a tip for landfill, an eyesore. I took the bend quickly, eager to leave it all behind. Yet, even though this suburb was my Egypt, it was Aurelie's Promised Land at the same time. As I turned onto the main road heading south-west to my place, I regained my composure. I smiled to myself, knowing that my dear old friend, who had brought laughter into my life when I needed it most, had found beauty and love in a place where I thought it wasn't possible.

***

'So, Ruhi, Jake. You will need help when the baby comes,' Pa stated over a Sunday family lunch at my parents' place a few weeks later.

'Um...' I looked at Jake and Maya, who were sitting opposite me at the dining table. '...At this stage we'll be okay. I'll let you know if we need anything when the time comes.'

'Ya, that's fine. But I can definitely come and give the baby bath, give coconut oil massage, cook for you, all that,' Ma said.

'No, that's okay. Jake and I want to be doing those things ourselves. If you're keen, I guess the biggest help would be picking up some groceries for us from time to time and potentially even taking Panda for walks, if you're up for it.'

Ma shooed my ideas away with her hands. 'Eh, hoga! Jake can pick the groceries on his way home from work. What help do you need *with the baby?*'

'Nothing at this point, Ma. I appreciate you offering, but Jake plans to take a month off work and play an equal role in the baby's care.'

Just as I imagined my answer was sinking in, slashing through Ma's visions of taking to her grandchild with water, soap, towels, coconut oil and food, and causing her to wilt, Pa scrunched his eyebrows and progressed to the next item on his agenda. 'So, how soon after the baby is born will you be coming here to live?'

I laughed.

'At the beginning of September, maybe?' he asked in earnest.

'Wait. Are you serious?'

'Yes. You know that's what all women do in our culture. Her husband sends her back home to live with her parents after she has given birth.'

'Pa, I live ten minutes down the road. And even if I didn't, my home is with Jake. Also, he doesn't "send" me places.' That last bit seemed lost on Pa.

'Ya, Jake can come live here too then!' Ma chimed in.

'But why?' I asked, becoming exasperated.

'Because it's tradition. We will do everything for the baby and you can relax,' Pa said.

'Yes! When I had you, I barely did anything,' Ma said, radiating excitement. 'I just fed you and slept. Sybil, Helen and your Ajji did everything else. They gave you body bath, head bath, changed your nappy, played with you. Everything!'

'But *I* want to be doing all those things for my baby.'

'Why? When we can do those things for you?' Pa asked.

'Because it's my baby. That's how I'll bond with him or her,' I said. It wasn't supposed to be a jab at Ma, but deep down I resented the fact that she palmed me off to other family members while she chilled out – and rejoiced in that fact. Of course she was entitled to down-time but after all the years of being made to fit around her chaotic schedule, being left in other people's care without being able to look forward to quality time with my mother where my own interests were validated (as opposed to following her around at the shops), I couldn't care if my choice to spend quality time with my kid stood in the way of her wanting to do the same. *Sorry, but you don't get to skip a generation then decide you want to bond with your grandchild.* Maybe Ma twigged; she gave me a blank look, opened her mouth as if to say something, and closed it.

Pa broke the silence. 'Anyway, I've told your Ma to take annual leave when the baby comes so that she can be with you every day.'

At this point, my capacity to remain patient and polite had almost been reached. Fury mushroomed inside me. I couldn't believe that Ma had already booked her annual leave when I was still working out how to delicately inform her that I didn't even want her at the *hospital.* It took so much concentration to stay calm and collected when I responded.

'No, that's okay. You don't need to take time off work,' I said. 'Jake will be at home with me.'

'Yes, I can come help! You and Jake can relax while I look after the baby!' she said.

My jaw tensed up so much that my teeth felt like glass about to break. I decided to leave it for the moment and deal with it later. They just weren't getting it: Jake and I *wanted* to participate in the ordinary, day-to-day activities with our daughter. She wouldn't be able to talk for a while, so we wanted to learn her cues and all the other ways she'd communicate with us in the meantime.

In Ma and Pa's eyes, our ideas were fanciful and couldn't possibly outweigh generations of tradition. Ma couldn't comprehend that she hadn't *earned* the right to come over and spend time with us whenever she liked. Really, I didn't think she had any desire at that point to spend much time with Jake and me – it was about having access to her grandchild. As for Pa, he seemed content to contract Ma out to us, in lieu of actually connecting with us himself.

Pa changed the subject, probably also hoping to cross this bridge at a later stage. As far as I could see, my parents weren't counting on my relationship with them changing for the better; they were counting on me eventually finding myself desperate for their help with the baby. I was determined not to let that happen. I wished they'd embraced the opportunity I presented and worked with me on filling the gaps in our relationship to build up trust again. Instead, they decided that any 'help' was going to be on their terms only, which was fine, as long as I had the right to decline without being harried. I understood that they were enthusiastic grandparents, keen to spend precious time with their grandchild, but I didn't appreciate the way they were bypassing their relationship with me to forge a new one with my child and continue preserving the charade of happy families.

Also, if my parents were not empathetic or intuitive to *my* needs as an articulate adult, I couldn't expect them to be attuned to those of my daughter. I wasn't sure of what role they would play in my daughter's life, but it was not going to be the one they envisioned. At some point, I was going to have to break it to Ma that she wasn't invited to the hospital during my labour, or to our house every other day thereafter.

Maybe I was harsh in some ways, but there was still too much between my parents and me that had corroded our relationship over time and that hadn't been dealt with openly.

13

Funeral plans

Late in my pregnancy, Jake would regularly come home to find me sprawled out on the daybed, hands on belly, binging on bread and episodes of *Offspring* simultaneously. It was a relief for Jake to see me move away from *Suits,* all of which I'd consumed at lightning speed. 'Why do you watch this shit? It's so terribly written!'

'I'm tolerating it because I need to know if Donna and Harvey get together.'

'Why? Harvey's a dick.'

Fewer arguments were had as a result of my newfound affinity for *Offspring.* But Jake also had concerns about me watching a show full of birthing scenes – especially given the plot hinged on occasional accidents, emergencies and tragedies.

He was right to be worried. I had developed an irrational but very real fear that I would die in childbirth – especially after the episode where a mother was in the transition phase of her labour and felt that something was not right. The medical staff reassured her and encouraged her to keep breathing. She drew in a deep breath and never exhaled; her respiratory system had failed. Shortly after, her baby was born. In an instant, without warning, the new father lost the love of his life. Widowed, he had to continue the parenting journey without her. His whole world went cold, except for the warm little baby he held. It was one of the most harrowing episodes of any TV show I'd ever watched, and I spent the rest of the afternoon sobbing.

Naturally, my next course of action was to get my affairs in order. By the time Jake got home, I'd organised an appointment with our solicitor to finalise and sign off on our wills and I'd completed the necessary research regarding my funeral. After Jake had changed out of his work clothes, he moved into the kitchen to wash some dishes while I served up dinner.

'So, babe, when I die...' I began as I heated up our food.

'What? Why are we talking about this now?'

'Just listen! For my funeral, I don't want anything fancy or expensive. I was a minimalist while I lived so I'll be a minimalist in death too.'

'You do realise you're already talking about yourself in past tense?'

'Shoosh!' I turned around to face him, arms akimbo. 'Instead of an extravagant ceremony, I'd rather you used the money for yourself and for our kiddo in here,' I said, now patting my belly with one hand.

'Yeah, okay.' He shook his head.

I continued as I grabbed our cutlery. 'I would like my body disposed of in the most environmentally friendly way possible. These days I hear that cremation is not great for the atmosphere, but I'm down for that if it's the best you can afford. If you decide to bury me, don't worry about a coffin and all that hoo-ha. There are these burial suits you can buy online. I've looked it up and bookmarked it in our browser for you. The brand is Coeio. C-O-E-I-O. Got that? It has mushroom spores in it, which help your body decompose quickly. So you can just chuck me in one of those and put me in the ground. Maybe plant some flowers on top, but don't go overboard with an elaborate tombstone or anything.'

'Okay...'

'And when it comes to the eulogy, feel free to keep it simple. I don't want you to have to say anything I haven't heard before. Say it all while I'm alive. Also, at the service, people can wear what they want. It doesn't need to be all black. But then, it doesn't need to be balloons and colours either, if you don't want it to be. You know I'm not a fan of balloons anyway. Most of the time, they're just tacky. So yeah, just keep it chill, like me, when I was alive.'

'You're still alive.'

'Yes, yes, yes, okay, Captain Obvious! So! I trust you one hundred per cent to parent our child. You'll be a magnificent dad. Don't second-guess yourself. I guess I would just hope that you tell our kid about our crazy stories, take her out in nature, help foster her spirituality and show her how to practise gratitude rather than taking things for granted. Also, when it comes to you and a second chance at love...' Jake rolled his eyes. 'I trust you. Go for it, if it's right for you and our daughter. Maybe just steer clear of my sister – that'd be weird. It's nice that you're pretty much best friends but maybe just keep it that way.'

'Are you done yet?' The microwave beeped.

'Unless, of course, you can't help it and you're seriously in love with Maya and like, *every* other alternative is unviable. I don't know. I won't even be alive for it so if you absolutely *must* be with my sister, then so be it. Good luck to you both with all the awkwardness.'

I checked Jake out as he leaned back against the kitchen bench and sighed as he dried the last of the dishes.

'You're so hot. Let's have sex tonight,' I said, moving plates to the dining table. 'Anyway, can you remember all of that or do you need me to write it down?'

'Wait, what?'

'Will you remember everything?'

Jake wiped his hands and turned to put his arms around me.

'Yes, I'll remember,' he said. I ended up writing it all down anyway a few days later.

On that night though, Jake knew not to bring up the possibility that I could one day end up having to plan his funeral, depending on who went first. A few years ago, I had informed him that I'd been praying and put in a request with God for either me to die first, or both of us at the same time in our sleep, like Noah and Ally in *The Notebook.* I knew Jake would be devastated if I died first. But if I was the one to lose him, I would be distraught *and* mentally unstable. Jake had always been the saner of us. Case in point: he was not alarmed by me discussing the logistical fallout of my impending death.

I always believed that Jake loved the ludicrous things I had to say. Jada Pinkett-Smith once said that she and Will kept married life sexy by changing things up all the time. In that regard, I was a natural as far as conversation went. I kept this man on his toes! On the other hand, sex had become somewhat predictable because I only had so many positions I could manoeuvre my pregnant body into – still glorious, though, as I was reminded later that night.

Jake fell asleep as his daughter woke up for night-time shenanigans, which evidently included bhangra practice along my uterine wall.

'I hope I make it through this with you, buddy,' I whispered to her.

Jake and I ended up (eventually) laughing at my over-the-top response to the *Offspring* episode, but I still quietly battled negative thoughts about how our journey would pan out. I'd enjoyed the best ten years of my life since meeting Jake and I was sure that our time together would soon come to an end. Obviously I'd die one day but I was convinced that I wasn't going to make it to old age: my volatile, emotionally unpredictable childhood had led me to believe that nothing wonderful lasted. Ten years together was already a long time and if ever Jake was unusually late coming home from work or the supermarket I often braced myself for the worst. It was only a matter of time before my life itself would be 'taken away'. In addition, my tendency to have panic attacks put me on edge about my chances of surviving the ordeal of labour. And so, without an iota of medical evidence, I declared myself a prime candidate for respiratory failure during childbirth.

I lay awake imagining my demise. When I'd arrive at the hospital, I'd be given an injection of some sort, triggering my phobia of needles. A panic attack would ensue and I would struggle to breathe. Eventually, I'd take my final breath and cark it. Then Jake would have to open this book up to this exact chapter (deliberately titled for his convenience) for guidelines on what to do next.

Considering I never attended a funeral until my mid-twenties, as a child I was acutely aware of death and the fragility of life. If you think this sounds profound, let me assure you that it was not. It was a direct result of my parents allowing me to watch macabre films like *Independence Day*, *Titanic* and *Armageddon*. I had countless nightmares about my own death at the hands of aliens, a foundering ship, a meteor, or all three.

Ma took almost eight-year-old me to the cinemas to see *Titanic* when it came out in December 1997; she shoved the popcorn in front of my face while Jack worked on Rose's nude portrait and for the duration of their vintage-car boink. Though my eyes were covered for all of the kissing and sexy bits, they were open for all of the dying and drowning bits. After every vivid nightmare, I braved the dark corridor to my parents' bedroom in the middle of the night (and had to wait outside until they unlocked it), petrified that tomorrow may never come. And one day, it almost didn't.

Raksha Aunty was living with us at the time, after emigrating to Australia with her husband. One time, while she and Ma were bathing Maya, who was just a few days old, a thick little toffee lodged in my throat. I could barely breathe as I cried out for Ma. I have no idea how I managed to talk but tears rolled down my face as I pleaded,

'I'm too young to die, Ma! Don't let me die!'

Ma, already in a panic, became doubly shocked. In her retelling of events, her thoughts went from, *This is so scary – I need to save my kid,* to, *Where did she learn that?!* Ma handed Maya to Aunty then started hitting my back. When that did nothing, she held me upside down. She tried everything but I continued to choke and cry. So she ran me over to our Turkish neighbours' place, where my best friend at the time, Ibrahim, lived (friends who were boys were allowed until I was midway through primary school). In Pa's absence (he was at work), Ma went looking for Ib's dad because she believed that men were the ones to call on in a crisis. Ib's dad wasn't home, but his mum, whom I affectionately called Anne (pronounced *Ah-neh* – 'Mum' in Turkish), was. Together, she and Ma made me chug a small bucket of water, which conquered the toffee and saved my life. I've since learned that offering water as a remedy to choking could actually worsen the situation. Nevertheless, I was grateful their quick thinking paid off this time.

The toffee incident cemented my lifelong premonition that I would die young, but this fact didn't dampen the joy of life for me; if anything, it heightened it. I became a curious mix of fatalistic and wildly romantic. If it wasn't for my doom-and-gloom outlook, I may not have chased after love the way I did. When Ma made me close my eyes during steamy movie scenes, I could still hear the soul-stirring music, the pillow talk, the breathing. After all the Bollywood love stories I'd watched and all the ballads I knew by heart – *Suraj Hua Maddham, Saathiya, Kuch Kuch Hota Hai* – I was a sucker for love.

When I felt it with Jake, I went all in and never looked back. With death around the corner and my arsenal of romantic lyrics and poetry overflowing, I was destined to drown someone in my passion before I left this planet.

***

In July 2007, the rift between my parents and me was visible but at a standstill. The peace and quiet of Saturday mornings hovered like a brief mist in the Echo Chamber House, before Ma woke up and sleepily but rambunctiously charged down the stairs like a miniature tank, ready for action. Until then, the only sounds that came from downstairs were the susurrus of Pa reading the paper and preparing chaha. Our move to the new house three years earlier had marked a change in our family dynamics. One of the most prominent differences was that Pa had cooled off a bit with the hitting and beating. It hadn't stopped entirely, but it was less frequent. There was no announcement or line in the sand. It just died down.

This shift meant that Pa and I began to get along a little better, which was partly why I went to him, and not Ma, when I started dating Jake in Year 12. My other motive for going to Pa was that, while there was an equal chance of both parents being upset about the news, Ma was less likely to react rationally or think it through before deciding to take action. I had arranged for my conversation with Pa to take place when Ma would be out shopping later that morning.

When she was gone, Pa called out from the bottom of the staircase, 'Ruhi, your ma is gone. I'll be ready at the dining table.'

This was the first formal conversation I'd asked to have with either parent. Nothing had ever been so important to me. Heart pounding and palms sweaty, I walked out of my bedroom with Maya, who'd promised to see it through with me.

'You'll be alright. I'll help you when you don't know what to say,' she said. She was eleven years old.

'Why is Maya here?' Pa asked when we took our seats.

'Um...'

'For moral support!' Maya piped up.

'Okay, tell me, Ruhi.' Pa took a sip of his chaha and folded his arms on the table.

I tried to speak, but the words stuck on my parched tongue.

'Ruhi has something important to tell you,' Maya offered.

'Yes, tell me,' Pa said.

I cleared my throat. 'So ... something has happened...' I stopped in my tracks again. It was impossible to progress.

'Yes, Ruhi. What has happened?' Pa asked.

'Um ... I ... I made a friend.'

'Okay?' Pa chuckled.

'Yeah, so basically ... I made this friend. And ... something happened...'

Pa laughed at my awkwardness by that point, completely bewildered. His eyes softened when he smiled. The wrinkles around them gave me a warm feeling, something I'd started to experience more often since moving house.

'Is that all?' he asked.

'And ... ahem.' I cleared my throat for the fifteenth time. 'It's a boy.'

There was no going back now. It was out in the world and I was about to suffer the early death I'd predicted. Pa still looked lost.

Maya ripped the bandaid. 'She has a boyfriend, Pa.'

What the?! I didn't know whether to punch her for being bold with such delicate information or to hug her for being braver than me – *or* to duck for cover as Pa turned Super Saiyan. Seriously, the kid should have been awarded Young Australian of the Year for her masterful diplomacy throughout this difficult conversation.

Pa was quiet. Strange. I sensed he had a lot of questions but was struggling to cut through the shock. He went to speak, and then seemed to have trouble completing his sentences and questions. Maya to the rescue.

'Tell us his name, Ruhi...' Maya prompted.

'Um, Jake.'

'When and where did you meet?' She knew all the answers but asked for Pa's benefit.

'At my friend's seventeenth, two months ago. Zam used to know him from primary school and she introduced us.'

I was hoping that dropping Zam's name would win some favour. Rather than impressed, Pa was dumbfounded. He teared up.

'What's wrong, Pa?' I asked.

'No, nothing.'

'Tell us, Pa,' said Maya.

'I just hadn't expected you to grow up so quickly,' he said, wiping his wet eyes with his fingers. It was the most vulnerable we'd ever seen him, except for the day he had picked up the phone in the Stone Fruit House to learn that his father had suffered a fatal heart attack. Like that day so many years earlier, after shedding his tears, Pa shut off again. In those rare moments, I would grasp for this sensitive, overwhelmingly *human* incarnation of Pa, wanting to ask all of my questions, but he forever eluded me. Apart from these wispy moments of clarity, Pa's inner self only came through when his anger boiled over.

His tenderness surprised me. His advice was to keep the news of my boyfriend under wraps from Ma for the time being – none of us could predict how she might take it. Our doctor had warned that Ma's cholesterol levels posed risks to her heart health, and Pa was concerned that the stress of learning about Jake might make matters worse. He told us he wanted to lay some groundwork before I told her the news and that everything would be okay.

Two weeks later, Pa advised that Ma was ready for me to broach the topic. I appreciated him approaching the situation with such care; however, it soon became clear that he'd either done a poor job of preparing her or that, no matter what he tried, my budding romance was destined languish in a basket labelled *Things That Can Only Happen Over Ma's Dead Body.*

When I approached Ma, she was sitting in the lounge, in her designated spot on the couch. The lights were switched off as she watched one of her Hindi TV serials, broadcast via a gigantic satellite dish erected behind the house without council approval. Ma's hair was pulled back tightly in a small bun and drenched in oil. She looked like an Indian gang lord, ready to pick up the phone to her gundas and order an assassination. I stood in the far corner of the room, leaving as much distance as possible between us.

'Your father says you have something to tell me,' Ma said. Her eyes remained on the TV straight ahead.

Knowing that Pa had my back gave me confidence to say the words more easily than I had with him. I told her about Jake. Her head slowly swivelled on her neck, like an owl, as she turned to me with a cold expression. Her beautiful, big, brown eyes narrowed. She didn't yell or panic, as was her usual way, which just made her reaction all the more menacing. I glanced at Pa with a look that said, *What the hell is happening here?* Ma responded with a murderous voice, like a Sith using The Force to control my mind. 'You are going to break up with him and you are never to speak to him again – do you understand?'

I looked at Pa. 'But Pa, you said—' I spluttered.

'No arguments,' Ma cut me off. 'Just do as I say.'

Meanwhile, Pa's spine apparently dissolved; either that, or he actually changed his mind in the ten seconds that had lapsed since I'd told Ma.

'It's best that you listen to your mother, Ruhi,' Pa said.

WHAT? TRAITOR! 'No,' I said. 'This isn't some sort of fling. I actually love him and—'

'*Love?!* You're too young to know what love is! Finish your studies, then we can talk about love,' Ma interrupted.

'What?! Five years from now?' I protested, not knowing that I was actually about to spend the best part of a decade at uni.

I could tell that Pa was confused and was looking to Ma for direction, which was unlike him. I wasn't sure why he had been cool with it at first, only to suddenly hop on board Ma's bulldozer. I could only guess that he might have initially felt guilty about imposing the same rules upon me and Jake that Ajji and Ajja had on Ma and Pa.

'But, Ma! I thought you would understand – after what you had been through with Pa!'

I'll never forget her next words, completely void of compassion: 'You thought wrong.' And that was that.

My relationship with my parents had been making headway – if only limping, stumbling headway – up until that moment. It was inevitable that at some point we would come to an abrupt halt. That moment had arrived, only the halt was more like a fiery car crash. Off a mountain. Into a ravine. And then the car exploded. Just like in the action movies Ma loved so much.

I was devastated, not only because I was being told that I wasn't free to love who I wanted to love, but also because Ma had not shown me one ounce of goodwill. She didn't even feign interest in hearing me out or bother to learn a single thing about this young man I was besotted with. I decided that she and Pa were hypocrites and I'd never allow them to hear excitement in my voice again – which, up to that point, hadn't been a common occurrence anyway. The things that gave me true joy in the world, outside of Ma's and Pa's ideals, were seldom visited upon by my parents. They didn't know my favourite books, movies, music, interests and hobbies, let alone any details about this person who meant so much to me.

Ma kept speaking but her words slid off me. I was hurt beyond my ability to respond.

'You are never to see that boy again. Do you understand?'

Silence.

'You are going to break up with that boy tomorrow. Understand?!' she said again. *That boy,* dim and distant.

I was too exhausted to argue. So many of Ma's and Pa's decisions involving me seemed founded in fear and a need for control. I could understand that it must have been scary to raise kids in another country so unlike their own – Maya and I doing things they never would have done themselves ... Except that they had done the *exact same thing!*

The difference was that Jake and I actually told our parents *before* we got married and had a kid. *Yeah. I said it* ... to you, dear reader. I said it to you. Not to Ma. She would have torn me a new one if I had.

Ma got Sybil Aunty and Ajji to talk some sense into me over an international call. On speaker, they pleaded with me to listen to my parents and to believe that they knew what was best for me. I blocked them out and stared at my hands as their impassioned voices shot through the room and past my ears. In the Echo Chamber House, the only people allowed to use their voice were the ones whose views mirrored my parents'. When we hung up, Ma asked over and over if I had registered what she was saying. I was still non-responsive. It was too late in the evening and, frankly, I was ready to call it a night in every possible sense.

'See, we don't know what these Australian boys are like and we just don't want him to break your heart,' Pa said. But it was too late for that; a pair of Indians had beaten the Australian boy to it. I kept my face turned away until Ma grew tired of addressing a wall.

***

A few months later, Ma and Pa discovered I was making plans to move out on my own. Before I could, they emptied an entire cement-truck full of guilt on me.

The rapid-fire questions all riffed off the same theme: *How can you even think of leaving? What will others think? What will they say about our family?*

What will our relatives think if you leave us before marriage? Are you still seeing that boy? We sacrificed everything and came to this country for you and your sister to have a better life and this is how you repay us?

It was an abomination in our culture for a girl to move out before marriage, unless she was required to for work. I ended up staying put for the same reason that I stuck it out at university: the fear of what my parents might do to themselves if they couldn't live with the shame and social implications of their daughter's choices. Still, I didn't buy into their diatribes about everything they'd sacrificed to migrate to Australia. My parents made sacrifices for Maya and me – there was no doubt about it – but I wanted them to own that choice and admit that they did it for themselves as much as for us. Sure, I'd led a life of greater privilege and opportunity than I might have in Dharwad, but I didn't want them to forget that Ma was obsessed with the idea of becoming a 'foreigner' and living in a Western country, and Pa probably wanted to escape the veritable shit-storm whipped up by their love marriage and love child.

Of course, not long after my parents arrived in Australia, disenchantment set in alongside their admiration for their new home. If they were speaking to family and friends in India, they praised Australia's cleanliness, the comparatively low levels of corruption in the justice system, the pristine drinking water, the gorgeous city and the fantastic local amenities. But when they chatted with friends in Melbourne, they spoke openly about racism in the workplace, their view that the Australian education system was inferior, and the apparent lack of propriety in local youths.

'Ayo, have you seen the short dresses and skirts these girls wear here? And the bikinis they wear at the beach! Are baap re! How can these girls be so shameless?' I'd hear aunties say, Ma among them. I'd chuck on the radio and my parents would ask, 'What garbage is this? How can they call this music? How can you listen? You can't even understand any of the words they are saying!'

One of the deciding factors when they applied for permanent residency, and eventually citizenship, it seemed to me, was the belief that Maya and I would be safer in Australia. It was a fair call and one that I was grateful for; however, their idea of safety for their daughters only covered *physical* safety. As long as they could see that my body was intact, it didn't mean much to them if everything inside me was broken.

Instead of moving out, I commenced my own quiet resistance. I distanced myself from my parents as much as I could while still under their roof: I washed my clothes separately; I mostly bought my own food; I worked as much as possible to stay away; and when I wasn't working, I hung out at the university library, often catching the bus home late at night. I spent a couple of evenings with Jake every week and lied about it, saying I was at the library alone or with friends. On those nights, he drove me home and I lied again about catching the bus. When I was home, I kept my bedroom door shut. Ma and Pa opened it when they walked past, saying, 'How many times do we have to tell you to keep this door open?'

'How many times do I have to tell you that I am studying and your loud conversations and TV shows are distracting?' I'd retort.

I avoided asking any more favours of Ma and Pa. My theory was that as long as I depended on them, they held onto the right to tell me what to do with my life. Over time, the frequency of my lies reduced, only because I barely spoke to my parents anymore and gave them as little information as possible about what I was up to. I was polite with them but never offered anything authentic. They sometimes spied on me, but Jake and I were ever so careful, always looking over our shoulders. Other times they tried to trick me into outing myself.

'One of your aunties said she saw you walking around the shopping centre with a boy,' they sometimes said to test me.

'Which aunty? And where was this alleged sighting?'

'Don't worry about which aunty. She didn't want me to say. Tell us the truth – are you still seeing that boy?'

'Nope. The fake aunty must have been mistaken.'

'Ruhi. If I find out you are seeing that boy again—'

'I know, okay? I have to go study now.'

Then I'd go upstairs and text Jake about it on the spare phone he gave me, which I kept hidden and silent in the secret pocket of my old school blazer. After two years of hiding our ongoing relationship from my parents, they found out that I was still seeing 'that boy' – and not because we slipped up.

It was my nineteenth birthday. I spent the day in the city with Jake. He organised a picnic at Birrarung Marr and booked a ride on the Melbourne Star. When the time came to go home, something in me snapped. I couldn't do it anymore. I didn't want to keep having to say goodbye to him, not knowing when we'd squeeze in another time to meet, how we'd manoeuvre it and what fresh excuse I'd have to come up with. The meticulous planning it took just to spend time with the person I loved most in the world suddenly became more than I could bear.

That morning, I'd told my parents that I'd be out with a girlfriend and would return around four o'clock in the afternoon. Instead, I decided not to go home. By six in the evening, I had over twenty missed calls from Ma and Pa. My friends texted me saying that my parents were calling them to find out where I was. Of course, my friends covered for me but they said my parents had gone into panic mode. I ended up returning their calls around eight o'clock. Realising that I would have to face them sooner or later, even if only to collect my belongings, I agreed to go home on the condition that they would accept my relationship with Jake, whether they liked it or not. The truth was out: yes, I was still seeing 'that boy'. Ma was beside herself. Pa had always been suspicious, so while he wasn't shocked, he was livid.

As soon as they picked me up from my friend's house where Jake had dropped me off, we drove straight to my cousin Jia's house. Our parents were best friends and Jia's dad, Sunil Uncle, was Ma's cousin. For a while in primary school I used to sleep over at their place every Friday night. Jia and I would try to wake up at six o'clock every Saturday morning to watch *Sailor Moon* and *Dragon Ball Z* on Cheez TV. When I tried to do the same at home, Ma and Pa told me off for my dharidhrathana, which loosely translated from Kannada meant 'idleness leading to poverty'. 'You're watching TV first thing in the morning? Chi! Go do something better with your time!' It was at Jia's house that I was also introduced to pancakes. Her mum, Vaani Aunty (who gave me the puberty book) would prepare breakfast for us, and I lost my mind when I tasted maple syrup for the first time.

But there was nothing sweet about our visit this time. We drove to Jia's so my parents could vent and consult with hers on what to do with the miscreant who had once been the promising baby they'd brought out from India. Jia and I stayed downstairs with the adults while our younger siblings were sent upstairs to play. Ma and Pa had a massive whinge about my actions and looked to Aunty and Uncle for guidance. They'd endured a similar process with Jia and her boyfriend at the time, former persona non grata in their household.

Aunty and Uncle told Ma and Pa something they didn't expect to hear: they were better off coming to terms with Jake and me being together.

'See, people in Australia are moving forward. Even people in India are moving forward. They are more accepting of boyfriends and girlfriends these days, especially in the modern cities,' Vaani Aunty said. 'But people who came out of India many years back, like us, are still stuck in the old ways.'

She encouraged my parents to set some rules and boundaries for their own peace of mind and get on with it. And so they did: that evening at Jia's house, all four parents collaborated on a new set of policies. I wasn't to talk about Jake around our Indian community. He wouldn't be invited to any family events

– 'Finish your studies first, then we'll see,' my parents told me.

If anyone saw us together out and about, I was to introduce him as my friend. No kissing. No holding hands. Initially, I was only to see him once a month, which I negotiated to once a week with the assistance of Jia and Vaani Aunty. Whenever my parents proposed an absurd addition to the rulebook, Vaani Aunty shot me a hold-your-horses look, her expressive eyes reassuring me that I needed to keep my cool and agree for the moment; there would be time to renegotiate later when everyone had calmed down. This proved difficult in the immediate future with Ma and Pa's protean set of regulations, but it was better than having to lie and hide.

My parents took a while to settle down. Ma didn't speak to me for the next two months, which was a bit of a relief to be honest; it was the quietest she'd ever been. Still, it wasn't exactly a heartwarming feeling to know that I'd offended my mother into complete silence. Pa took each day as it came. We spoke minimally. I often heard him through the walls, consoling Ma when she locked herself in their bedroom in the evenings.

Tensions loosened with time. Nearly a year went by. In December, Pa travelled back to India on his own to visit his mother when she was sick. In his absence, Ma agreed to meet Jake for the first time and invited him to lunch. My usually dazzling mother wore a maxi cotton nighty and coconut oil in her hair, which she combed back into a bun. Perhaps her lack of effort was a form of protest; I suspected an internal conflict between her stubborn reservations and her curiosity about Jake. I was glad she brushed her affectations aside to meet him. All the layers were peeled back.

At first, Ma was polite with Jake, but she didn't pretend to like the situation one bit. Over the course of the afternoon, I watched her forced smile morph into a genuine one. Jake, never usually the type to offer or entertain flattery, thanked Ma for the meal and even went as far as to compliment her on her excellent cooking. She watched him eat about six chapatis with her creamy baingan bharta and channa palle. Ma was thrilled, and since then, her life motto has been, 'I must feed Jake.' Soon Ma was the one trying to persuade Pa that Jake was 'a nice, respectful boy' over the phone. She wanted Jake to meet Pa when he returned from India. Pa took a while to warm up to the idea, but when they finally met, he took a quiet shine to Jake. Like Pa himself, Jake was reserved, he used words sparingly and, when he did speak, it was well thought-through and often humorous.

One of my favourite things about Jake was how he interacted with Maya. He was a good listener and when he was finally grafted into our family, he always made sure Maya was heard. The rest of the family often talked over her and shoved her opinions to the back of the line – but not when Jake was around. Whenever Maya was mid-conversation with Jake and *someone* interrupted to ask, 'JAKE, DID YOU LIKE THE CHAPATIS? DO YOU WANT MORE?' he would respond with, 'Just a second, Ma. Maya was saying something.'

Since they first met when Maya was eleven years old, she looked up to Jake like he was her own big brother. When Maya started at the university where Jake worked, they carpooled on days she had classes. On one particular forty-degree day, she had to run around the university buying second-hand books. By the time she'd collected them all, she was flustered, faint and no longer able to bear the weight of all the books in the heat. So she called Jake and waited on the lawn at the centre of the campus. He met Maya where she'd almost collapsed, picked up half of the load and walked her to his office, where they dumped the books until the end of the day.

I bawled my eyes out whenever Maya told me about her adorable interactions with Jake. I loved the way he never threw himself at my parents. He was respectful of our culture and didn't criticise Ma and Pa for seeing him as a challenge or an obstacle. When our circumstances could have torn us apart, we grew closer. In 2012, after six years of dating and four years of practising my HR and team-building skills on Jake and my parents, we finally got married.

***

I'd often heard it said that you never know just how much you can love someone until you've held your baby in your arms. I doubted this would be the case for me. I was sure that my heart would explode like a piñata full of glitter when I got to see my baby, but I'd already experienced this kind of deep and overwhelming love.

For me, it existed in the relationships I had with Maya and Zam, and then I'd experienced it in a new kind of fullness ever since I first loved and felt loved by Jake. The dysfunctionality within my family projected pain and difficulty onto our relationship. The fighting, controlling, manipulation, blackmailing and threats were frequent potholes on what seemed like an endless road. But we made it, Jake and me. We made it. And we looked forward to soon sharing our immense love with our daughter.

Fingers crossed I wouldn't die first.

14

Atithi Devo Bhava

अतिथि देवो भव

Breathe. Okay. Alarm clock – 4.30am. Ugh. Saturday? Sunday? Saturday. No point in going back to sleep. I must have gnashed my teeth so hard that I woke myself up from another nightmare.

I busied myself making pancakes for breakfast, comforted by the quotidian nature of the undertaking and its even ratios; 1:1:1:1. One cup of self-raising flour, one of pinch salt, one cup of soy milk, one egg. These unremarkable real-life calculations countered the distress of seeing The Man from the Hospital in my sleep again. As soon as it was a decent time to make a call, I picked up the phone.

'Hi, Ma. How are you?' I asked.
'Ya, good. Slept well?'

'Yeah ... listen, I'm just going to get to the point. You know what happened in India all those years ago?'

'Hmm ... which...' She pretended to root around for the right memory, but I knew the woman; sharp as a butcher's knife, she understood exactly what I was talking about.

'I'm going to tell Pa. Tonight.'

'WHAT?! GONE MAD OR WHAT?!'

'It's up to you whether or not you want to be there but, regardless, I'm telling him.'

'EH! WHY YOU WANT TO DO ALL THIS NOW?!'

'I'll explain tonight.'

'Please, Ruhi. Don't do this. Let's talk about it some more. You're seven months pregnant. Why you want to open up all of this again? That too, now?'

'Ma, this is not a negotiation. I thought I'd do you the courtesy of letting you know. This is not about you or about getting you in trouble. This is about what I need to do for my own peace of mind. If you want to be there, I'll see you tonight, but you don't have to if you're not keen. Bye, Ma.'

'EH WAIT, RUHI!'

'Ma ... I'm hanging up. Bye.' I was actually probably more reluctant than her to talk about what else had happened in Dharwad (other than the incident with Pathravalli). But it needed to be done.

That night, we gathered in my parents' family room. I shared a single-seater armchair with Jake – he sat on the armrest holding my hand tight. Ma occupied her usual spot on the couch opposite us. Pa sat on his floor cushion in front of her. Maya was on a chair a couple of metres away. She knew what was coming.

Everyone waited for me to say something. I had thought through exactly how I was going to handle this, but when the time came, I was paralysed by my own disgust at having to somehow describe what had been done to my eleven-year-old body. For a few minutes, not a single sound disturbed the room. The only thing that emitted itself into the still, darkened lounge – it was where we watched movies, so the overhead lights were rarely used – was the light inside my parents' display cabinet where Ma stored her collection of crystals and mementos from her travels. Since Ma first left Dharwad, she had flown to almost every continent with Pa, covering more and more territory as us kids got older. They'd achieved so much together, as evidenced, in part, by their souvenirs. But for every tall, lit-up, glass cabinet that enshrined the most prized trinkets in one's life – most of the households in my extended family had this particular kind of furniture – there were usually one or two drawers at the bottom, holding things that were not for exhibition. Sooner or later, they would be opened.

***

January 2002. The summer school holidays back in the Stone Fruit House.

I was about to turn twelve years old and was ready to start high school. We'd just returned from our trip to India. Outside was a cloudless sky and sunlight streamed in through the windows: all the trappings of a lovely day. Our street was quiet and so was the house. Ma was pottering around in her room and Maya was playing in hers while Pa was at work. My bedroom window was open, but no breeze came through. All that wrinkled the stale soundlessness was a ticking clock. I sat hunched on my bed, petrified. But I knew what I had to do. I stood up and headed for Ma's room.

She was organising her dresser and acknowledged my presence with a grunt. Filled with trepidation, I somehow managed to push my voice through my tightening throat.

'Ma, something happened while we were in India that I have to tell you about.'

'En atha?' she asked. *What happened?*

I stared at my parents' unsightly bedhead for a few seconds. A radio complete with nightlights and golden buttons and speakers was built into its grey-velvet upholstery, like a bejewelled elephant. This furniture choice embodied the general design motif of our home – somehow both aggressively multi-functional and ornate. It epitomised the haphazard, detached style of decorating that failed to make that house feel like a home; just another thing Ma brought home because she liked it, not considering whether or not it cohered with her previous choices.

'Someone did bad things to me,' I said.

'Huh? What things?'

'Like...' I was struggling. My under-equipped vocabulary and inability to identify my private parts were always going to make this conversation tough.

'They um ... they ... *touched* me?' I said, borrowing a word from the film *Hum Dil De Chuke Sanam.* When Amrita asked her daughter, played by Aishwarya Rai, if the man had touched her anywhere – 'Kya usne tumhe kahi chhua hai?' – it was the only time I'd understood the negative implication about a physical exchange between a male and a female.

'What?! Who?!'

'Saul Uncle,' I said.

'WHAT?! WHAT ARE YOU SAYING?!'

'He told me not to tell anyone. I'm not trying to get him in trouble but I felt like it was wrong.'

'WHEN DID THIS HAPPEN? WHAT DID HE DO?!'

'In the bedroom while you were asleep. And on the night bus from Dharwad back to Bangalore.' In a small voice, I explained to her the logistics of the incidents – vaguely describing which body parts were involved, what I'd been instructed to say, and how, in the lead-up, he'd taken me for rides on his new motorbike, told me I was beautiful and bought me lollies.

'Why did it take you two weeks to tell me this?' Ma's brow furrowed and she turned away momentarily, fixing her eyes on her floral bed sheets as though their pretty petals might somehow soften the shocking situation before her. 'Why didn't you tell me while we were in India where I could have done something about it?!'

'I don't know!'

She asked more questions. I answered them. Then she got on the phone to our family in Dharwad to tell them everything, without considering how that might make me feel. It was no longer my story, but ours. It was all up to Ma now to 'fix' the situation. At least I knew she believed me – not because she told me so, but because I overheard her reasoning in Kannada with her sister that I was a naive young girl, incapable of fabricating such things. She enlisted Helen Aunty and Sybil Aunty as overseas proxies to execute justice on her behalf, and mine.

Apparently, they tracked down the perpetrator and yelled at him. I was also told that they hit him with their shoes. Then they called us back within the hour. Ma answered, and I could hear a commotion on the other end. Then Ma handed the phone to me. It was Saul.

'Look, Ruhi, I don't know what you're saying. Anything I did was simply showing affection like uncles do. You know? I don't think I did anything bad. But *if you* felt awkward, I'm saying sorry now, okay?'

When I'd returned to Australia and it had all sunk in, the memories made me want to set myself on fire to be cleansed. So his less than half-arsed apology made me feel worse. He knew exactly what he was doing and there was nothing familial or friendly about it. I didn't know how to respond.

'Um, okay. Thanks.'

After hanging up, Ma's eyes searched mine for answers. She paced the room with the cordless phone in the hand she placed on her hip, while her other hand stayed on her forehead. I knew she was distressed. Looking back, the next time she opened her mouth, it would have been great to hear her say something like, 'Ruhi, I am so sorry that happened to you. Your father and I are here for you if you need to talk about it. We're going to report this to the authorities to make sure it doesn't happen to anyone else. If you would like to see a counsellor, we can organise that. How are you feeling? What do you need? We'll make sure you never have to see that man again.'

What came out instead was, 'Don't tell anyone about this, *especially* your father.'

***

Ma broke the silence: 'Shall I tell what happened?'

She wanted to move us along. I didn't like that. I didn't want her to butt in and try to rush me through decades of shame and secrecy. This time, I wanted to tell Pa what happened myself, but I couldn't find the words in any of the three languages I grew up with to convey what was inside me. So I buried my hands in my face and permitted her to go ahead. Her gaze shifted to Pa.

'See, when we went to India many years ago, Saul did something bad to her. He was young. He was stupid. I called Dharwad and told them. He got in a lot of trouble from Mommy, Helen and Sybil. Ayo, they even hit him with their chappals!' She was proud to confirm this fact, like it made it all better. 'I practically gave him a beating over the phone. He said sorry afterward. That time, I told Ruhi not to tell you anything because I was worried about what you would do to Saul if you found out, but now, she wants you to know and has come here to tell you. That's all.'

Though my relationship with Pa had been strained through the years, I knew that, underneath the angry crust, he would always have my back. I believed that if he had found out about someone in our community sexually abusing me, he'd have made them sorry they ever did.

When Ma first told me that I wasn't allowed to tell Pa, it didn't sit well with me but I couldn't articulate, back then, why that was the case. There was a visceral urge in me to let my dad know about this, perhaps in search of justice. After fifteen years of holding it in, I could finally puke it out.

'What did Saul do to you, Ruhi?' Pa asked. As I considered his question, my deepest, ugliest fear of having a daughter became clear to me.

It had always bothered me that, when Saul first began to cross boundaries, my eyes were open and I stayed where I was next to him. Was I so desperate for someone else's attention, interest and affection that I was willing to pay that kind of price for it? My guilt and self-admonishment didn't subside until years later, when Ivana asked me this question: 'Regardless of whether the victim seems to consent or not – they can't consent, they're a child – but even if they *seemed* to welcome your actions, would *you,* at the age of twenty-six, molest an eleven-year-old kid?'

My response was, without hesitation: 'Never.'

'So when your mother writes it off as "a young boy's stupidity" that might have made sense if we were talking about a twelve-year old. That kind of behaviour in a twenty-six-year-old, an adult, is predatory.'

I agreed, but while I technically no longer saw myself as culpable for Saul's actions, underneath I was still scared I might raise someone so *screwed-up* (for lack of a better term at the time) that she would *let* an abusive man take advantage of her, instead of screaming for help. The challenge, I realised then, was to raise someone who would scream – someone with enough self-worth to raise hell if another person violated her boundaries, someone who knew what her boundaries were in the first place, someone who would never engage in victim-blaming, like I had done to myself. I also had to do the hard work of drawing my own line in the sand and addressing the problem of my own decaying self-esteem.

This feat was easier said than done when your own mother was the sort of person to minimise, dismiss and then bury your experience of child sexual abuse. Ma's succinct and callous summary of the events already had me in tears that night. I didn't know what more I could say without over-dramatising it to them.

'What Ma said,' I answered Pa, taking a deep breath. I filled him in on some missing information, including the phone apology. I wondered how he felt, only learning this massive secret fifteen years later. He seemed to be taking it in his stride, but I couldn't say what was going on inside his head. The pain that came on next caught me off guard. I didn't know what it was like to be kicked in the stomach by the hind legs of a bull, but I imagined that what I felt next came close.

Pa was the one whom I expected to come to my rescue, to bring balance and justice, to set things right with Saul, to be my imperfect knight in shining armour who only abused me for 'my own good', and not for his own pleasure, as Saul did. He opened his mouth to speak again and when he did, his tone was void of any aggravation or passion.

'Look, what happened was not right,' he said. 'Now, Saul has a family. He has settled down. Let's not do anything drastic. Ruhi, a lot of time has gone by. What would you like your mother and I do about it? Of course, I will make him apologise to you again, properly. But what can we do to move forward from this?'

Move forward? You only just got here! Where is all the rage he summoned when I fumbled at school? When I disobeyed him? Where is all the fury I physically absorbed for years? Why isn't he mad?

'Okay, first of all, I *don't* want an apology from him. In fact, I don't want to engage with him *at all.* I have two reasons for bringing this up now. One: when members of our extended family come to visit us after the birth, I don't want him anywhere near my baby. And, two: I want you to tell his wife what happened. If not, I will tell her.'

'BUT, WHY?!' Ma asked.

'Because I feel that it's necessary to notify the one other adult who is responsible for the safety of their young children, given that he was ever willing to molest a child.'

'Eh! Don't use words like "molest".'

'Why? That's what it's called.'

'No,' she said, shaking her head. That was how Ma tried to own the last word. As long as she finished an argument with *no* and shook her head, no counter-argument had a hold on her. It simply would not and could not be true.

***

Ma took a similar position when I was in Year 11 and Pa hit me across my head for the first time, as opposed to the usual smack across my face. I was about to leave for church. He was infuriated by something I had done or said and he didn't hesitate to let me know.

Up to this point, in my role as eldest (and apparently delinquent) daughter, I'd learned to anticipate his frequent outbursts. But at the age of sixteen, when I'd finally settled into a semi-permanent personality and a more enduring group of friends, I started to entertain the idea that I didn't deserve to be beaten at home anymore.

For twenty minutes, I locked myself in the bathroom to click my bones back together and put my skin back on. Then I went to church with Ma. I wept silently through the entire service and when it was over, I approached the events coordinator, Bethany, whom I'd never met before. Ma followed me and stood a couple of metres behind me. She knew about my run-in with Pa that evening and probably wanted to make sure I didn't say anything about it. Though Bethany was a stranger to me, her face was like a smiling moon drawing me in. I needed someone to talk to. Conjuring a smile, I said hello.

'Hi! I've seen you around these past few weeks. Welcome! What's your name?'

'Thanks. It's Ruhi,' I said, my voice no longer steady, nor my eyes dry. 'Um, would it be okay if I talked to you about something in private?'

'Oh, of course. Let's go in this room over here, Ruhi,' she said. Ma walked toward us. 'Is this your mum? Would you like her to join us?'

'Nope. No, I really don't,' I said, turning my back on Ma as I walked into the room.

'Hi, would you like to grab a tea or coffee and we'll let you know when we're ready?' she suggested to Ma, who nodded even though she didn't want to.

When we went inside, I told Bethany what happened. She copped my life story in less than half an hour and held space for me to express my pain. She put her arm around me and offered some helpful words of encouragement and advice. Ma waited outside the room, peering in through the thick, sound-proof glass doors. Shortly after, Bethany invited her back in and gently set down the law.

'Ruhi told me about what is going on at home,' she said. 'I understand that, while there are cultural differences, which I can appreciate, it is in fact, against the law for your husband to hit and shout at Ruhi. We call that abuse and it can't continue.'

Understandably, Ma was taken aback.

'See, my husband is only doing what he thinks is best for our daughter. Yes, he is harsh sometimes but he is not a bad man,' Ma said. For the record, I agreed with her.

'I hear you,' said Bethany. 'And I'm not saying he is a bad person. I don't think Ruhi is saying that either,' she looked at me. I nodded. 'But the abuse needs to stop.'

'Please don't call it "abuse". He is not *abusing* her.' Ma's voice cracked and the sound of helplessness trickled out.

'Hitting a minor is physical abuse,' Bethany explained politely. 'And if he does it again, the police could get involved. Whatever your husband's motives are, I need you to communicate the seriousness of his actions to him.'

Ma broke down crying, defending Pa. 'He's not a bad man. He is a good father,' was her mantra, tears rolling past her mouth.

Bethany put her hand on Ma's shoulder. 'I know this must be difficult to hear. But there are other ways to communicate his feelings without hitting your daughter.'

On the way home, Ma kept her face turned away from me. I'd betrayed our family. When we got back, she skipped dinner and stayed in her bedroom for the rest of the night. I heard the muffled sounds of her conversation with Pa through the wall. Though I couldn't decipher their exact words, I knew she had relayed the conversation with Bethany because when Pa left their bedroom and passed me on his way down the staircase, I sensed a new kind of distance between us as he avoided eye contact with me. It was as though we had gone from being father and daughter to defendant and plaintiff, just waiting for our day in court. It seemed he was the one dreading the sound of my footsteps around the house now: one wrong move and his own daughter could report him to the police. It was not a feeling of power that I enjoyed wielding.

Pa never hit me again after that night. But Ma still could not, would not, wrap her head around the word 'abuse'. As long as she kept shaking her head and chanting, 'No, no, no, no,' it wouldn't become reality.

***

When I called Saul a pedophile, Ma had the same reaction. Except that time, I heard a bitterness in her voice as she spat, 'Don't call him that!'

'That is the term applied to anyone who molests or sexually abuses children,' Maya said to Ma, who continued to shake her head and look away. *No, no, no, no.*

'Okay, let's stay focused,' said Pa, as though we were talking about Harbhajan Singh's hat-trick instead. 'Ruhi, why are you bringing this up now? And what do you expect us to do?'

Ma interrupted. 'Okay wait, I just want to tell one thing. Ruhi.' She looked at me, about to try another angle. 'I am not saying that what happened is right. It is one hundred per cent wrong and we all agree. But this is not a special case. This happens all the time in India. Actually, it happens everywhere but the men are especially like that in India. That doesn't make it alright, but it is very, very common back home. Even with small things – small things like catching the bus. The men on the bus will try to touch you. I went through it. Helen and Sybil had to face it. That's why women carry safety pins on public transport. To chuch dirty men with. That's just how things are in India. Saul was a big idiot for doing what he did. But he was young and stupid. He shouldn't have done what he did but I'm telling you, it's common.'

'Why are you telling her that now, Ma? What point are you trying to make, exactly?' Maya asked.

I butted in before Ma could answer. 'Ma. He was twenty-six when he did it. That's pretty much my age *now.* If Maya had kids, how do you think it would go down if I did to them what he did to me? And why are you so intent on trivialising what happened? Someone copping a feel on a bus is horrible, but it's not the same as an uncle grooming his niece during the day and taking advantage of her at night when one is looking. More than once!'

I couldn't believe that I had to explain this concept to two intelligent adults – my own parents! People who were meant to have my back.

This bullshit conversation was beginning to fatigue me. And everytime Maya or I called them out for saying something inappropriate or insensitive they fell back on their classic tool for deflection: 'Look, we all know my English isn't as good as yours. You are taking the wrong meaning from my words and holding me to them like a lawyer.' Of course, their English was excellent and when we gave them an opportunity to clarify what they meant, in Kannada if they wanted, they preferred to change topic.

Jake stepped in.

'Either way, he's not coming to see our baby,' he said.

Silence.

'Does anyone want a drink?' Ma finally offered. All of us refused except for Pa. When she returned with two glasses, one for herself and one for Pa, she addressed Jake in the gentlest way she could.

'But Jake, it's not nice to stop him like that,' she said. 'Saul is our family, how can we say yes to everyone and exclude him?'

'Easily? He sexually abused your daughter.'

To Jake, Maya and me, there was nowhere left to go from that statement. To my parents, no bridge was far gone enough to burn when it came to extended family. Their stubborn kids just didn't want to see it.

'Okay, look, it's been a big night. Why don't we put an end to it for now, think about it, go to sleep and pick it up again in a couple of days?' Pa suggested.

How can you sleep? I wondered.

'Yep. That's fine,' I said. 'But in the meantime I want to make myself *extremely* clear. I *do not* want Saul to know about our discussion under any circumstances. I would like us to talk through it further, try to get on the same page, then figure out what to do next.' I looked directly at Ma. 'That means that in your conversations with him, you *do not* bring this up, Ma. *Please.*'

'Ya, I won't. Sheh! Why would I?!' she asked.

'Because it's precisely what you've done in the past. I ask you not to mention personal details of my life to friends or extended family and you do it anyway, even when you've promised not to.'

'Okay, maybe I have done before. But I won't again and I haven't done for a long time.'

'Ma! Just last month...'

She cut me off. 'I know how serious this is! Please don't worry! I am not going to say anything to him.'

Later that night, I lay in bed with Jake, each of us with a hand on my belly feeling the kicks, flutters and bum rolls of our active little pumpkin. Something had changed inside me as I began to embrace motherhood, and not just the size of the ever-growing resident fetus, of course. But she wasn't just a fetus; she was already my baby girl whom I silently vowed to cherish and protect. Becoming her mother made me realise that the wife of Saul was also a mother to some precious young children only barely out of toddlerhood.

It recently occurred to me that if Jake had sexually abused a minor before we'd met, I would have wanted to know about it, especially for the safety of our children. That is why I resolved that Saul's wife needed to know. Their marriage was none of my business, therefore I wasn't going to hold myself responsible for whatever transpired as a result of her knowing. But I felt a strong sense of responsibility to their children – they were the vulnerable ones.

I'd accepted I couldn't take my story to the police; it happened overseas and so long ago. Ivana advised that if I wanted to raise it with the Department of Human Services so someone would check on the kids, I could. But I knew Saul's wife was a reasonable woman and, judging by the way she and her husband griped about each other to my parents, even threatening to break up at times, I figured she already thought critically enough of him to assess whether or not her children were a target. I decided I would be the one to tell her if Ma refused to, like the time she couldn't say no to Saul when he came to visit my father in hospital.

My phone lit up on the bookshelf next to our bed. It was a text message from Maya: *Ma just got off the phone with Saul. She told him everything and warned him that his wife might find out.*

I wasn't surprised but I still wanted to punch a fucking hole through our brick wall. Of course she was going to tell him everything. He was her favourite sibling. Her baby brother.

INTERMISSION

We have a saying in India: 'Atithi devo bhava' in Sanskrit, meaning *The guest is god;* 'Mehman bhagwan hota hai' in Hindi; and 'Eh! Hogabyadri! Namma kooda oota madri!' in Dharwad Kannada (a less formal version than Bengaluru Kannada), which roughly translates to *Eh! Don't go yet! Stay and eat with us!*

One of the most beautiful qualities that is widespread across Indian cultures is the universal duty of hospitality toward house guests. It's why Ajja let beggars sit on our porch in Dharwad and served them chapati and palle. It's why, when we migrated to Australia, Pa's old friend Soundaraj and his wife, Pallavi, invited us to live with them until we found our feet. It's why my parents kindly offered free lodging, home-cooked meals and shopping and sight-seeing trips to the countless other relatives and friends who arrived in Melbourne, either to tour or to stay.

Ma and Pa took care of others without expecting anything in return.

When we lived in a three-bedroom house, the third room was reserved for guests. When we lived in a four-bedroom house, the fourth room was for guests, and when the summer holidays came, the whole house became a playground for our cousins. When Helen Aunty and Manoj Uncle came to Melbourne, they stayed with us in our house for over a year until they bought their own property. Same with Raksha Aunty and Venkatesh Uncle, and many other couples. One time, Ma invited a former student of hers to live with us for a fortnight. She was proud of him for having become an accomplished obstetrician. Over lunch one day, after she and Pa ran all of their health concerns by him, Ma mentioned that her doctor had discovered fibroids in her uterus that needed to be removed.

'Aunty, I can do a hysterectomy for you, next time you come to India,' he said.

'You can take out my uterus for me?'

'Ya, of course! Why not, Aunty? It's much cheaper back home.'

'Ya! Okay! Thank you!' And that was that.

Maya and I were used to random guests dropping by to stay with us. It was part of life, and so it was no different when newlywed Saul and his wife came to live with us. By then, I was a busy uni student and he was besotted with his wife, so there weren't any weird vibes coming my way apart from awkwardness, which I was glad for. Still, it was beyond belief that he was allowed to stay in the same house as me after everything that had happened. I raised it with Ma before they came to stay, but she wouldn't have a bar of it. We were obliged to take care of family and friends who came from overseas. Plus, Saul had his new wife by then and had turned over a new leaf apparently, so there was nothing to worry about, I was told. Ma had declared the incident resolved and Pa still didn't know what had taken place.

Strangely, I hit it off with Saul's wife. She was young, fun and we got along well. I still hated him, but put on my friendliest face because Ma had warned me not to let Pa suspect anything. Saul, Ma and I pretended nothing had happened and we lived together in harmony for a year or so. One day Saul's wife confided in me about how desperate she was to have a child but, alas, her husband wanted to wait until they'd settled down with jobs. I remember thinking it was the first sensible thing to ever come out of him. So it was a shock to hear my own response next.

'Just grab a tiny needle and poke some holes in the condom,' I joked. Now that was fucked-up. I'd heard someone throw around that phrase on the radio or in a movie and decided to use it with her. Why? *Why?* She was both surprised and tickled, and I laughed along but deep down I knew I'd gone too far trying to foster the friendship, or something that resembled one. What a vile, deceptive thing to say; I was ashamed for a long time afterward and eventually had to forgive myself for allowing something so insipid to come out of my mouth *and* for forgetting who I was speaking to.

Ma ended up having a fight with Saul when he bought a brand-new car while he still owed my parents a lot of money. I couldn't understand how she continued to be surprised every time her shitty little brother found a new way to spite her or his other sisters. A few months went by before he and Ma made amends. In that time, Saul and his wife found a new place to stay – a property on the other side of the city that he bought off Tina Aunty. Somehow, Saul ended up pissing them off too. Ma and Pa didn't entertain guests from overseas again for a long time after Saul and his wife left.

So, atithi devo bhava? By all means, treat guests like gods – even if, sometimes, they leech money from you. Even if, sometimes, they are pedophiles. At some point, you'll get a free hysterectomy out of it.

15

God vs. family counselling

Jake and I decided to go to church on a Sunday several weeks and several unresolved family discussions after the night we told Pa about Saul.

A guest speaker took the pulpit that day. He told a story about a holiday house that he and his wife had been building for over twenty years. Every time they went back to the house, they worked on it some more. One day, a tradie accidentally started a fire and the whole thing burned up within two hours. The couple was devastated and ended up seeing a therapist together to process the grief.

In one of their sessions, the speaker's wife said something along the lines of, 'It was the only place where I felt truly safe in the world,' which was an interesting statement to their psychologist. When probed further, she revealed that she'd been molested in the home of a relative when she was a child. She hadn't told a soul before – not even her husband. When he heard his wife tell that story for the first time, he looked at her and said something like, 'I am so sorry this happened to you. But if it took the fire to unearth the pain of your past, I would have set the place on fire myself years ago.'

His words struck deep into my core. I wept. I wept through the rest of the service and the forty-five minute drive home.

'He said he would burn the thing down all over again, just for her to find healing, babe!' I howled in the car. At home, Jake brought me lunch and a cup of tea. He rubbed my back, asking if there was anything he could do to help.

'My parents are burning nothing for me! I'm not even mad at Saul. I technically forgave him ages ago during a prayer night at our old church. I don't think about him and I don't care to have anything to do with him, frankly. I'm upset at Ma and Pa! Why are they so apathetic? Ma wants to look out for her little brother; I know that. But Pa? Even Pa is acting like this is hardly an issue. And how can they be worried about hurting *Saul's* feelings when everyone else gets to see the baby and he doesn't. Like, what the actual fuck?'

'Yep. If it was someone else and not Ma's brother, they'd be treating the situation very differently,' Jake said.

'Yeah! One hundred per cent! And you know what makes me feel worse? The fact that Ajji, Ajja and my parents spent so much time and money in a court case in Dharwad to fight my grandparents' neighbours over the boundaries of their property. A piece of land is *that* important to them. Yet no one went to the authorities or called on the justice system for me!'

Jake sighed. He was hurting for me. For the rest of that day, my face was sore, my head ached and my eyes were bloodshot and swollen. By evening I felt like I was losing my mind.

'Come with me,' Jake said. 'You need some fresh air.'

'No, I don't feel like going anywhere.' I was glued to the daybed under my Gryffindor blanket.

'I know. And when we get home, you can stay here all night. Take a few minutes, put on a jacket and come with. Trust me.'

He walked with me down to the beach. On the shore, the water was still and as clear as glass. Looking across to the horizon, the silvery expanse before me was liquid steel, reflecting the grey sky like a long, wide mirror with one gilded edge that caught the vivid orange sunset in the west. I took my shoes off and walked toward the cold water. My feet sunk into the wet sand. As the slow tide washed over my ankles, I felt pulled back down into my humanity again. I breathed deeply and began to feel drunk and heavy with a sense of calm.

Jake's hand curled around mine. 'Still feel like banging your head against the wall?'

'No,' I laughed. 'Thank you. I needed this.'

'I know. You're welcome.'

***

We managed a total of four family discussions about what to do regarding

Saul. At least, that's what my parents focused on. For me, it became less about Saul not visiting the baby – Jake and I had resolved not to open the door if he showed up – and more about my parents' allegiance to him.

After much persuasion from Maya and me, my parents agreed to a family therapy session with Ivana. Although Pa drove us there in his car, it felt more like I was dragging my parents along the gritty asphalt of Nepean Highway by their hair, as though I was torturing them. When we got there, Ivana welcomed us and addressed my parents as Sir and Ma'am. I hoped they would notice how courteous she was and warm to her quickly. Instead, Pa was impassive and Ma let Ivana know early on that she doubted her professional ability to help the situation in any way.

'I don't believe in counselling and all this. I believe in God,' Ma said. *Thanks for that, Ma. I don't think they have to be mutually exclusive.* I knew she was hurting. The man who abused me was the same boy she played with as a child. He even looked like her, but with a rounder nose, a squarer head and less sculpted, meatier hands. They were similar in other ways too; both of them could confuse the crap out of you, thanks to the way their conviviality, cunning and ability to schmooze marbled together under a layer of chocolate icing.

Before Ajja died, he lamented to Ma over the phone how his son – his youngest child, the pride and joy of the family – ignored his studies, disrespected his parents and generally gave them a hard time. After Ajja was gone, Ma took it upon herself to always guide and protect her little brother in their father's absence. He was the same little boy whom Ajji and Ajja had waited many years for; their precious son who finally arrived after all their daughters. Especially Ajji; so ardently had she longed for a son that when her third daughter, Sybil, was born, Ajji was so completely shattered about bringing another girl into the world that she refused to look at her baby for days. It was only upon the insistence of her nurse sister that on the third day she finally glanced at the unwanted child.

Eventually she got over it. But Saul! He was the miracle boy – the boy whom Ajji breastfed for four years because he was special, while her daughters, in comparison, only got a year or so at the breast. Together with my dad, Ma paid for a significant portion of her brother's wedding and helped him and his wife move to Melbourne where she could properly take them under her wing. It was a beautiful thing she did for him, if you ignored the messed-up parts of the story.

It must have been difficult for Ma to sit across the room from her headstrong daughter, torn between her loyalty as a mother and the desire to protect Saul from potential ruin. She thought I was punishing him with threats to tell his wife, even though Ma insisted he was a changed person.

'How do you know he's changed, Ma? What if you found out he did the same thing to his own daughter?' I asked.

'I know him. He is a good man now. He is heavily involved in his church, playing the piano and giving his time to God. And he is a family man now.'

'Well, according to you, he was a good person back then too. And I suppose the fact that he played the organ for years in his church in India meant that he couldn't have abused me simultaneously? Except that he did.'

'No, no. He was different then. Now he is changed. That much I know.' *Alrighty then.*

As much as Ma didn't like my accusations, she was especially bothered by the fact that Jake and I had forbidden Saul from seeing our baby – ever. According to her, it was rude of us to treat a family member like an outcast. Also, his poor wife had done nothing wrong, and yet we were making her miss out on seeing the baby she had excitedly waited for, apparently (we rarely saw them after they moved to the other side of Melbourne into Tina Aunty's old house).

Ivana began our session by thanking my parents for their time and willingness to participate.

'You don't have to thank us; we are her parents,' Pa interrupted. 'We will do whatever it takes to help her.'

'That's great to hear,' Ivana said. 'I'm sure Ruhi is encouraged to hear that from you as well.' I nodded with her.

I had centre stage first. I reiterated to my parents that, although it took me several years, I had processed the trauma, forgiven Saul and bore no ill will toward him or his family. My plan to tell his wife my story was not a quest for revenge. Rather, I wanted to do what I could to protect his own kids. I didn't have any desire to tell others in our extended family, as I didn't think it would achieve anything useful, especially given that all of my cousins, other than Saul's children, were adults by then. If he had changed, great. But none of us could be sure and, regardless of what Ma kept telling herself, there were children at risk. Furthermore, I didn't want to relive the trauma by seeing him again and I certainly didn't want his disgusting hands near my child. My parents doubted my claims about forgiving him but I expressed my view to them that it was possible to forgive someone for their actions – let go of the desire to get even – and still feel grossed out by the thought of them because of visceral memories you have of their transgressions against you. I told them that I believed it was possible to forgive and not forget, to forgive and still have boundaries against seeing them ever again, to forgive and wish them and their loved ones well in your heart, from a distance.

'But why now?' Ma asked. 'You were fine when they came to Melbourne and he lived with us. You were fine seeing him at family parties all this time. Now suddenly you don't want to see him?' I noticed for the first time her bland clothing and conspicuously make-up free face. For Ma, this was the look of mourning.

'Did I have a choice, Ma? You forbade me from telling *anybody.* Then you invited him to stay with us while he settled in Australia, without stopping to think about how I would feel sharing my home with them!'

After some back and forth, Pa stepped into the ring with his blinders on, and a focus on *being positive* and *moving forward.* He looked at Ivana and asked what he could do to facilitate that process. Ivana suggested that the best thing they could do to help me was to be there, actively listen and empathise with me.

'Okay, how long do we have to listen for?' he asked.

'For as long as she needs.'

'So, we have to talk about this forever?' Pa said, now fretful.

'For however long she needs.'

Pa's head jerked backward and he dropped eye contact with Ivana, turning to look at me. 'But I don't understand what that will achieve. It makes her upset. It makes us all upset to talk about it, so why talk more? It happened so long ago, in the past – why do we have to ruin our present day by constantly talking about it?'

'Ya, we just want this to be over,' Ma said.

A jug of water sat to the side of the room, still mostly full. Eventually, Pa offered me some.

'No thanks, Pa.' In that moment, I preferred to stay dehydrated. I didn't want a light at the end of the tunnel or a silver lining or *any* kind of relief.

The situation was so full of shit and I wanted it to stink hard enough so my parents would finally inhale its miasma and call it what it was. All I wanted was for them to acknowledge my pain with a few moments of silence and genuine solidarity. Only when my parents had erected a plaque that said, *Here lies some fucked up shit that our daughter went through. We hereby give our word that no Sauls will hurt her or this family again on our watch* – then and only then would I be content to move on.

I wanted the ugly truth exhumed and out in the open, to be touched only by the air, rain and dung beetles; to rot away before our eyes. But my parents wanted to keep it buried. I'd known this was how Ma felt for years: the few times I'd tried to dig it up, she had shushed me. But I still couldn't believe that Pa was standing beside her, shovel in hand, ready to cover the hole with dirt again. It's not that I wanted him to be angry at Ma – I just believed that he would understand and support my decision to distance myself from Saul. But he didn't. He couldn't. It went against his deeply held family values. I could see in his eyes how fatigued he was by the session. The level of discomfort was too much for him.

'The other thing that hurts is the fact that you are constantly prioritising him over me—' I said, before Ma interrupted.

'No we are not! You are our daughter! Our number-one priority. How can you say something like that?!'

'And you refuse to hear me out properly!' I said. 'Your actions don't match up with your words. And we keep talking in circles; you two are forever trying to make me change my mind about *him,* rather than respecting what *I've* said. And by the way, I *can't believe* you still want him in your life, *knowing* what he did. Pa had the excuse of ignorance all these years but now that you know too–' I pointed at Pa, 'I don't understand how the two of you can *still* insist on inviting him to your parties and going to his place all the time. This man, who sexually abused me. How can you even be around him? And Pa, I believe in forgiveness like you do, but forgiveness doesn't always lead to reconciliation. *No one is required to keep hanging around their abuser.*'

That, right here, was my *aha* moment (*Oprah! I made it!*). The truth of my own words smashed me in the face: there I was, sitting in the company of two people who had abused me physically, psychologically and verbally, all in the name of parenting. Lord, the excuses I made for them over the years! Ivana had even taken to pointing out the disclaimers I'd insert before every parent-related story I told, my go-to being 'They're good people, but...'

A few months before the family counselling session, I had caught Pa shaking his head in pity as he watched an interview on TV. The interviewee was talking about how they were abused by their parents as a child.

'Very bad, very bad,' he said. 'It's just a child.' I was surprised by his reaction.

'Pa, I'm glad that you can look at this now and feel that those parents went too far. But you do realise that you pretty much did the same stuff to me when I was little?'

'Eh. No. I smacked you every once in a while but it was nothing like what they are showing here,' he said.

'So, do you remember that time when you said I was overweight and you forced me to run laps of the court in front of our house while you counted? I hated it so much and didn't want to do it. And you'd heard from one of the uncles a few months before that he'd successfully "disciplined" his daughter by making her take off her clothes before he hit her with a belt. So when I refused to go running, you made me take off my clothes and threatened to throw me out onto the street naked. You said that you'd only let me put them back on when I agreed to go running. So I did and I cried the whole time.'

'What?! That never happened, Ruhi. Sheh! How do you come up with these things? I don't remember anything like that. No, no, no.'

Just like that, history was rewritten. He and Ma invalidated my lived experience often. There were several times when Maya and I questioned our own sanity. It was what we experienced through our senses versus the words of our authoritarian parents.

In this case, it could be that Pa genuinely forgot about it. It may even be that he suppressed it. Either way, how was I supposed to carry on in a relationship with a crumbling foundation, when my parents weren't willing to even recognise it, much less repair it?

***

While Ma and Pa were content with a 'working system' where we saw each other once a week and conversed about surface-level details, such as electricity prices and weekend plans, I was unwilling to continue a relationship that only felt as deep as a puddle.

Just weeks away from going into labour, I needed to focus. I was done expending emotional energy on people who disregarded my feelings. After twenty-seven years of unsuccessfully trying to secure my parents' approval in any permanent way, I was done. So I told Ma and Pa that I would not be seeing them or answering their calls until after the birth.

My decision injected fresh tension into our already-struggling family dynamic. Pa said he understood my need for space – sort of. The way he put it was, 'Your generation is very different to ours' – translation: your generation is a bunch of spoiled kids without a moral compass – 'but if that's what you want, what can I do? Have some space, do what you need, we just want you to be happy.'

Ma texted me a few times, asking if she could come by and drop off a meal. I thanked her for the kind offer but declined each time. She showed up to our house twice asking to see me. Jake went outside to meet her at the front gate, thanked her for coming and explained that I was resting inside and wasn't keen for visitors. The second time it happened, he came back inside to find me crying on the bed.

Later, Maya told me that Ma drove home in tears. Pa left a message to say that it was fine if I wanted to cut him out but not do it to my poor mother who was desperate to see me.

16

Following in the footsteps of Blinky Bill

'Pa, what's your favourite colour?'
'I like all the colours, Ruhi.'
'No! If you had to choose one, what would it be?'
'Maybe, red.'
'Okay and what's your favourite TV show?'
'You know I don't watch much TV. But I like comedies.'
'What's your favourite food?'
'Oh. I like every food there is. All food is good. We should always be grateful for the food we have. We can't be picky with it.'
'What's your favourite animal?'
'All animals are nice. God made them all. How can I choose a favourite?'
'But if you had to choose one?'
'What kind of questions are these?'

'Just answer the question, Pa! *Please*.'

'Yawa. Okay, maybe a bird.'

'Why?'

'*Are!* You made me choose something so I chose a bird.'

I glared at him.

'Okay, they can fly. That's why.'

Content with his answer and knowing he was out of reasons, I walked away and packed my usual hobo knapsack, using a potato masher from our kitchen as the stick and one of Pa's handkerchiefs for the sack. Blinky Bill walked around with a hobo knapsack. Blinky Bill also carried a sandwich in his sack, so I packed a sandwich in mine. The other items that went into my knapsack changed every time, depending on what I could find around the house. I had to think hard about what to take, because I could only carry so much. This time I packed a small mahogany buddha statue brought into our house by an uncle from Thailand; a tiny silver key to my piggy bank; and an apple.

With my knapsack on my shoulder, I followed Ma along the corridor of the

Stone Fruit House. The sound of our bare feet peeling off the plastic carpet protectors was the backdrop to our conversation: Ma's narrow, elegant feet adorned with anklets, toe rings and burgundy nailpolish, followed by my small pudgy feet, smooth little replicas of Pa's.

'Did you know I would look like Pa?'

'No! No one knew! When you came out, everyone said you were his carbon copy. If not for his *meeshee*, there would be *no difference. Yella* nindh appa nang eithi. *Enu* thagiangila! *Everything* of yours is like your father's. *Nothing* is removed! Your fingers. Your toes. Your mund moog!' She pinched my 'blunt nose' affectionately. 'Nice, thick, black, wavy hair. *Everything! Ayo!* Big, big eyes! Round, round face! *Round* eyebrows! His whole family has the same eyebrows! The whole village!'

'So I looked like my cousins on Pa's side?'

'No. You were cuter. So chubby. SO fat and cute. After you were born, none of us ever left you on the floor. Everyone wanted to carry and hold you all the time! *That's* how cute you were.'

'Did you know I was going to be a girl?'

'No no, we only found out after you were born. I wanted a boy but, ayo, your pa was so happy when the nurse gave you to him! He wanted a girl so badly! In those days, they didn't give the baby to the mother straight away. They always gave it to the father. So they took you away, cleaned you and put you straight in your Pa's hands. He was over the moon!

'I was so tired. After some time I asked the nurse if I ended up having girl or boy, still hoping it was a boy. She said, 'Girl.' I felt little disappointed. Everyone in India was asking, 'When will your son be born? When will you give us pedas?' Because when a boy is born, the family gives everyone peda and when a girl is born, the family distributes jalebi. Everyone wanted me to have a boy. And even when I thought about it, I thought it would be nice to have a boy. But the minute I saw you ... finished! No more desire of boy. But your pa, he always knew you would be a girl. He used to say to me,

"I hope we have a girl and I hope she looks like you."'

'Did it hurt to have a baby?'

'Ayo! You gave me so much pain! Some children give lots of trouble to the parents.' She chuckled. 'I was sitting in our house, in Ajja Ajji's house, watching my favourite TV show that time. It was called *Nupur* with Hema Malini. I *still* remember! I was wearing a maroon nighty with small white flowers. That time I had bought lots of nighties with buttons in the front so I could feed you easily after you were born. My hair used to be so thick and long in those days. I used to tie in a *looong* plait. Just before, your Pa had taken me for a walk that evening. He took me for compulsory walks every day because people told us it was good for the mum just before giving birth. Then after that, I came home and sat down to watch TV, *then suddenly* I felt tummy pains.

'My aunty was a nurse and she lived nearby so she came and checked and told me the baby was coming! That time we didn't have a car. Only Ajja's Luna scooter. And they would say it was not good for pregnant ladies to sit in auto rickshaw. Ajja had a friend – his name was Mohammad – and he owned a car, so he drove me, your Pa, Ajja and Ajji to the hospital in the middle of the night.

'The doctor said that by early morning, the pains would increase. But it took so long. I tried to sleep in the hospital bed but ayo, I couldn't sleep, it was so painful. In the morning, the doctor checked and said it would still take longer, so he left me and went home. I got so angry! I said, "*Are!* How the hell can he just leave and go?!" So I started walking out of the hospital toward his house!' Ma laughed. 'Your Pa came running after me and took me back to the room.'

'And then?'

'Then ... they told me baby was taking too long to come out. Your head was too big! You sat there with all that intelligence in your head and got stuck! So they said they might have to do caesarean. Then they induced me.'

'What's that?'

'Gave injection to make baby come out faster. Then big big contractions came, but still they prepared me for operation. They decided to try one last thing with the vacuum suction. I saw the anaesthetist come into the room. He started taking his shoes off to prepare and *suddenly* you came out. You must have felt the vacuum cleaner, got scared and came out quickly!'

I enjoyed watching Ma roar with laughter when she told these stories. Sometimes she'd stop to say that she liked seeing me laugh like that too. She continued: 'Because of that vacuum, you came out with a conehead. You should thank your Ajji. She sat every day for forty days and rubbed your head with coconut oil. That is how it became so nice and round.'

'What was Pa doing when I was born?'

'Pa was walking up and down, up and down the ward. He was so stressed. Ajja and Ajji were with him. But when you came, they were the happiest people on Earth. Ajja bought jalebis and distributed to everyone! In the hospital, at the church, all their friends, everyone! I wanted your Pa to give you something special so he went out and bought a gold chain for you on the same day you were born. After ten days in the hospital, Ajji held a special prayer and welcomed you into the house. Then two days later, we had your christening and I wore my wedding saree. Usually they wait forty days but we couldn't wait because your Pa had to return to Jeddah.'

'Why did Pa have to leave again?'

'Because he had a nice job with good money that helped our family. Ajji and Ajja didn't have much money for hospital fees and all. But then he had to leave again soon after your birth. He didn't want to leave us. We sat and cried together when he had to go back to Jeddah for work.'

'Why couldn't we go with him?'

'Legally, we couldn't join him until he was in Saudi Arabia for two years. It was *so* hard to stay without him. The only reason I could do it was because I had my mommy and poppa. We couldn't even go with your Pa to the airport. Paapa. *Poor thing.* Unwillingly, he went alone from Dharwad; had to go in the bus by himself without wife or baby daughter. Had to go in the plane by himself to another country. Imagine what he must have felt. He held you all the time before he left. Then he gave you poppie on your face and left.'

Pa walked in from another room and joined the conversation.

'Ya, I didn't want to go. I felt very bad. But I had to.'

Ma interrupted. 'Then he had an accident while playing cricket. He fell, broke both of his legs then came back in wheelchair! Ha!'

Pa continued. 'When I came back I enjoyed playing with you. You were my timepass. Sitting on my tummy and jumping all the time. When I had to go back to work again, my flight was delayed so they put us up in a hotel overnight. I had spoken to my friend, Soundaraj, who was applying to come to Australia and I thought, *Why not?* There was a writing pad and a pen in the hotel. I took it and wrote a letter to the Australian High Commission saying I was thinking about taking my family to Australia and that I would like to know what the formalities are. I *still* remember the address by heart: 1/50

G Panchsheel Marg, Shantipath, Chanakyapuri, New Delhi, and the postcode was 110021. I don't even think I had a stamp! I just posted it. And the rest is history. It was all God's plan.'

Ma picked up the story again. 'When we were leaving India, you *would not* come with us. We had to snatch you away from Ajji Ajja. Ayo! It was so horrible. You were so attached to them.'

'But wasn't I just a baby? How did I know we were leaving them forever?'

'You didn't know we were going overseas, but you knew we were going somewhere without Ajji Ajja. When we finally dragged you away and put you down to walk next to us, you *ran* back to Ajji Ajja. They loved you so much. Ayo, I can't tell you how much they cried that day. I had never seen them cry like that.'

I started tearing up, even though I didn't remember it happening.

Ma continued. 'Your first word was "Ajja", remember? You were *everything* for them. You were their first grandchild. They were so proud of you. They played with you all day, every day. You were closer to your ajja and ajji than you were to Pa and me. We somehow managed to pull you away, even though you wouldn't stop howling for them. Later, your ajji told me that your ajja sat and cried like a small child. No one could console him. He was so heartbroken.'

My eyes welled up even more, picturing this man whose affections for me were bottomless but whom I barely had any recollection of. It was so strange to think that he lived in a place and time that briefly intersected with my own existence. His blood ran through me and his heart had been given over to me so entirely; I wanted to do something, to offer something in return for the tears he shed for me, but I knew not how.

Ma finished the story. 'Then after we came to Melbourne, you were stuck to me. Wherever I went, I took you. Anywhere I went, you were with me.'

***

Many years later, as I neared the end of my pregnancy, I thought back on this conversation and imagined an open handkerchief before me. On it, were my parents' and grandparents' generous spirits, their bravery, their kindness, their sacrifices and a sandwich stuffed full with the sound of their laughter. There was a lot that I left out, on purpose. I had to think hard about what to take, because I could only carry so much. I closed my eyes, tied up my imaginary knapsack and flung it over my shoulder as I entered into life as a parent.

17
Birth and death

Delicate blossoms along our street signalled the arrival of spring. My heart felt calm. There was still a chasm between my parents and me, but I'd decided not to let my thoughts wander to that area of my brain until after the birth, when I'd have the emotional capacity for it.

All of my nesting had culminated in a single trigger-happy day with the labelling machine. The baby's room was nearly ready: I'd positioned the grey Soft Mat that my parents had purchased in the centre; the timber cot and change table were against a wall; and the cupboard was stocked with supplies. I placed my old globe on the chest of drawers opposite the cot. Curling around the base of the pastel green and blue globe was a miniature wooden train; a gift Maya had brought back from her trip to Switzerland earlier that year. I'd made a floral dreamcatcher, which hung from the ceiling over the change table.

And in the corner was a rocking chair and matching rocking footstool.

Our daughter was going to have the room with the best view: a window to the sky and massive trees overhead. From there, I could see dozens of birds flitting from tree to ivy-covered fence to tree. Bethany, the kind woman from church who had listened to my story, now my good friend, had given us a homemade gift that we'd hung on the wall by the window. It was a piece of wood with soft purple, pink and white flowers and foliage arranged in the first initial of our baby's name, which only she and a handful of other people knew.

Over dinner a few weeks earlier, Bethany had suggested that maybe I was going through grief, mourning the people I wished my parents would be. Just as they wanted me to be a certain kind of daughter, I had my own expectations that they weren't living up to. On all sides, there was disappointment and refusal to accept things for what they were. Beth suggested that it was perhaps time for me to let go of the image I was clinging to of parents who understood me better; only then could I accept the people my parents were, then and there, and decide on what kind of relationship, if any, I wanted with them. Ivana had said the same thing. I wasn't capable of changing other people, just as my parents couldn't change me. The more energy I put into forcing my perspectives on them, the less I'd have left for my daughter and husband who were both my first priority.

Looking back on my childhood, I could see that as much I had experienced a life of privilege, I had spent a great deal of it grieving – only I'd kept skipping over the anger stage of grief. That anger had finally caught up with me in pregnancy. And for the first time, I was learning how to let it burn outside of me, rather than holding it all in while my insides turned to ash. I made peace with the three lines in the ultrasound that told the obstetrician our baby was a girl. With my heart and bladder both full, I greeted my first contractions in September.

***

'She's here! She's beautiful!' Voices rang around me.

Then, there she was, hovering above my face in the hands of the paediatrician, who wrapped her up like cocktail-samosa filling in its triangular pastry. My daughter was unlike anything I had imagined and far more adorable than her cute little extraterrestrial three-dimensional ultrasound photo had let on. Her skin was creamy and her closed eyes were perfect crescents with long lashes running along them. Her cheeks were pink and her hair, dark brown. Surely, she had descended to Earth from the place where snowflakes and sunbeams and cherubs were made.

After the birth, Jake said he was going to take her to the nursery while they sewed me up. I nodded feebly, but with complete faith that he knew the drill. Later, I bawled my eyes out when I learned that Jake had taken off his shirt to hold her close and give her 'skin on skin contact', as we'd learned about in our prenatal class, while they waited for me to emerge from surgery.

In the stark white operating room, I could see only the ceiling lights. I'd never felt so desperate to sit up before, except for in those nightmares where I was completely paralysed, screaming inside. I was lying on my back for about an hour in that room, almost catatonic with both arms splayed out to the sides; the screen between my lower body and the rest of me meant there was no room to keep my arms beside me. The hospital staff kept reassuring me that we were almost done.

As I waited, my leaden body lost all warmth. What started as a slight shiver turned into a strong, uncontrollable shudder. *I knew I'd find myself here. Now Jake is going to have to enact my funeral wishes. It'll suck if I die right here but, man, I am one organised woman,* I thought.

'I'm c-c-cold!' I yelped.

The anaesthetist explained that feeling cold was a normal side effect of the epidural. One of the assistants, seriously an angel sent from heaven, covered my upper body in a thick waffle blanket. It didn't stop my trembling but it made me feel so much better. Eventually the shakes died down and, after what felt like an eternity, I was good to go.

Yay! I've made it out alive ... Not so fast. They wheeled me into the recovery room where I had to wait under observation for another forty-five minutes. The anxiety of not being able to sit up was building. I remembered learning in prenatal classes that it's ideal for a baby to be fed within the first hour of their arrival. I was itching to see my baby. Also, when fifty minutes had gone by and I hadn't been collected, I started to lose my mind a little. The lack of control over how and where I used my body was doing my head in. When one of the nurses asked if there was anything she could do for me, I requested to sit up but was told that it was advisable to stay horizontal – something to do with blood pressure. I also inquired about when I'd be taken back to my infant, and without making any phone calls, she kept reassuring me that someone would grab me soon. I was about to have a nervous breakdown.

Then I heard a familiar voice and then saw a kind face above me, smiling down: my Angel Nurse – he was back! He asked me how I was doing. I told him I was fine, aside from my aching desire to sit up.

He giggled and said, 'No problem, let's get you sitting up!'

After some delicate manoeuvring, I was back in the land of the vertical.

'Your daughter is doing well,' Angel Nurse said. 'She's so cute. I just went to see her and your husband before coming down here. Hey, would you like an icy-pole?'

'Yes, please! I would love one!' I just about wept with gratitude. 'You know what? You are the best – seriously the best.'

He chuckled and we had a great chat that took my mind off my prior frustration. I discovered that Angel Nurse was from the Philippines and had two daughters and a wife. They'd been in Melbourne for a while and loved it but missed their family back home. I knew what that was like – except my parents were still in the same city. Angel Nurse then excused himself to attend to another patient.

I appreciated the recovery room a lot more once my torso was vertical. I was the only patient there, surrounded by several empty white beds. As I looked out the window, I finally felt like I was coming back to Earth. It was a grey day, Jake's favourite kind – a good one for his daughter to arrive on. I imagined him holding her in the antenatal ward, enjoying the scenery outside, where the clouds hung low over rooftops.

I looked around the room and noticed a clock. *Wait, what? Two hours?! It's been two hours since I've seen my baby!* Another nurse came in to check something at the desk and I gave her my best puppy-dog eyes. When she proceeded to the door, clearly not there to collect me, I had to stop myself from throwing my icy-pole stick at her and yelling, 'TAKE ME WITH YOU, BITCH!'

Eventually, someone finally wheeled me up to our room and I got to see my tired Jake and my new best mate, whom I'd spend every waking and sleeping hour with over the next few

weeks – and possibly well into her adulthood, or as long as she'd let me.
***

Six weeks went by and we found our rhythm. Breastfeeding no longer felt like I was trying to shove a soccer ball into the mouth of a turning clown head at a fair. Jake was better rested than he had been a few weeks earlier, but his hair had grown out while we were holed up in our baby bubble. He looked like a tall, sexier version of Lord Farquaad.

Mentally, I was in a healthy place. We started inviting over members of our extended family to visit. When our daughter was born, Jake had sent out a text to announce her arrival and let people know that we would notify them when we were ready for visits. Nobody kicked up a fuss about it except for my parents, whom we invited to the hospital for a visit on day three anyway.

They were delighted to meet their granddaughter but the rest of the visit was transactional and awkward. They were bummed that Zam had seen the baby before they did, and that we only called them the day after the birth, rather than inviting Ma into the labour room to cheerlead me through it. I didn't see much of my parents for a while after that. I knew they hated it, but I just didn't have the time or willpower to deal with our baggage *and* care for my newborn.

Months passed. When I felt up to it, I called Ma and Pa to say that I was willing to keep the communication lines open provided we kept seeing a family counsellor. I wasn't going to spend any more emotional energy on running around in circles, so I let them know I needed an impartial mediator in the room for those more heated conversations. Ma agreed, but said she didn't want to go to Ivana again – when she'd asked about Ivana's religious views in the last session, she wasn't satisfied with Ivana's answer about having a spirituality other than Christianity. So, I agreed to see Arlene with them, a Christian counsellor from my parents' church. I looked forward to seeing her as I knew her from my time at the Echo Chamber church and

I was very fond of her and her husband.

Our first session came around quickly. Jake looked after our daughter at home while I met with my parents in the counselling room of Arlene's house. We'd started with a prayer then spent the first half of the session catching Arlene up on everything that had happened thus far. Then we just sat, blankly looking at the coffee table, the walls and, reluctantly, at one another. Ma sat cross-legged on the couch opposite me. Pa stood up in the corner next to Ma; he wasn't able to sit for long due to his back problems. Maya had dialled into the session as it was too far for her to drive on a weeknight.

I could feel a headache coming on. Tears were gradually drying on my hot cheeks. I'd expressed again that I was sick of being told to 'move on' from my trauma, and I'd told my parents how it had hurt me to witness what I saw as indifference on their part. The last time I'd spoken to Pa on the phone, he'd said, 'An idle mind is the devil's workshop,' – a jab at how I'd quit my job, which he theorised had given me an unnecessary amount of space and time, leading me to wallow in problems that I'd fabricated.

'Do you have anything to speak into that?' Arlene asked Pa.

'Uh ... not really. What do you want me to say?'

When Ma opened her mouth, offering to help him, Arlene held out her open palm and said, 'No, he can answer for himself.' Ma, who had already butted in a few times before, nodded.

'Well,' Arlene helped him along, 'your daughter just said that she's hurting for the reasons she explained. Do you have anything you want to say to her in response?'

Pa beat around the bush at first, then asked Arlene if what I was putting them through was 'normal'. Ma interjected yet again, trying to coax an apology out of Pa for the sake of keeping the peace – and gaining access to their granddaughter.

Pa brushed her off. Any apology at that point would have been insincere anyway. Instead, he defended himself and the role he had played in my childhood trauma. He said that my life had been easy compared to his. He agreed that *maybe* he was a little harsh, from time to time, but insisted that he only hit me to 'put me on the right path' and make me a 'better person' – and only when I did something wrong.

'I did something "wrong" about ten per cent of the time, Pa. The rest of it was more about your unrealistic and over-the-top standards,' I said.

The room went quiet again.

'Are there any healing words you would like to say to your daughter before we wrap up?' Arlene asked Pa. He looked lost, unable to cobble together a sentence. Arlene changed tact.

'Tell me what you love about your wife.'

'I don't know.' He shrugged.

'How about I go first and you can follow my example?!' Ma offered. She didn't wait for his reply. 'I love that you are a responsible man. I love that you are hardworking and that you care about your family. You play with the kids nicely and you are knowledgeable. Okay, your turn now.'

Pa glanced at her, then around the room and then at Arlene.

'I love that she is a beautiful woman, on the outside and inside,' he said. 'I love that she is also hardworking. She comes home after work and she cooks and cleans. She is lively and joyful. She makes everyone laugh and she is a generous woman.' My parents shared a brief smile.

'It's nice for Maya and me to see and hear you say those words to each other,' I said.

Arlene asked if I wanted to have a turn. I started with Pa. Like him, I looked at Arlene as I answered her question, rather than addressing him directly.

'I love that my dad is a helpful person,' I said. 'If anyone he knows calls at any time of the day or night needing his help, he'll be there for them. I love that he was brave to marry Ma and travel across the world with his young family. I love that my dad doesn't hoard good things for himself. If he ever comes across a helpful article, online talk or piece of advice, he'll share it with people around him. I have to agree that he's a hardworking person and I appreciate the sacrifices he has made along the way to provide for his family.'

I didn't look up to see Pa's reaction to my spiel.

'I love that Ma is so giving of herself,' I continued. 'I love that she's outspoken and friendly. She plays pranks on people and makes us laugh. She's courageous and willing to try new things. She hates cooking but she still cooked for her family every day for almost thirty years. She is also hardworking, like Pa. And I love that no matter what happens in a relationship, she's not too proud to make up after a fight.'

Ma smiled and wiped away a tear. Maya and I started but didn't bother finishing our lists as we didn't have any new material to share. 'We don't need to do this because we tell each other every week!' I laughed.

Everyone had a shot. When it was Pa's turn to tell me why he loved me, he said, 'She's a good girl. She's helpful and she's caring.' That was all he had to say about me: a generic three-adjective analysis. I had hungered for his approval like a famished elephant and he fed me like a bird.

***

A week after our first session with Arlene, Ma said she wanted to go for a walk with me. Midway through, she turned to me and reached for my hands.

'Ruhi,' she began. 'I am sorry for all I did and said to hurt you. I should never have asked you to keep what happened with Saul a secret from your father. And for all the times I put you in between your father and me – I shouldn't have done that.' She started crying. 'The last time I said sorry to you, I just wanted to move on from the situation but I thought about it and realised you needed to do it in your own time. Now I am saying sorry genuinely. Please accept my apology. Please forgive me and give me another chance.'

'Thank you for saying that, Ma, I appreciate it.' I wasn't sure what had brought about her change of heart but I welcomed it, either way. I wondered if maybe she was just saying what I wanted to hear so that I would let down my guard and allow her to see her granddaughter more often. But I wanted to give her the benefit of the doubt.

'And any time I do or say something that upsets you, you simply tell me, okay? Don't hold it in because you worry about how I will feel. If I don't know the problem, I cannot change.'

'Thank you, Ma. You can tell me when I say something to upset you too. But I have to say,' I asserted as gently as possible, bracing myself for a dismissive response, 'I've tried that before with you and you sort of don't like it.'

'No, no, no, everything is changing now, I promise, but once you tell me something, you need to give me time to change. I cannot change straight away because I'm getting old now and my habits have been there a long time.'

'Of course, Ma.'

'And don't worry – I won't call Saul anywhere near you.'

'I appreciate that, Ma. More than you know.'

'Also, Maya told me you are feeling sad and you're missing your cousins and aunties and uncles because we keep inviting Saul to family parties,' she said.

'Yeah I am, Ma ... I don't understand how you won't prioritise my invitation and leave Saul out.'

'Ya, I understand now.' She surprised me again. 'So, in future, I'll let you know about parties first and I just won't invite them.'

'Thanks, Ma.'

'Also, I told Saul that he had to tell his wife about everything ... But I'm confused because, for a while, he didn't want me to say anything to her and now he's telling me that she knew about it since before they got married. Something is not adding up,' she said. 'But if you still want to tell her, you can and I won't stand in your way.'

'Thank you, Ma. I will call her later,' I said. I was floored; my mother had come so far.

'Listen, before you go, you should know your Pa is very upset. I've never seen him cry like this before. He also complained of chest pain and arm pain. I am worried because I don't want him to have another heart attack.'

'No one does, Ma.' I lost some of the warmth in my voice. She had a tendency to use guilt as a way to push for her preferred outcome.

'Can you talk to him and try to make peace?'

'That's exactly what I'm trying to do in counselling. And this should remain between Pa and me. Please don't be the messenger between us.'

'Okay, okay,' Ma said in response to my terse request. 'So can I come over twice a week now?'

Good old, gung-ho Ma. Even though she had been unusually softly-spoken for most of our conversation, that over-the-top enthusiasm and inability to take things slow could never be entirely suppressed.

'Why don't we just start with once a week for now and ease our way in?' I smiled.

***

A few months on, visits from Ma were going swimmingly for the most part. She did use the 'things-take-time-to-change' line to excuse her behaviour at times, which frustrated me. I still noticed her doing things I'd asked her not to, like taking photos of the baby (I didn't want them to end up in Saul's phone because I knew she couldn't resist showing her granddaughter off).

But at least I could talk to her about those things and rely on her to come to the table. It became clear that she valued her relationship with Jake and me, and especially the bond she'd developed with our daughter. I realised that I needed to do some work on myself too, particularly when it came to managing my expectations of her. Our relationship was far from perfect, but I wanted to honour her willingness to try with my own.

Pa and I had been estranged for those few months, until late one Friday night. Maya and Jake were with me in our lounge and my daughter was sleeping when the phone rang. It was Pa. He'd tried calling Maya's phone but it was on silent. His tone was steady but urgent when he told me that he and Ma had been involved in an accident. I put the phone on speaker and Jake and Maya huddled around to hear what happened.

On the way home from visiting an aunty, a four-wheel drive had collected Ma and Pa as they crossed the road at a pedestrian light, knocking them both to the ground. Pa had staggered to his feet to find his wife lying still and unconscious. They sustained some superficial injuries but were mostly fine – though I could tell my usually cool, collected Pa (when he wasn't having an outburst) was shaken when he called from the hospital. Ma had come to by then and would make it through the ordeal with just some bruising. Maya left my place to pick them up from the hospital as soon as she heard. I stayed at home knowing my baby would soon be up for a feed.

I was concerned for them but also somewhat unperturbed during the call. As I reflected on it later that night, I asked Jake if I was a monster for not having been flustered by my parents' accident, for remaining unfazed by the news. I wanted them to be okay, and I was glad that they were. I had no idea how I might have reacted if they weren't. But I felt awful when I caught myself shooing away thoughts that sounded like, *Maybe life would be easier if they didn't make it.*

'That doesn't make you a monster, babe,' Jake said. 'I think it's just a natural response after all you've been through with them lately. It's clear how much you care about your parents and I'm sure if they weren't okay, you would probably be distraught. You were so worried when your dad had his heart attack, remember?'

I grunted, unconvinced and still concerned about how much evil lurked within me.

Ma and Pa recuperated from their injuries and a couple of months went by before our next counselling session with Arlene. By then, Pa was insisting that he could only make appointments on weeknights and weekends, which he knew was precisely when Arlene didn't work, except for in special cases. She made that exception for our first appointment, which I emphasised to my parents had been a once-off.

Of course, I knew Pa just wanted to get out of it. He barely touched his personal leave entitlements as a rule and didn't see family counselling as a reason to start using them. A few months earlier, I'd have cried about his apathy, but I didn't care anymore. I finally accepted that he could come if he wanted to, and if not, fine. No counselling meant no contact. Until I could see that we were all learning some skills in active listening and empathy, I wasn't going to put time in anymore outside of our sessions.

My hopes were dwindling when I arrived at Arlene's place on an October afternoon for what would end up being our final family counselling session.

Arlene began by asking what each of us hoped to achieve from the session. She motioned for Pa to answer first.

'I don't have any problems. I'm here because she asked me to come,' he said, glancing at me.

'I'm here to look at how we can better connect with one another and perhaps have a relationship again that works for all of us,' I said.

Then Ma spoke. 'I had a good conversation with Ruhi recently and have told both my daughters that if they ever want me to come to counselling in future, I will be happy to. It's important to work through our problems.' She was trying and failing to hide a proud grin.

The next two hours resembled a game of tennis – except that Pa and I were playing on entirely different courts, serving balls into the void and hoping for a rally. I knew Pa felt the same frustration that I did.

'I struggle to be in the presence of my dad and, now to a lesser extent, my mum.' I said. 'I can't have an authentic relationship with him because, if I'm honest with him about the details of my life, I feel assessed and judged on each decision, rather than having any sort of emotional connection with him.'

'Can you give us an example of that?' Arlene asked.

'I don't have a recent one with my dad as we haven't spoken for a while, but I can share a similar instance with my mum, just to demonstrate what I mean?' I offered. Arlene nodded.

'Okay so, the other day, I was excited to tell my mum that Maya and I had booked a holiday to Bali to celebrate my birthday. Instead of being happy for us, her initial response was, "Oh. Why would you go to Bali? Why don't you go somewhere nicer, like Greece? And how much are you paying for your trip? Woah – that's too much just for Bali!" It just brought the mood down and I kind of regretted sharing my good news. I expressed to her that I wished she had been pleased for me, even if she wouldn't have chosen to go herself. She thought about it, and then came back and apologised, saying, "I know we are different people. This will be a good holiday for you. I am happy for you and I know you will have a nice time with your sister." It meant a lot to me that she changed her approach like that, but I feel like my dad wouldn't get it. He's only happy for me if it's something *he* values, like when I got top marks at school or got promoted at work.'

'So you expect me to just be happy about everything you do and not say anything about it?' he accused.

'No. Not at all. You're entitled to your opinions. But if you want to have a relationship with someone, I think it means moving beyond your judgements. If your child makes a decision that you don't agree with, you can still let them know that you love and support them regardless. Also, you always *have to* give your unsolicited opinion on *everything* I do. I'd like it if you waited until I asked for it, in future. It'd be great if both you and Ma worked on that, actually.'

'Okay. So now I have to jump up and down with happiness even if you're doing something I don't think is right.'

'No, Pa! Why can't you just be happy that I'm happy, even if the information I'm sharing is not something that necessarily matters to you?'

He shook his head and paced up and down the room.

'Pa, I'm making an enormous effort to have a relationship with you and you're barely contributing. You make it so hard to book an appointment with

Arlene and you complain about the time and money spent on counselling, like it's a waste. It's nothing compared to other things you invest in. The other day, I invited you over to our place to celebrate your birthday with your kids and granddaughter and to share a cake that Jake had baked for you. It was nice that you came but you watched the clock the entire time until you finally left only two hours later. And for what? To go to *Saul's* house and spend the rest of your evening there, celebrating your birthday with them by talking them through their marital problems! How can your priorities be so out of whack? This, *here,* is what I wish you would invest in. Maybe you should be working on your own family's problems first.'

His nostrils flared and his eyes widened. 'This is *so wrong!* This is *so bad* that a daughter has to go through a counsellor to speak to her own father! You're right, I don't want to be here. This is *very wrong!* I'm sorry, Arlene, I can't do this anymore. Bye.' With that, Pa put his hands together as a final

Namaste in Arlene's direction and stormed out, Ma trailing behind.

I thanked and apologised to Arlene as I left too, then strode out to my car. Halfway there, Pa came marching toward me, furious in a way he hadn't allowed himself to be during our sessions.

'This is *killing me!*' he yelled. 'You know that? It *kills me* to come to counselling! I am *never coming* again!'

'Yeah, okay. I'm heading home. Bye.' I got in my car and shut the door. Standing on the curb, he discarded his stoic facade.

'Look at that!' He laughed and clapped his hands in derision as he walked toward my window. 'Same thing as always. She just walks away and closes the door when it gets hard!'

I wound down my window. 'No! *I am here! I am here* in counselling. *You're* the one walking away because it's too hard! *Okay?*'

'We almost *died* the other day when we got hit by a car! Imagine if we *actually* died! Would you have felt happy, knowing that this is how you treated your parents before they died?!'

'Yes, as a matter of fact.' I was surprised at my own composure. This was new. 'I'm proud of myself knowing that I've done everything in my power to try and resurrect our relationship. I'd have no guilt if you died. I've done my best.' *Uh-oh.* My chest started pounding after my short-lived moment of Zen. I became shaky again. 'And actually, *you're* the one walking away from *me*! And I'm not going to ask you back anymore. Goodbye.'

I drove home. It felt as though something or someone had just died in my arms.

I had been trying to open a door that wasn't going to budge, at least not in the time I'd hoped, because my dad was holding it shut on the other side. I wasn't one to lose hope easily, but that moment crystallised things for me: even if I wanted to hold on to the dream of a healthy, functioning – warts and all – family, the time had undoubtedly arrived for me to pry my hands off the door handle and walk away.

In that moment I remembered something I had heard Pa and his friends say when I was a child. I recalled him sitting with tipsy uncles at an after-party-pity-party in the backyard, woefully speculating about their futures.

'These kids yaar, they won't care about us when we get old. They'll be busy with their own lives. What will become of us?' an uncle asked.

At the time, I felt so sad upon hearing their collective outlook on the future; away from their families in India and abandoned by their children in another country. Back then, I silently vowed never to let my parents feel that way when they grew old.

By the time I pulled up into our driveway, I was numb and out of tears. *Maybe a lonely dotage will be Pa's own doing,* I thought. *Or maybe my presence in his life won't make a difference to whether or not he feels lonely.*

18

Birds

A few weeks later, still in a state of torpor, I was reluctant to leave the house. Thankfully, Zam's birthday was coming up and I'd planned a surprise for her that required me to ditch my pyjamas.

I picked her up from her flat in Melbourne's northern suburbs at seven o'clock in the morning. As she walked toward my car, I could see that she'd followed my instructions when she emerged in her shorts, backpack, tank top and hiking boots, with the sheen of sunscreen on her shoulders.

'Happy Birthday!' I gave her a massive hug.

For the next hour and a half, we caught up on each other's lives. I told her about the most recent counselling session with my parents and my dad's early departure. Having known my parents for half of her life, she was disappointed and felt for me. Zam was having similar problems with her parents, in that, we both felt that our parents barely knew who we were, partly because we had to hide it from them and mostly because they didn't seem to *want* to know.

'And what's the deal with our dads just wanting to let go once we're married?' I said. 'Unless I make the effort to call or text him, I won't hear from him for weeks on end.'

'Yeah, what the hell. My dad said something about that the other day. Apparently, once I get married, I am no longer his responsibility so I won't be seeing him as much. And I was like, "Um, I'm still your daughter and you're still my dad." Why wouldn't we just continue as is?'

'My dad used to say the same thing! In counselling with Arlene, I asked him why he always turned me down when I invited him to a one-on-one coffee with me. He used to come up with excuses but I knew there was an underlying reason. And he finally came out with it! Get this, right ... he doesn't want to catch up with me alone because he doesn't think I should be "separating" the family but inviting only him. I think he's taken the lessons from *Bhagban* a tad too far – you know that movie he loves where Amitabh Bachchan and Hema Malini are torn apart by their own kids?' I asked Zam as she snorted and rolled her eyes.

I continued: 'But here's the punch in the guts. Before our last sesh, Maya had told me that Pa seemed a little fragile after the car hit them. So we decided that I'd check in with him and Ma regularly because I live closer to them. So I called to ask how he's doing and ask if he'd like to go for a walk together...'

Zam looked into her lap and rubbed her thumb and middle finger along her eyebrows, already anticipating that the next thing to come out of my mouth would be ridiculous.

'He knocked back my offer, saying he was alright. Then I spoke to Maya later that evening, knowing that she'd just driven down to spend the weekend at my parents'. And she goes, "Yeah, Pa and I went for a nice walk together this evening. He really opened up about how he's been feeling since the accident." What the hell? I mean, I'm glad he could open up to her – it's not a jealousy thing – but I think it just confirms that I am the problem child to him. He might "love" me but I actually don't think he "likes" me. I know I can sometimes be abrasive and, yeah, I can dial down my need to be the moral police at times, but he actually doesn't seem to enjoy the idea of being alone with me at all. It's like *all of me* is outside his comfort zone.'

We were out of the city now, driving along the undulating roads that led to Ballarat. The vibrant green hills were freckled with tiny grey sheep in the distance.

'Okay, no more of that!' I announced. 'We can continue that depressing conversation another time! Let's focus on the fact that you're twenty-eight now. How are you feeling about it?'

'First of all, the conversation is not depressing. You're my best friend and it's never a bad time for you to update me on your life. And I'm feeling good actually! Apart from the hardships with my family, I feel like I'm where I need to be. Things aren't perfect but I think

I'm the best version of myself so far, with room to get better. I'm figuring out who I am. I feel close to God. So, yeah, I'm doing great!'

Zam and I arrived at our destination and searched for the right parking lot.

'Werribee Gorge! Dude! I've been planning to come here for months and just haven't had the chance. How did you know?'

'I didn't.'

Once we gathered our backpacks and belongings, I escorted her over to a group of people standing in a circle under the gumtrees by the dirt car park. We were the youngest ones there. Most of the group were middle-aged and some were elderly but they all looked fit.

'Welcome to our second Walking with God in Nature day of the year. Looks like everyone is here now,' said a tall man in cargo shorts and a wide brimmed hat. 'My name is Trevor. Today, we are going to be hiking through Werribee Gorge. We will begin and end with a reflection but we ask that you please remain silent while we are walking. Please go at your own pace; slow down if you need to. There's no hurry. Take in the surrounds. Pay attention to what you can hear, smell and see. And feel free to stop whenever you need to.'

Zam looked at me with her eyes full of eagerness and gratitude. The organisation running the day was a centre of Ignatian spirituality in Melbourne; I'd participated in spiritual retreats with them before and had told Zam about how gentle and uplifting the experiences were.

Trevor continued: 'Please take a slip of paper and pass it on. When they've all been handed out, I'd like each of you to read your sentence out loud. Then we'll begin our walk.'

As I heard the first few sentences being read out, I recognised the beatitudes from the Sermon on the Mount. Except they sounded a little different.

Blessed are those who know their true place in the universe.
They will find peace.
Blessed are those who recognise and value the interdependence of

all created things. They will live in friendship with creation.

Blessed are those who delight in the company of nature. They will always have a song in their heart.

Blessed are those who tread lightly on the Earth. They will experience freedom of spirit.

Blessed are those who delight in rain, sunshine and surf. They will feel the touch of God.

Blessed are those who talk to trees and animals. They will hear the voice of God.

Blessed are those who protect and defend the weak and voiceless. They will be remembered by future generations.

Blessed are those who mourn the suffering of our planet. They will understand the heart of God.

Blessed are those who hunger and thirst for what is right for all creatures. They will walk with Christ.

I opened my eyes and felt like my chest had been cleared of all the clutter I had brought with me that morning. I looked around, marvelling at the artistry of nature, the beauty of the planet we lived on and the people in it, even in our brokenness. I focused on everything that was real around me and I let go of the worry inside me; especially the fear of things that hadn't yet happened and might never happen. I was reminded that I was an infinitesimal part of everything that constituted that moment on our planet and an even smaller part of history. Yet I was known and loved.

We began our walk and I spent the first thirty minutes panting up a hill with my head down. Then I remembered the purpose of our hike, which made me slow down and even stop at times to just stand there, feel my feet on the earth and let that particular pocket of nature imprint itself upon my memory. I slowly filled my lungs with the fresh air of Werribee Gorge. I basked in the songs of cockatoos, rosellas and kookaburras.

The harsh beauty in front of me, made up mostly of ashbrowns, ochres, olive-greens and greys, was so unique to the bush on this land, specifically Wadawurrung and Wurundjeri country.

I felt confronted by it as I climbed, as though it spoke to me, asking, *Do you like me?* If I had the choice to be in the Werribee Gorge or the Daintree Rainforest, I'd have chosen the latter, lusher, more tropical option. But something about this landscape was challenging me to expand my palate, as though I'd miss something vital in life if I wrote it off as too dry, straggly, lifeless. There *was* life, but it was hiding. I looked up at the trees. They were old, branches broken off and trunks hollowed out. I'd recently read about these trees, how special they were; it took more than one hundred years for them to hollow out and although the trees looked dead, they were full of life as animals made their homes in them. They had jagged edges where branches had fallen, and the branches that still hung on jutted out at strange angles. We reached the summit on one side of the gorge and sat in silence, looking out over the edge of the cliff.

After lunch, we walked by the river. I spotted a superb fairy-wren for the first time, in all of its sapphire glory.

At the end of the trail, Zam and I took off our shoes and soaked our feet in the water as we sat on rocks among the reeds. *This is the part of you I like most,* I silently said to the gorge, promising to visit again. At the end of the day, we gathered in small groups and Trevor asked each one of us to share what we appreciated most about the hike.

'What stood out to me today,' I said when it was my turn, 'was how untethered and at liberty the birds were. Sure, they have to collect food and, sure, evolution plays a part in how they go about their business, but no one has them on a leash telling them where to go, how to be, what to do. I want to be more like that.'

The spiritual director in our group, Paul, took a moment to absorb my words, as he did for everyone else in the group. We were at ease in our collective silence as he reflected on each of our responses before answering.

'It sounds like freedom is quite important to you,' he said.

'Yeah,' I pressed my lips into a thin line and willed myself to hold back any tears. I gave Zam a look. *I don't know why I'm this emotional!* I said with my eyes.

Paul thought for a while longer then asked, in his soft, wizened voice, 'Did you notice all the eucalyptus trees?'

'Yes, I did. They're incredible.'

'The eucalyptus is a very drought-tolerant tree. It is intent on surviving. If it doesn't get enough water or if part of it isn't in good health, it will drop entire branches so the rest of the tree can keep going. I just find its resilience glorious, don't you?' He paused. I nodded. 'Even in hardship, it won't give up on reaching toward the sun.' He smiled with wrinkly eyes as he left me with that thought. Like he'd placed a lump of gold in my lap.

How did he know? Or maybe he didn't and he was just following an invisible current. Like the one that led me to take Zam there that day.

***

A year went by, and I was still estranged from Pa. Then one day, my piano arrived. When we set up this tall, white, second-hand, vintage, gorgeous beast of a piano in the corner of our lounge room, the first person I thought of was Pa. It reminded me of the white pillowcase Maya and I bought him for his birthday a few years earlier, as a joke but also as a kindness, because he had been lamenting the new sheets Ma had bought for their bed.

'How can she make me sleep in red and orange sheets? Such hazardous colours! How will I sleep?!' he had complained. We were all in stitches when he received the white pillowcases with genuine gratitude and relief.

More than anyone, Pa loved to hear me play piano as a child. Before he thought music lessons would get in the way of other 'more important' academia, it was the one thing we delighted in together. 'Play "Malagueña"! Play it again. See how beautifully she plays, everyone!'

When the piano removalist left, I serenaded Jake and our daughter as they twirled together to the music – music that wouldn't reach my father's ears. Instead, Ma told him about it when she saw it during her visit the following week, just like she told him I'd taken up writing.

The distance I maintained from my parents enabled me to drop the branches that didn't serve me and grow new ones. I spent the time away from them searching deep within and finding the little girl who lived inside me before she was twisted, folded and scrunched up to fit into a box that wasn't made for her. I started to become the painter she'd been in kindergarten, drawing blue and yellow squares on a sheet of butcher's paper. I became the curious five-year-old who'd sat in the dirt and scratched away at it with a coin to reveal soil that looked like powdered gold underneath. I became the writer who'd won third place in her Year 2 creative-writing competition, despite struggling to write many essays later in university. I became the kid eating improvised pancakes and licking maple syrup off the plate. I became a wild bird of the gorge. I became a freely running river and I became a eucalyptus tree.

***

The following year, I booked my flights to India. I planned to go back to my motherland without my parents for the first time. I had a long list of things to do: suss out where I could return to with my daughter and husband; buy chudidhars for my daughter and myself; get lost in textiles, architecture, art and poetry; find gifts for my parents; go trekking in North West and North East India; and scratch the ground to see what I could find.

My baby was two years old by then. She was brave, intelligent, empathetic, affectionate and, although we inevitably had an influence on her, she was mostly an unadulterated version of herself. We asked her lots of questions, let her play freely and took an interest in her observations of the world. We danced to Bollywood songs with her. Sometimes I sang her to sleep in English, sometimes in broken Hindi or Kannada. Every few days, she'd ask to speak to Ajji and Ajja. When they Facetimed, I never made an appearance and hardly engaged in conversation, but I was happy to foster their relationship with my daughter as they seemed to enjoy one another's company so much.

I received a note from my daughter's playgroup saying that the end of year wrap-up was around the corner and parents were to send a plate of food with their kids to share on their last day. My go-to for this sort of thing would normally have been homemade muffins or cupcakes, but this time I taught myself how to make kalakand with cardamom and rosewater swirled through its creamy crumbs. My daughter couldn't get enough of it and I could not express how proud I felt as her mother, trying to give her access to half of her heritage and succeeding – for now.

I did end up talking to Saul's wife. It was a weird phone call. She appeared to be aware of the abuse, but still in denial about its nature, regurgitating Saul's own words to me over the phone and declaring it nothing more than affection shown by an uncle to his niece. 'I know what it's like to be pregnant too,' she added. 'These hormones make us extra emotional about things from the past, but they'll eventually balance out.' She couldn't be moved, so I gave up. I wished her all the best, hoping their kids were safe and thriving, and we agreed to part ways until I felt comfortable to be in their presence again. I didn't tell her that such an outcome was unlikely in my view. The sad part was that I'd miss out on getting to know Saul's children, my youngest first cousins. But that was my call. If I ever bumped into them in future, I'd only have kindness to offer them. And maybe one day we could meet up without their dad in the picture.

***

My thirtieth birthday arrived. For once, I had zero plans. I ate breakfast with Jake, Panda and our baby girl and waited to see what the rest of the day brought, which turned out to be two surprises: Maya and Zam. They both popped over for lunch, and afterward the six of us had a dance party in our lounge, Panda included. I was freeboobing it in my pyjamas sans underwear but these people didn't care. I didn't feel the need to dress up for any of them, and it ended up being one of the most sacred birthdays I'd ever had. I spent it in a room full of honest people who had witnessed one another's brokenness, healing, shame and victories. Between us, there was nothing that needed covering up or burying. I'd never felt more like myself.

Before she went home, Maya handed me an envelope. 'Pa wanted me to give this to you.'

Later that afternoon, I sat at my desk and read it.

Happy B'day, Ruhi.

God blessed us with a beautiful daughter 30 yrs ago. I still remember the days, you being carried on my shoulders, holding your hands & walking. And one day, you even poohed on my white shorts.

It has been a wonderful journey, raising you, playing Monopoly with you and thank god for what you are today. I am really proud of you and you are already a 30 year old beautiful woman, and wife and caring, loving mother.

We have had challenges but thank God for his help in guiding and bringing you through them.

I pray God that you continue what you are, growing strong in his faith and continue to hold his hands. And I am sure he has plans for you and he will always be with you throughout your journey.

God bless you always, along with husband & baby

Best wishes for your journey, further on for many more years.

PA & MA

At first, I nitpicked at his words, particularly his signing off as 'Pa & Ma' when the card was clearly only from him. Then, I read it again, this time as a fellow parent, knowing that our paths aren't linear, predictable or easy by any means. Thinking along those lines softened my stance a little and I felt a small spark of connection through the ink on the card, written elegantly by my father's hand. There were a million imperfections when it came to our relationship, but now that it had been hollowed out, and with this gesture from my father on my birthday, maybe we could start building something new. And maybe not. I'd have to wait and see. I didn't know how I was going to reply, but I knew it would come from a thoughtful, considered place. I wanted to respect my father and myself at the same time. I didn't want to just appease Pa or push for a happy ending before it was due, if at all. Maybe, in the same way I found one part of Werribee Gorge that I wanted to revisit, Pa's writing in the card was the river I could sit by, taking in the beauty.

I was then distracted by a small voice growing louder and louder as it neared the bedroom. The sliding door opened.

'Mum! Mummum! Mum!'

'Yes, my love?' I answered my daughter.

'Shide! Shide!' she said, pointing to the front door.

'You want to go outside?' I asked.

'Ow yeah!'

'Okay, I'll come with you!'

'Yeah! Yeah!' She was so excited.

'Where are we going?'

'Park!'

'Alright, let's get our shoes on and go to the park.'

She rushed outside as soon as we had what we needed.

'We'll be back shortly, babe!' I called out to Jake. He walked out to the porch to give us both a kiss before we left.

'Okay, let's go, baby!' I said to my tiny adventurer.

'Go! Go!' she shouted with glee and led the way.

Our destination was a three-minute walk away and she knew the way by heart. I followed her from behind. It was my favourite time of the day. In our home we called it Golden Time: that short period just before the sun started to set, when it hovered above the horizon and went from a hot yellow to a gleaming gold, casting long shadows. It was especially spectacular when we were down at the beach.

I adored the way my daughter's small, pudgy hand with indented knuckles had to touch every fence post, every bush, every brick and every flower that she passed. This time, I stretched out my right arm and followed her lead, taking in all the different textures under my fingertips. We were both fairy-wrens. With our wings stretched wide, we were ready to experience everything with the wonder and awe of two new beings in this world.

Author's Note

Dear Reader,

I want to share with you why I wrote this book. I also want to offer some clarity on what this book is not. Of course, you will also draw your own conclusions about what this book means to you.

This book is a personal, crafted memoir of *my* experience aspiring to the Good Indian Daughter ideal. I am aware that a certain image is conjured in the minds of many non-Indian people when they think of Indian women. I've come across people who think we are 'all the same'. I also feel that many Indians – elders, in particular – perhaps as a result of our collectivist culture, fall into patterns of generalisation, to the extent that they forget our individuality – and importantly, the individual talents and dreams of each girl and woman they see themselves as responsible for (this is often the case for young, Indian sons too).

While I've found, through my relationships with women of Indian and more broadly South Asian descent, that many of us have faced similar challenges around expectations to play the Good Daughter role, I am not seeking to represent other brown women with this book. The way I've lived out the role of the Good Indian Daughter and then rejected it is different to the way other women have navigated this dynamic in their lives, depending on their caste, class, religion, location, gender identity, sexual orientation, family situation and the different patriarchies they face, among other factors. Our experiences are not homogenous. And many brown women will not find themselves on this type of trajectory at all.

    I think one of the most miraculous things about books is when a reader is gifted with words to describe feelings and experiences they've never been able to articulate themselves. To have these words, to hold them next to indescribable blobs in one's mind and suddenly see these amorphous thoughts or emotions take form, is such a quiet but powerful way of uplifting and emboldening. Other writers have done this for me, and I hope my book will do the same for some of its readers.

I have written about my trauma in this book. My trauma does not define me. And this book is not a 'trauma testament' for people – especially white people with a saviour complex – to take as evidence of their own culture's superiority. Every culture has aspects worth celebrating just as they have qualities worth critiquing. I hope I have done a fair job of critiquing and celebrating the cultures I grew up with in those small pockets of what is now known as India and what is now known as Australia.

So, what do I hope my readers will make of the trauma I've written about in this book? To borrow Roxane Gay's words in *Hunger,* 'I do not want pity or appreciation or advice. I am not brave or heroic. I am not strong. I am not special. I am one woman who has experienced something countless women have experienced ... I hope that by sharing my story, by joining a chorus of women and men who share their stories too, more people can become appropriately horrified...' Because it is horrific, the number of hoops that daughters with experiences like mine and worse than mine have to jump through, the number of people we have to please, the abuse we are expected to remain silent about – and in many cases to keep enduring – and to continue standing after it all just to be accepted; to be respected. To be conditionally 'loved'.

I'm done being *good* for other people. And while I enjoy the feeling of strength that comes with that declaration, at the same time I feel heartbroken knowing that not everyone is in a privileged enough position to be able to say that and act on it. Other women facing similar pressures to be good daughters have been systematically pushed to the fringes or held back by a society that deems their social circumstances (caste, class, religion, etc) as lesser. Many do not have access to the resources that have allowed me to live a life of my own charting. Meanwhile, there are those who *do* have the resources to create, to speak up, to write, but they are silenced when their work is recognised as a form of dissent.

Michaela Coel summarised these conflicted feelings so eloquently in *I May Destroy You,* and I ask her questions of myself: Are my experiences in this book 'a walk in the park when other girls are currently being stoned to death for having mobile phones, are bleeding to death after genital mutilation, are looking at a womb irreparably destroyed by militias systematically raping them during times of civil conflict and war? Are these facts a humbling reminder not to be so loud about my experiences, or are they a reminder to shout? Can my shout help their silent screams?'

I do not take my position as an author lightly. I could not have written this book if it wasn't for countless women (womanists, feminists and women who are lifting others as they climb but prefer to call themselves neither of the above) – those who are prominent and those who have worked behind the scenes – paving a road ahead of me where there was none before. I could not have written it if it wasn't for the sacrifices my parents made to provide me with an education and a safety net. And while I don't know if I would have become an author if my parents had not emigrated to what is now known as Australia, I must acknowledge that I could not physically be here, writing at my desk, without the horrific violence that colonial invaders inflicted upon the Indigenous owners and custodians of this land. I am still working out what it means to be an immigrant (whose country of birth has also been wrung out by colonisation) here on the lands of the Kulin nation, what it means to be a storyteller here, what it means to actively pay my respects to elders, past, present and emerging and what it means to respect this unceded land that I inhabit, not because it was granted to me by its rightful owners and custodians, but by other means that are viewed as acceptable and legal by systems put in place by the colonisers.

Also, dear reader, I want to be transparent with you about the fact that Ruhi Lee is my pen name and the name I prefer as a writer in public. It is not my birth name. Taking on this pseudonym was a decision I thought long and hard about, and discussed with my parents. That I have written this book and am releasing my story and my family's story into the world is, understandably, terribly uncomfortable for them. While I, personally, have nothing to hide as an author, I want to honour their request that I respect their privacy. You'll probably see me at events or catch photos and videos of me online. If you do recognise me from another era when I had a social life, I ask that you please keep it to yourself – again, out of respect for my parents.

Lastly, dear reader, if this book has horrified you, it's done half of its job. I ask you to look around you to identify the hurdles your own society has placed in front of people in your life who are daughters and to ask those daughters what, if anything, you can do to support them. If you are one of those daughters, please remember that you are not alone, help – though it may prove difficult to get – is available, and *you matter.* The other half of this book's job was to make you laugh. I inherited my father's love of comedy and my mother's knack for it. Hopefully, this book has brought a bit of joy and laughter. If it hasn't, you are also not alone. I once had someone read thirty pages of the book and ask me, 'Do you think this is funny? Because it's not.' So that makes two of you, at the very least.

    Yours sincerely,
    Ruhi

Acknowledgements

Ma, Pa and Ajji. Thank you for answering my numerous questions about our family's history and traditions and for helping me translate from Kannada and Hindi to English. You did all of this even though it would have been easier for you if I had never written this book. *All these apples are yours.*

To all the women in my family – 'good' daughters and disappointing daughters alike – those who are still with us, those who have long gone and those to whom this world was too cruel, you've always been required to sacrifice so much and you still give/gave. I thank you and I am sorry.

To the custodians and elders – past, present, emerging and future – of Boon Wurrung country, where I write, I offer my heartfelt gratitude and solidarity.

Dilpreet Kaur Taggar, Tasneem Chopra, Intan Paramaditha, Kate Mildenhall, Pip Williams and Emily Clements – you marvellous women have all been so generous. Thank you.

Brad Aaron Modlin and James Brubaker of Southeast Missouri State University Press, thank you for granting me permission to include an excerpt of 'What You Missed that Day You Were Absent from Fourth Grade' at the start of this memoir; this poem means a great deal to me.

Samantha McNally from the Australian Bureau of Statistics; thank you for your time and patience with my questions and calculations. You saved me from the consequences of a couple of missing zeroes!

Zoya Patel and Mridula Nath Chakraborty, thank you for your support in the earlier stages of writing this book. Mridula, thank you for opening my eyes. Your advice was invaluable. Zoya, you are a pioneer to me; *No Country Woman* was the first book I'd ever read by a woman writer who had origins in India and had mostly grown up in this part of the world. Your book made mine feel all the more possible.

Many thanks go to Writers Victoria, Australian Writers Centre and ACT Writers Centre. As an emerging writer, I gained so much from the courses and workshops made available by these organisations.

In particular, I benefited hugely from the HARDCOPY program of 2019, run by ACT Writers Centre; Nigel Featherstone, Mary Cunnane and the wonderful team who worked behind the scenes. Thank you. My thanks also go to the participating publishers and literary agents who encouraged me to be more confident in my voice and who provided their thoughtful feedback on the beginning of my manuscript. I am grateful to the Ainslie and Gorman Arts Centre for hosting me while I participated in HC19; and of course, to my cousins, colleagues and friends who raised funds for me to travel to and stay in Canberra for the duration of the program.

Alex Adsett of Alex Adsett Publishing Services, thank you for your help throughout the journey. Meeting you and hearing you speak at HC19 made me feel confident that I would find people in the publishing industry who really cared about writers and not just book sales.

Many thanks to the folks at Campion Centre of Ignatian Spirituality; the work of this organisation instilled hope in me when I thought it was lost.

My counsellor gave me hope too. And a way out. Thank you.

In fact, I am grateful to every person around the world who makes it their life's work to assist others with their mental and emotional wellbeing. Bless you for shining so bright in the darkness. The same goes for many, many writers whose books, articles, screenplays and poems have inspired me from the very beginning. I can't list them here but God knows how indebted I feel to other writers and artists; even those I'll never meet in this lifetime.

Michelle Tom, Katherine Tamiko Arguile and Ashley Kalagian Blunt. Where would I be without you top notch writer-friends? (Probably still doggy-paddling in the lake of tears I cried after my first few consecutive rejections.)

A fellow author, who published their book with Affirm Press, once said to me that when it came to bringing this book out into the world, 'Ruby is everything'.

I found this to be true; thank you Ruby Ashby-Orr for being an incredible editor. My many thanks to the amazing Freya Horton Andrews and Karen Gee who also assisted with this process. I am also grateful to Martin Hughes, Lauren Ravida, Rosanna Hunt and the rest of the team at Affirm Press for believing in my work and for getting it out into the hands of readers. Karen Wallis, thank you for the awesome book cover.

My father-in-law is one of the biggest reasons I had time to put pen to paper. Thank you for all the babysitting and bagels, Dad. Thank you also for being my cheerleader, my literary-events-buddy and for listening to every episode of my now-deleted podcast. You're the bee's knees in *beeskneeslees.*

My heartfelt and eternal thanks to my best friend (Zam*), who is also my sister, and my sister (Maya*), who is also my best friend (and probably crying as she reads this). Thank you for your words of affirmation, ongoing support and for believing in me from the very first shitty sentence I wrote. Thanks also to my cousins, my sister-in-law and my girlfriends – you know who you are – all of you women are strong and delicious and you enrich my life beyond measure.

To my beloved husband and daughter, thank you both from the bottom of my heart. You two are beyond my wildest dreams. (And that is all I can say without being a hypocrite – seeing as I told my husband in the 'Funeral Plans' chapter that I didn't want him to say anything in his eulogy that he hadn't said to me in real life.)

God (?) – whoever, however you are–

ತುಂಬಾಧನ್ಯವಾದಗಳು

And you, dear reader, thank you, thank you, thank you.

Glossary

Terms are in Kannada unless otherwise stated. Several of these words are used in both Hindi, Kannada and other Indian languages. Many of them don't have a precise translation in English but I have consulted with my parents on finding the right fit and we have done our best. As with all words in Kannada and Hindi, there is no one correct way of spelling them in English and you might have come across other ways of spelling the words I've listed below.

Vowels remain constant in their pronunciation, as follows:

    a, as in art
    i, as in igloo
    u, as in look
    e, as in bed
    o, as in ox

Vowels topped with a macron, are elongated: ā, ē, ī, ō, ū

***

amla supari – sundried gooseberries; also known as *awala supari*

anda boorji – a scrambled egg breakfast/picnic dish containing onions, green chillis and coriander

are! – colloq. hey! (as an accusation)

are baap re! (Hindi) – colloq. Oh my God!

atta (Hindi) – wheat flour

ayo! – an exclamation expressing shock or dismay

baingan bharta (Hindi) – a smoky dish of minced eggplant that has been grilled over charcoal or an open fire

bella – jaggery

bissi – hot

chaha – tea (sounds like 'cha' when said quickly); *chai* in Hindi

channa – chickpeas

chappal – colloq. slippers (formal, *chappali*)

chi – colloq. yuck

chuchga – steel spatula

chuch – poke

chuddie – underwear

chudidhar – a traditional outfit comprising of a veil (*dupatta/odni*), a tunic and pants. Also known as *salwar kameez*. Technically a chudidhar or churidar refers to the pants only and a specific type where the cut of the pants is narrower. But my community uses the word chudidhar to refer to the whole outfit.

didi (Hindi) – big sister

dhrushti – colloq. a ritual usually performed by a woman elder to remove the influence of the evil eye (*ketta dhrushti*). Cotton balls, salt, dried chillies, mustard seeds, broomstick straw or any combination of these props are held in line with the forehead of the person from whom ketta dhrushti is being removed, then swept downward toward their toes and spat on, with the belief that the power of the evil eye is absorbed into those props before being burned.

dagga – also known as *bayan,* a musical instrument played alongside a tabla. The dagga is the larger, bass drum that creates a deeper sound than the tabla.

ghagra – also known as *langa, ghagra choli, lehenga choli* and *chaniya choli,* a traditional costume consisting of a skirt (usually floor-length), blouse and veil (*dupatta/odni*).

goonda – thug

gulab jamun – dessert: deep-fried balls of a dough made from milk solids, soaked in an aromatic sugar syrup spiced with cardamom, rose water and other ingredients depending on how one's family makes it

hai bhagwan – colloq. (Hindi) oh God!

harrak – colloq. torn, worn out (formal, *harraku*)

holas – colloq. dirty (formal, *holasu*)

hudugi – girl

idli – steamed rice cakes predominantly eaten in South India

izzat – (Hindi) honour, reputation

jalebi – sweet: deep-friend swirls of batter soaked in sugar syrup

kabaddi – a two-team sport played recreationally and professionally

kachra – (Hindi) rubbish

kajal – (Hindi) black eyeliner

kala – (Hindi) Black

kalakand – milk-based sweet

karriawa – derogatory term for a dark-skinned girl

khō-khō – a two-team game played in India, involving chasers and defenders

kothambari – coriander

kubsa – the name used in Karnataka for a baby shower. Also known as *seemantha*. Other names such as *godh bharai* are used in other parts of India.

kumkum – red powder (vermilion) used to mark the forehead during pooja

mangalsutra – a necklace, traditionally gold and comprising of black beads believed to ward off bad luck and danger, placed around a bride's neck by the groom during a wedding ceremony to act as an ongoing visual marker of her status as a married woman; also spelled *mangala sutra* and also known as *thali*

maryade – dignity, honour, reputation

nimma magalu – your daughter

paapa – poor thing

palle – a curry or stew of vegetables; sometimes in a gravy, sometimes dry

pallu – the part of the saree draped over the shoulder, also known as *seragu* in Kannada and *aanchal* in Hindi *peda* – Indian sweet

pooja – an act of worship; also spelled *puja*

poppie – colloq. kiss (formal, *muthu*)

reshmi – silk

sabasgi – dill

sambar – dish containing lentils and vegetables often accompanied by rice, idlis or dosas; also known as *saar*

summa kundher – colloq. sit quietly

tava – (Hindi) pan

uppit sheera – a breakfast dish made of semolina; uppit is the savoury component with ingredients like onions, curry leaves, ginger and green chillies while sheera is the sweet component often containing sultanas and cashews; the dish is also known as *chow chow bhath*

weeboothi – a bar of white, chalky powder used to mark the forehead during pooja

yaar (Hindi) – mate, friend

yawa – colloq. exclamation expressing exasperation

Sources

Chapter Ten: The Good Indian Daughter

Alkema, L, Chao, F, You, D, Pedersen, J, Sawyer, C.C., 2014, 'National, regional, and global sex ratios of infant, child, and under-5 mortality and identification of countries with outlying ratios: a systematic assessment', *Lancet Global Health,* 2: e521– e530.

Dandona, R., Anil Kumar, G., Dhaliwal, R.S., Naghavi, M., Vos, T., Shukla, D.K., Vijayakumar, L. Gururaj, G., Thakur, J.S., Ambekar, A., Sagar, R., Arora, M., Bhardwaj, D., Chakma, J.K., Dutta, E., Furtado, M., Glenn, S., Hawley, C., Johnson, S.C., Khanna, T., Kutz, M., Mountjoy-Venning, W.C., Muraleedharan, P., Rangaswamy, T., Varghese, C.M., Varghese, M., Srinath Reddy, K., Murray, C.J.L., Swaminathan, S., Dandona, L. 2018. 'Gender differentials and state variations in suicide deaths in India:

the Global Burden of Disease Study 1990–2016', *The Lancet,* p. e485.

Ismail, Shajahan, Sathyanarayana Rao and Wylie. 2015. 'Adolescent Sex Education in India: Current Perspectives', *Indian Journal of Psychiatry.*

Menon, N. 2012. *Seeing Like a Feminist.* Zubaan and Penguin Random House, India.

Pande, R.P. 2003, 'Selective gender differences in childhood nutrition and immunization in rural india: The role of siblings', *Demography,* 40:3, pp.395–418.

Scroll Staff, 'Dumka sexual assault: RJD leader blames item songs, ads and pornographic content for rape culture', *Scroll India,* Sep 30, 2020, accessed Dec 27, 2020 https://scroll.in/latest/980933/dumka-gangrape-rjd-leader-blames-item-songsads-and-pornographic-content-for-such-culture

United Nations Population Fund, 2020, 'State of World Population', p.48.

Varadhan, S, 'One woman reports a rape every 15 minutes in India', *Reuters,* Jan 10, 2020, accessed Dec 27, 2020 https://www.reuters.com/article/us-india-crime-women-idUSKBN1Z821W

Chapter Eleven: A baby shower fit for a queen who hates parties

Kacker, L., Varadan, S., Kumar, P. 2007. 'Study on Child Abuse INDIA 2007', Ministry of Women and Child Development, Government of India.

Bhalla, N, 'Almost 90 percent of India's rapes committed by people known to victim', Thomson Reuters Foundation, Aug 21, 2015, accessed on 28 Dec 2020, https://uk.reuters.com/article/india-women-crime-rape/almost-90-percentof-indias-rapes-committed-by-people-known-to-victimidUSKCN0QQ0QS20150821

Sengupta, N., '109 children sexually abused every day in India in 2018: NCRB', *India Today,* Jan 12, 2020, accessed, 28 Dec 2020, https://www.indiatoday.in/india/story/109-childrensexually-abused-every-day-india-2018-1636160-2020-01-12

'India sexual abuse: "Four child victims every hour"', *BBC News,* 1 Dec 2019, accessed in May 2020, https://www.bbc.com/news/world-asia-india-42193533

'Sexual Assault in Australia', 2020, Australian Institute of Health and Welfare, p.12.

Australian Institute of Health and Welfare 2018. 'Family, domestic and sexual violence in Australia 2018'. Cat. no. FDV 2. Canberra: AIHW

'Child Sexual Assault: Facts and Statistics', 2019, Braveheart Foundation Limited, p.28.

Chapter Twelve: Unsolicited advice

Bacon, L., Aphramor, L. 2014. *Body Respect: What Conventional Health Books Get Wrong, Leave Out, and Just Plain Fail to Understand about Weight.* Barbella Books, Inc.

www.ingramcontent.com/pod-product-compliance
Lightning Source LLC
Chambersburg PA
CBHW010718300426
44115CB00019B/2952